JOLTED

JOLTED

Why We Quit,
When to Stay,
and Why It Matters

Anthony
Klotz

EBURY EDGE

UK | USA | Canada | Ireland | Australia
India | New Zealand | South Africa

Ebury Edge is part of the Penguin Random House group of companies
whose addresses can be found at global.penguinrandomhouse.com

Penguin Random House UK
One Embassy Gardens, 8 Viaduct Gardens, London SW11 7BW

penguin.co.uk

First published in the United States by Viking in 2026
First published in the United Kingdom by Ebury Edge in 2026
1

Copyright © Anthony Klotz 2026
The moral right of the author has been asserted.

Penguin Random House values and supports copyright.
Copyright fuels creativity, encourages diverse voices, promotes freedom of
expression and supports a vibrant culture. Thank you for purchasing an authorised
edition of this book and for respecting intellectual property laws by not reproducing,
scanning or distributing any part of it by any means without permission. You are supporting
authors and enabling Penguin Random House to continue to publish books for everyone.
No part of this book may be used or reproduced in any manner for the purpose
of training artificial intelligence technologies or systems. In accordance
with Article 4(3) of the DSM Directive 2019/790, Penguin Random House
expressly reserves this work from the text and data mining exception.

Printed and bound in Great Britain by Clays Ltd, Elcograf S.p.A.

The authorised representative in the EEA is Penguin Random House Ireland,
Morrison Chambers, 32 Nassau Street, Dublin D02 YH68

A CIP catalogue record for this book is available from the British Library

ISBN 9781529146400

Designed by Nerylsa Dijol

Penguin Random House is committed to a sustainable future
for our business, our readers and our planet. This book is made
from Forest Stewardship Council® certified paper.

CONTENTS

INTRODUCTION
The Big Jolt — 1

PART I
WHY DO WE QUIT OUR JOBS?

ONE
The Lottery Question — 13

TWO
Everyday Events, Extraordinary Effects — 29

THREE
Getting to the Root of the Jolt — 43

FOUR
Carry On — 62

PART II
JOLTS AT WORK

FIVE
Direct Jolts — 79

SIX
Collateral Jolts — 89

SEVEN
Honeymoon Jolts — 98

EIGHT
Speak Up — 111

PART III
JOLTS BEYOND WORK

NINE
Crossover Jolts — 125

TEN
Remote Jolts — 137

ELEVEN
Positive Jolts — 151

TWELVE
Lean Back — 164

PART IV
WALKING AWAY

THIRTEEN
Preparing to Exit — 179

FOURTEEN
Turning Your Resignation Intentions into Reality — 189

PART V
HELPING OTHERS NAVIGATE JOLTS

FIFTEEN
Recognize Your Role in Others' Future Jolts — 207

SIXTEEN
Surface Jolts as They Happen — 217

SEVENTEEN
Shape the Effects of Jolts — 227

EIGHTEEN
Create a Positive Post-Jolt Relationship — 235

Epilogue — 245
Acknowledgments — 247
Resources — 251
Notes — 253
Index — 281
About the Author — 293

JOLTED

INTRODUCTION

THE BIG JOLT

In the autumn of 2020, I received an email from journalist Arianne Cohen, who was working on a story about how to quit a job. We scheduled a thirty-minute meeting but ended up chatting for over an hour. Toward the end of our conversation, I remarked that her article was going to be useful for all of those who were going to quit in the coming wave of resignations. Although it was an offhand comment for me, Arianne's interest was piqued. She asked me to explain.

Fumbling my way through an answer, I reflected on the MBA leadership course I was currently teaching in Houston. My students were early-career professionals working full time, while pursuing a graduate degree, during a pandemic (bless their hearts). As the students and I discussed their experiences as leaders and employees (in masks, with me behind a pane of plexiglass and half of the class on Zoom), something seemed "off" about how these hardworking, high-performing professionals were feeling about work. And it wasn't just them.

Late 2020 was still in the heart of the pandemic, but there was general optimism about the coming vaccines—hope that the jabs would let us get back to "normal." I shared that hope, but I also got the feeling that the world of work could never go back. Because, like my MBA students, almost everyone I talked to described how one or more events of the past year had caused them to reassess work and/or life.

You didn't have to look very hard to see that many people's jobs had become more challenging, and in some cases scarier, almost overnight. Frontline workers were doing their jobs with the added risk and safety equipment tied to the health threat of COVID-19. The same was true for medical workers, who were also faced with increased death and illness brought on by the pandemic.

Elsewhere, with schools and day cares closed, parents grappled with the impossibility of educating their children from home while working full time. Millions of people switched to remote work, forcing them to do their jobs in a completely new way. While many couldn't wait to get back to working in person, many others embraced the increase in flexible work and were (and some still are) dreading the eventual day when they would be called to return to their pre-pandemic offices, work schedules, and daily commutes.

The year 2020 also brought widely publicized acts of racial injustice and polarizing elections—events that caused people to pause and reflect on what they stood for and whether they were living those values.

Disruptive events were everywhere. Abrupt changes to people's jobs. To the boundaries between their personal and professional lives. To the space in which they work. To the social fabric of their lives outside of work. And they were happening amid lockdowns, when people's social calendars were empty, giving them the space to stop and think about life and work. The collective reflection caused by these widespread events should have led to a wave of people making major changes in their lives, including quitting their jobs. And yet, the actual resignation numbers in the economy were low.

For a researcher who studies work and quitting, the reason was pretty straightforward. With the economic harm the pandemic wreaked, 2020 was one of the worst times in history to quit your job. In times of uncertainty, most of us wisely shy away from taking risks like switching jobs or taking a career break. Thus, there was a sea of disruptive events, but only a trickle of quitting. The amount of actual leaving was dammed up by the economic and personal uncertainty associated with the moment.

But when the economy opened up and that uncertainty eased, I suspected that the pent-up effects of these disruptive events—which we will come to know as *jolts*—would unleash a significant and sustained flood of resignations across the US and beyond.

Two months later, Arianne interviewed me a second time, for a short piece in *Bloomberg Businessweek*. At some point in the conversation, I called my predicted wave of quitting "the great resignation" without giving it any thought. The resulting article came out on May 10, 2021. I was at home that morning when Arianne emailed me the link and said, "This is currently #3 most-read on the entire Bloomberg site (which is a rather large ecosystem!)." I shared the link on social media and it immediately began racking up more views than all of my prior posts combined. I went into the kitchen and told my wife about it and she laughed and said, "Are you going viral?"

A few hours later, a news website confirmed it: "Professor's Prediction Goes Viral."

One Event Away from Quitting

In the years since that *Businessweek* article, I have discussed the dynamics of the Great Resignation with audiences from corporate executives to undergraduate students. One such occasion took place on a below-freezing February evening in Pocatello, Idaho. The Idaho State University College of Business invited me to spend a few days on campus and share my research and ideas. This included conducting what they had dubbed a "Masterclass" on leadership and employees' relationships with work. The audience was forty or so professionals, made up of graduate students and leaders from the local business community. I began the session by asking them a question that we'll unpack further in the next chapter: If you won enough money that you could live comfortably without ever having to work again, would you *keep working*?

I had asked the Lottery Question at many presentations over the years, so I wasn't surprised that, as usual, the vast majority of hands shot into the air to indicate they would keep working. But after posing it this time, I got a brilliant suggestion from one audience member. "You should ask the question again, but instead of asking how many of us would keep working, ask how many of us would keep working *at our current jobs* if we won the big one." So I threw it out to the audience.

Ask yourself this question right now: Would you keep working *at your current job* if you came into enough money that you no longer needed to work?

The number of "yes" hands in the air in that Idaho classroom? About three! As I recall, when I asked what jobs those three people had, all of them were entrepreneurs. My takeaway? These Idahoans clearly felt positively about working, but not nearly as positively about the version of work they were experiencing in their current roles.

Following that wintry evening in Pocatello, I kept asking that follow-up question: If you won the lottery, would you keep working *at your current job*? Whether the audience was groups of students, executives, or frontline workers, time and time again, the yeses would plunge from the majority of the room to 10 percent or lower. A massive drop.

On the surface, you could say that the difference between the number of people who would quit *their jobs* versus quit *working altogether* if they won the lottery shows that for most people, there is a crucial gap between what they want out of work versus what their current job provides. And if given the financial freedom to do so, most folks would quit their current job to try to close that gap.

But there is also a broader, perhaps more helpful way to interpret this. *Most of us are one event away from leaving our job.* This insight, that quitting is often triggered by a single event, is one of the most underacknowledged realities in our work lives today. And as I'll explain, not acknowledging this reality can have serious consequences for our career success and overall well-being.

You see, at a high level, our relationship with work is characterized by a trade-off. We invest our time and energy in our jobs, and we get back not just financial compensation and benefits but ideally some happiness and meaningfulness—two components which, as we'll discuss later, make up "the good life."

The relationship we have with our work is often stable and rational. We go about our lives in a sort of autopilot mode, focused on doing our jobs and living as rich a life as possible outside of work. Most of us don't spend every day calculating whether we should keep working at our current jobs—whether the benefits they provide outweigh the downsides. This is a good thing. Constantly questioning and ruminating on work is bad for our mental health.

But over the course of our days and lives, positive and negative events happen. We get a pat on the back from a colleague after completing a difficult task, or we pitch an idea we're excited about only to have our boss reject it. We get in a fight with our spouse, or we watch our child make the game-winning score in their football match. These events cause emotional reactions in us. A burst of pride after the pat on the back, or embarrassment at the public dismissal of our idea. Sadness following our marital spat, or joy in our child's post-goal celebration. These ebbs and flows make up the fabric of our personal and professional lives, and the smile or the sting they cause often comes and goes without our dwelling on it. We coast along.

But every once in a while, a constellation of factors comes together to create an event that knocks us out of autopilot. A big or small event, inside or outside of our jobs, causes us to stop and reflect on our relationship with work.

Those events are *jolts*. Jolts thrust the trade-off we have with work to the front of our minds, for scrutiny. They put our relationship with work under the microscope.

Sometimes, the result of this reflection is minimal. Imagine you've been belittled by your coworker Charles. The incident was so unpleasant that the thought flashed into your mind, *I gotta find another job, away from this guy*. But after thinking about it a bit more on your commute home, you conclude that, Charles aside, your job is a good fit for you. Too good to walk away from. So, you simply lower your opinion of Charles and go back into autopilot.

But in other cases, jolts lead us to think more deeply. We seriously question whether the trade-off still works for us—whether the benefits of staying still outweigh the costs of leaving. When this happens, the jolt can spur us to action. To increase or decrease the effort we put into our jobs. Or to silently stew about our work until we burn out. Or to speak up and tell our manager that things aren't working. Or to abruptly and impulsively, or slowly and deliberately, walk out the door—away from our current job or from work altogether.

Jolts aren't good or bad. They can be treasures, spurring us to make career changes that place us on the path to the good life. Or they can lead us astray and cause us to make decisions that harm our careers and our happiness. Like quitting when we should have stayed. Or staying when we should leap. And let's be real. For many of us, quitting isn't an option. When this is the case, jolts can be a recurring source of frustration and dissatisfaction, reminding us of our stuckness. Or they can stimulate career growth, pushing us to find creative ways to improve our relationship with our current job.

Despite the impact of jolts on our behavior and our careers, when it comes to explaining why workers do the things they do, including why they stay or leave, we tend to overlook the significance and power of these one-off events. As a result, jolts often catch us, and those around us, by surprise.

The problem with underrecognizing jolts and their effects is amplified when you consider how common they are: Jolts play a role in over half of all resignations (which themselves, as we'll discuss, are more common than you might think).

Moreover, dealing with the effects of jolts can be a lonely process, filled with doubts and incomplete information. Questioning the health of your relationship with your job is often frowned upon at work, and those outside of work may not fully understand your situation.

How we deal with jolts and their aftermath has meaningful consequences for our lives. When unacknowledged or managed poorly, jolts can lead to choices that reverberate throughout our careers. On the flip side, by learning to recognize the events that jolt your relationship with work, and respond to them constructively, you can have more control over your career, and gain more satisfaction from it, than you may have thought possible.

And for leaders, the stakes are multiplied. Jolts can wreak havoc on the well-being and performance of workers and teams. And the frustration and quitting caused by jolts are not just disruptive but also contagious. At the same time, leaders are arguably in the best position to insulate workers from the negative effects (and amplify the positive effects) of jolts before, during, and after they occur.

The Jolts Toolbox

There is no playbook for how to navigate these disruptive events. Thankfully, there is research to guide us. This research piqued my curiosity when I first came across it as a grad student, and it led me to study resignations. Over the past fifteen years of studying the topic, I've found that this science holds the potential to help workers navigate jolts in ways that improve their lives. And yet, it's not widely known.

The purpose of *Jolted* is to explore the dynamics of jolts, how they can rapidly change our relationship with our work and our jobs, and how to best navigate these events when they happen.

We will begin by looking into what jolts are and why they're so common and impactful these days. Then we'll dive into the standard way we respond to them—a baseline reaction that sometimes leads us astray. I'll briefly introduce the four broad actions we can take to deal with a jolt, and unpack the first one: setting the jolt aside and *carrying on*.

Then, we'll turn our attention to specific forms of jolts—the six types of jolts you'll meet in your life. First up are three types of jolts that stem from work: those that happen directly to you (direct jolts); those that come from events that happen to those around you (collateral jolts); and those that strike shortly after you've started a new job (honeymoon jolts). I'll make the case that the second response to jolts at work—*speaking up*—is often the optimal response, but it's also politically tricky and prone to failure. To cope with that trickiness, we'll engage with the art and science of how to speak up following a jolt in a way that creates positive change for you.

We'll then move outside the workplace, to the types of jolts that involve our personal lives. These include not only jolts that span our work and home lives and happen directly to us (crossover jolts) but also those that stem from events in broader society, that trigger us to rethink our work lives (remote jolts). And then there are the positive events in our lives (positive jolts), which operate via different psychological paths than negative jolts, broadening our minds to different life possibilities. Dealing with these jolts of a more personal nature sometimes requires us to *lean back* from our work. We'll discuss the thorny issue of how to shrink the size of work in your life without quitting and without jeopardizing your career success.

When the first three responses to jolts—carrying on, speaking up, or leaning back—are insufficient or inappropriate for dealing with a jolt, the final option is to resign. To *walk away*. When it comes to quitting, people often depart in ways that lead to regret or that harm their career. But this needn't be the case. We'll open the black box of the resignation process and explore it, from deciding to quit, to planning your resignation, to executing your plan.

In the book's final part, we'll turn our focus away from ourselves and reflect on how we can help others navigate the jolts in their lives. We're often in a position to help those close to us cope with the negative sides of jolts and capitalize on the positive sides. While true for everyone, this is especially so for leaders. So, we'll examine how leaders and non-leaders can foresee future jolts, detect them when they occur, positively shape their effects on others, and maintain strong relationships even when jolts lead to separation.

This book is designed to give you a toolbox of evidence-based ideas and techniques for anticipating and navigating the jolts in your life and in the lives of those around you—to respond to jolts in ways that enrich your well-being and career success. I hope that when you finish reading, you'll be able to use these tools to enhance, maintain, and sometimes repair a career that brings you satisfaction and meaning.

I've written this not just to be a work book, but a workbook. Many times, I'll invite you to pause and think about your job in a certain way. My hope is that this book is useful not only the first time you read it but will serve as a reference whenever you experience a jolt. Let's get to work.

PART I

Why Do We Quit Our Jobs?

CHAPTER ONE

THE LOTTERY QUESTION

How our answer to a dream question explains the effects of jolts on our relationship with work.

During the Great Resignation, as worker shortages caused major headaches for companies, there was a flurry of stories about businesses that had taped handwritten signs on their front doors explaining that they were closed or had reduced service because "no one wants to work anymore." Today, the statement still makes occasional appearances on business fronts and gets directed at pretty much every new generation that enters the workforce.

As an organizational psychologist, I try to understand how people feel about their jobs and why they feel that way. So when these news stories flash across my screen, the question that enters my mind is: Has something happened that has changed people's collective feeling about work, for the worse? Does, all of a sudden, no one want to work anymore?

It turns out that the phrase *No one wants to work anymore* dates to at least 1894, throwing some cold water on the *anymore* part. But who knows, maybe people's desire to work has been declining for the past 130+ years. Or perhaps "no one" has *ever* wanted to work, and those who post these signs are just reflecting that reality.

I don't come to this question as a blank slate. I have experience as an employee and manager in big and small companies. As an academic, I have a good grasp of the science of how people feel about their jobs. And

I get a steady stream of insights from the students and professionals I encounter in my work. My answer to this question, based on these different sources of evidence, is that *it depends*. Work can absolutely be a lasting source of meaning and happiness for some people. So much so that it can lead people to want to work even if they don't need to. There are plenty of people who can afford to retire yet keep working.

But critically, work doesn't provide happiness and meaning by default. Lots of elements need to be in place for work to have a positive effect on our lives rather than a drain on our well-being. While some jobs provide these elements, a glance at global employee engagement reports reveals that many jobs fail to be a force for good in workers' lives.

So, there's this tension between what work can be and what it often is. Applied to the century-old refrain of *No one wants to work anymore*, this tension offers another potential explanation for understaffing. Maybe the issue isn't that *people* don't want to work but that *jobs* increasingly don't work for people.

In studying these ideas, I eventually found a pretty compelling answer. It came in the form of another question—one that has been asked repeatedly since 1972 as part of the General Social Survey (GSS) in the US. Approximately every two years, the GSS asks a representative sample of people the same questions. The participants are different every time, so the survey results provide a snapshot of American attitudes at that moment. And these snapshots can be combined to give us a test of the statement *No one wants to work anymore*. The question that caught my attention has been dubbed the Lottery Question:

> **If you were to get enough money to live as comfortably as you would like for the rest of your life, would you continue to work or would you stop working?**

Note that the potential answers are "continue to work" or "stop working."

If, in general, people don't want to work anymore, then the GSS data should show that a steadily decreasing number of people have answered "continue to work" over the past fifty years. I looked into the data and found three insights.

Most people want to work. The first insight echoes what I mentioned in the intro. About 70 percent of Americans report that they would *keep working* even if they never needed to again. That percentage is a far cry from *no one*.

And it's not just Americans. The International Social Survey Programme runs a similar, less frequent survey on a global scale. Within their survey is a statement that gets to the gist of the Lottery Question: *I would enjoy having a paid job even if I did not need the money.* Participants from thirty-seven nations rate their agreement on this question from 1 = Strongly Disagree to 5 = Strongly Agree. Across the almost 50,000 people who answered this question in 2015 (the most recent survey), the mean response was 3.5. While there are differences among countries, the mean is above the midpoint for almost all of them, suggesting that most respondents agreed or strongly agreed. So, it's not just the States; most of the world's workers would enjoy having a job even if they didn't need the money attached to it.

The overwhelming majority of people *do* want to work.

People want to work as much now as they used to. The second insight came from the trend line of GSS responses to the Lottery Question from 1972 to 2018. It's as flat as a board. Don't get me wrong; this percentage fluctuated during those decades, from a high of 77 percent "continue working" in 1974 to a low of 65 percent just six years later, in 1980. But the slope of the trend line across the past five decades is pretty much zero. This absence of a meaningful downward angle casts serious doubt on the *anymore* part of *No one wants to work anymore*. On the contrary, these data suggest not only that most people *do* want to work but that the proportion of those who *don't* want to work hasn't changed for over a half century.

The pandemic caused fewer people to want to work ever again. The final insight is the most meaningful and timely one. In reporting the GSS numbers above, I left out the most recent versions of the survey. In the last year the GSS was conducted *before the COVID-19 pandemic*—2018—the percentage of respondents who said that they would *stop working* if they found themselves with all the money they wanted was 28 percent. When the survey was again conducted across 2020–21 (i.e., during the pandemic), that number had jumped . . . *to 38 percent*. That represents a 37 percent *increase* in the number of people reporting that they would quit working if they financially could. If you extrapolate that shift to the entire US workforce, it means that from 2018 to 2021, roughly 17 million more workers would quit working if they could. The survey was repeated in 2022 and 2024. The "stop working" percentage was 35 percent in both years, still far above what it was in 2018.

Taking these recent findings into account, the percentage of the population who do and do not want to work is *almost* unchanged since 1972. While the results still show that, overwhelmingly, most people want to work, these recent data also point to a moment of validity in the *anymore* part. Far fewer Americans wanted to work in 2021 than they did only a couple of years prior.

This jump in people who said they would *stop working* if they struck it rich aligned with a surge in workers actually quitting their jobs in 2021 and 2022. At its peak in late 2021, the Great Resignation saw workers in the US resign from their jobs at rates around 30 percent higher than in 2019 (a year that itself had the highest rates of quitting since recordkeeping began in 2000). The increases in the number of *stop working* responses on the GSS and the number of Americans resigning from their current jobs point to a shift in how people feel about work's place in their lives. And while this shift was most pronounced in the US, evidence suggests that it also occurred globally, with resignations reaching historic heights from the UK to Japan.

Keep in mind that this shift away from wanting to work occurred alongside the most worker-friendly job market in recent memory. Salaries were skyrocketing and nearly every company was hiring. Remote and hybrid work arrangements were plentiful. If anything, we should have seen a record high percentage of workers reporting that they would keep working if they won the lottery, not a record low percentage. What was going on in the hearts and minds of workers?

Answering that question requires digging deeper into our relationships with our jobs and, in particular, what causes us to leave them. Management researchers and leaders alike have been studying such "employee turnover" for over a century, and for most of that time, they would have had difficulty explaining why so many people wanted to stop working altogether amid one of the best job markets in history. They were trapped in an incomplete way of thinking about why employees quit their jobs—a way of thinking that still dominates today.

Pushed, Pulled, and Jolted

Throughout much of the history of the study of quitting, researchers focused on two reasons we quit our jobs: how satisfied we are with our current job, and what alternatives we have to that job. This very sensible approach provides really good insight into why and when we leave our jobs. If your job satisfaction declines, you increasingly feel *pushed* by growing unhappiness to consider leaving your job, right? At the same time, if attractive alternatives to your job become available, you feel *pulled* away by better opportunities, toward greener grass. These two forces work in tandem. If you're very content with your job, even highly attractive alternatives may fail to pull you toward resigning. On the flip side, if you're highly dissatisfied at work but have no other options for making a living, you won't feel much of an inner push toward the exit door.

This push-pull perspective has a great deal of intuitive appeal, and for good reason. It does explain why people quit their jobs in many cases. It's so intuitive and powerful that it remained the primary perspective in the academic turnover literature for most of the twentieth century. And in the minds of many leaders and pundits, this push-pull type of thinking still holds—that employees quit in a rational and calculated fashion, when the toxic parts of their job outweigh the good and/or when they become aware of better alternatives.

This perspective explains why my prediction that a wave of quitting was on the horizon seemed ridiculous to many. As one Forbes piece entitled "Why the 'Great Resignation' Is Greatly Exaggerated" questioned: "Will they quit en masse to spite their employers? No, they won't. In surveys, respondents can be brave and talk tough. When asked if people will quit their jobs if they're forced to go back to the office, they may honestly say 'yes' at that time. Given a little room to think about the reality of this decision, they'll quickly realize it's not such a smart decision to depart without another job offer in hand." This quote perfectly illustrates push-pull thinking—that people won't quit a job unless things get really bad at work or unless they have a good alternative.

But push-pull thinking doesn't tell the whole story. As reflected in a recent trend first observed in China and dubbed "naked resignations," people with no good alternatives frequently quit. On the opposite end of the spectrum, people who love their jobs regularly leave for other jobs. People who can't stand their work and have good alternatives sometimes stay. And in the worker-friendly job market following the pandemic, more of us than ever reported that we wanted to walk away from work altogether. Such "irrational" behavior flies in the face of push-pull thinking. It can leave leaders scratching their heads, and it did the same to academics for a long time. However, this started to change as researchers began to unearth the impact that *one-off events* have on us and our relationships with work and our jobs.

This unearthing began when researchers started examining how companies deal with unexpected events, such as crises. In 1982, management professor Alan Meyer observed that just as earthquakes disrupt the structures of buildings, external events shake companies. He used the term *environmental jolts* to describe them. Studying the real-world case of an unexpected doctors' strike and its effect on hospitals, Meyer explained different ways that companies respond to jolts and showed that those responses impact how they perform in the future. As we'll see, the same is true for the jolts in our lives. There are different ways to respond to them, each with different implications for our future well-being and success.

Around this same time, the academic study of entrepreneurship was born, and there was a race to explain what leads people to make the leap from traditional jobs into entrepreneurial ventures. Many of us dream of being our own boss, but due to how risky it is, relatively few are willing to make that dream a reality. In 1975, management professor Albert Shapero wrote an informative and entertaining article in *Psychology Today* based on his study of hundreds of new ventures. He offered an insight that, to him, explained why so many of the entrepreneurs he studied entered self-employment in the first place. "The simplest route [to entrepreneurship]," he said, "is falling on hard times." That's it. He called entrepreneurs "displaced persons" because he saw most of them as people who had entered self-employment reluctantly. He went on to list all sorts of *events* that jolted the entrepreneurs in his study from their "nice, familiar niche" in their former jobs into launching a new venture: being fired, being passed over for a promotion, experiencing an organizational change, or (in a positive twist) being pitched a business idea by a friend.

A few years later, Shapero and colleague Lisa Sokol expanded this explanation by discussing why actual refugees seemed particularly likely to become entrepreneurs. They explained that most of us are pinned into our current life trajectory by pressures from family obligations, financial responsibilities, and *plain old inertia*. Breaking out of this autopilot and charting a new course rarely happens purely as a result of our initiative; there has to be a "powerful force" that jolts us into switching life paths. For the refugees they studied, these inertia-breaking events tended to stem from religious persecution or political oppression. Similarly, for the nonrefugee entrepreneurs that Shapero and Sokol studied, it was a displacing event, most commonly a single negative occurrence, that jarred them loose from their traditional careers and opened their eyes to an unrealized desire to start their own businesses.

These early studies laid the groundwork for a breakthrough in our understanding of quitting, in 1994. Thomas Lee and Terence Mitchell, two researchers at the University of Washington, published a paper that directly challenged the push-pull perspective. Importantly, their theory included push-pull turnover causes, wherein people slowly become dissatisfied at work, eventually reaching a point that leads them to start a job search or to quit without another job in hand.

But the basis for their "Unfolding Model of Turnover" is that the road to quitting often begins with a jarring event, "any expected or unexpected change . . . that shakes an employee out of a steady state or challenges the status quo with respect to his or her thinking about the job." These events—which they referred to as *shocks*—can be positive, negative, or neutral. The key element is that, like winning the lottery would do to most of us, they snap us out of our usual mode of thinking about our relationship with work. Anyone who has experienced or witnessed a midlife (or quarter-life) crisis has seen or felt what happens when someone living life in autopilot is suddenly jolted out of it.

Over the past three decades, researchers have found support for the predictions of the Unfolding Model. In one study of nurses who had recently quit their jobs, half the cases involved a jolt. In a subsequent study of around 200 people who recently left accounting firms, researchers found that just over 40 percent of jolts came from events at work, 40 percent came from opportunities outside of work (e.g., an unexpected job offer), and 20 percent came from jolts in workers' personal lives. Such findings, that at least half of quitters report that a specific event jump-started their quitting process, have been replicated in studies around the globe. As one example from Australia: Management researchers studied exit interview transcripts of over 200 people who voluntarily left an Australian marketing firm. In over two-thirds of cases, it was a jolt that triggered the turnover process. Even among those who didn't experience a jolt, many reported there being a "final straw" that pushed them over the edge to quit.

The takeaway from the Unfolding Model and subsequent tests of it are clear. As stated by management professor Brooks Holtom (who studied turnover alongside Lee and Mitchell for decades), "precipitating events, or shocks, cause voluntary turnover more often than accumulated job dissatisfaction." Put another way, when employees are asked whether there was a specific event that caused them to start thinking about leaving, the answer is often yes.

I first came across the Unfolding Model in my doctoral studies. At the time, I had worked as a manager for the prior decade, in a large organization and then in an entrepreneurial venture, and also gotten my MBA. I thought I had a pretty good grasp on what motivates employees to stay or go. My thinking was firmly rooted in the idea that the negative parts of our jobs, like low pay or an incompetent boss, are what push us to quit, along with the appeal of better alternatives that pull us away. End of story. But as I learned about the Unfolding Model and reflected on the times I had quit jobs, my employees quit jobs, and my peers quit jobs, I realized that in many cases, a specific event had kicked off the process. All this time, I had understood only half of the story.

After learning about it, I kept thinking about the Unfolding Model and my own resignation stories, those of my friends, family, and former colleagues, and of my former employees. In many of these stories, a pebble-size event had started the eventual avalanche of reflection leading to a person's resignation. And moreover, the avalanche could have been avoided or made less disruptive if it had been recognized by the person experiencing it and by those around them.

You may take a moment now to reflect on your own life and the lives of those around you, and think of the jolts you've experienced. Those events, big and small, that have knocked you and others out of autopilot.

Once you shift your mindset to looking for these specific events, you'll start seeing jolts and their most dramatic effect—quitting—everywhere. A legendary football coach has a revelation that leads him to announce his resignation in the middle of a winning season. The deaths of a family member and a close friend cause a future first lady to walk away from a lucrative career in corporate law. The most famous voice in television quits a new show after a producer tells her to tone down the emotion when she says her name. A terrorist attack thousands of miles away spurs a star athlete to leave sports behind and join the military. Reaching a milestone birthday causes an actor to reassess life and walk away from show business.

These are some of the stories we'll visit in this book—the types of stories that, along with the Unfolding Model, inspired me to study resignations. I'm not interested only in why employees quit, though; I'm enthusiastically curious about *how* people quit their jobs. This curiosity stems from my own work experience. To me, deciding whether to quit a job was often tough, but equally difficult was figuring out the best way to do it. And I could tell I wasn't alone because I observed people resigning in ways that unintentionally burned bridges or that added unnecessary rockiness to their career transition. Adding to my interest is the fact that poorly executed resignations are harmful to the employees left behind and impactful to firms. And finally, quitting is more common than most of us realize. In the US, the generation currently exiting the workforce switched jobs, on average, 12.7 times between the ages of eighteen and fifty-six. While promotions and terminations account for some of these switches, there's a whole lot of quitting going on as well.

Despite the complexity, stakes, and prevalence of jolts, pretty much no prior research had studied what happens *after* you make the decision to quit. How do you go about resigning? Who do you tell? How much notice should you give?

So, I began studying resignations—what happens after a jolt leads you to make the decision to quit. Whenever people ask what I study, I tell them, and then we're off, talking through the twists and turns of different stories of quitting. It turns out, people generally love telling their quitting stories. Better still, these events are memorable, so the stories they tell tend to be reliable and accurate. And finally, because resigning is such an unusual process, with few rules or precedents, the stories are usually pretty juicy.

I'll dive more into the stories and research later in the book, but for now, what's relevant is this: I found that what drove people to quit their jobs in positive ways (e.g., giving lots of notice, training their replacement) versus negative ways (e.g., badmouthing the company on the way out, giving little notice) often related to the jolt that triggered the turnover process in the first place. Whether someone is a bridge burner versus a courteous leaver isn't caused by whether they're a bad or good person but by the events that happen to them inside and outside of work.

Pretty early on in my studies, something started nagging at me. I was largely ignoring those who had experienced jolts and yet did *not* quit. These stories never make headlines. Yet they're just as important. People who wanted to leave but decided to stay loyal. People who simply couldn't quit for one reason or another and, having been jolted out of autopilot, had to figure out how to preserve their well-being while continuing to work in a deficient job. Those who decided to stay and work to fix the relationship and the problems with it, rather than starting over. And those who stayed and ultimately regretted doing so.

Quitting is just one option when jolts occur, and it's often not the best one. In those post-jolt moments, it's critical to understand all your options and how to choose the best one. This is especially true given that jolts aren't only common and impactful, but they're becoming more so.

Making the Wrong Career Decision Is Easier Than Ever

People often take hasty, rash, and incorrect action in the wake of a jolt because taking immediate action, especially quitting, feels both more urgent and more simple than ever.

First, the urgency. How many times over the past few months have you looked at your phone at work and read news of a disaster? COVID-19 didn't just cause a pandemic, it amplified an ongoing "infodemic" in which we are inundated with news and stories about bad things happening around the globe. Terms like *doom scrolling* and *revenge bedtime procrastination* are now permanent fixtures in our vocabulary. And while the pandemic is in the rearview mirror, the infodemic is not; we're continually alerted to surprisingly pleasant or (much more often) shockingly sad or unjust events taking place in the world.

In addition, over the past few decades many of us have experienced a slow but steady erosion of the boundaries between our work and personal lives. For most of us, gone are the days when we head off to work and mentally disconnect from the outside world during our workdays. As the comedian Chris Rock humorously observed, "My father used to leave for work at 6:30 in the morning and come home at 8:30 at night. And during the day, he and my mother had absolutely no contact at all. None, okay? That's what a relationship used to be. The kids could have been dead, but he wouldn't have found out until he got home." Rock contrasted that with how we work today, where right after we leave home for work in the morning and throughout the day, we are in almost nonstop contact with those outside of work, and receiving news from the "outside world."

And for many of us, gone also are the days when we leave work at the end of the day and don't deal with it again until we physically return to the workplace the next morning. Thanks to technology, work follows us home in the forms of formal (e.g., email) and informal (e.g., group chat) communication related to different aspects of our jobs.

And then there's the effect that jolts can have on our careers and lives. Jolts often trigger emotional reactions that interfere with our decision-making. And if there's ever a time when you need to be able to think lucidly, it's when you're determining whether your relationship with your job is healthy, and what steps to take (if any) if it isn't. The wrong decisions in the wake of jolts—quitting a job when you should have stayed, keeping silent when you should have spoken up, or remaining loyal to a company that doesn't deserve it—can have lasting consequences for how happy you are in your career and whether you reach your desired career potential.

And despite the stakes, making a bad career decision is easier and more tempting than ever. It's all just a click away. It's easy to see how technology has transformed the dating market; it has done the same thing to the job market. The ease of applying for other jobs in the wake of a jolt was captured in mid-2023 when for a brief moment, the term *rage applying* went viral. Imagine that your boss has just taken credit for one of your ideas, or your company just made their vacation time policy more restrictive. In the not-so-distant past, such an event may have jolted you into looking for another job, but you'd have to wait until you had the time and energy to do so, at which point your feelings of anger or unfairness may have subsided. Not anymore. Rage applying involves pulling out your phone and applying for multiple jobs with a few clicks and swipes, in the immediate wake of the negative event. And if that leads to an interview, it can be conducted virtually, as soon as that same day.

Beyond the ease of applying for different jobs, more than ever people can seek out different types of work. There are now all sorts of alternatives to traditional work, perhaps most notably gig work (i.e., when jobs are divided into small, short-term tasks and then contracted out to workers via some sort of [usually online] platform). The reality for most of us is that we cannot up and quit our jobs, because we need the pay and benefits that come along with it. But millions of workers have experienced being part of the gig economy, learning how to supplement or temporarily replace their income. For these individuals, the bar for quitting is lower, because they have the ever-present ability to generate some income as they conduct their job search.

Moreover, the increased availability of flexible work has lowered commute-based hurdles that used to restrict our job searches. Not long ago, we could apply only to jobs located within a reasonable five-day-per-week commute and that were somewhat convenient for our personal and family obligations (e.g., kids' school and extracurricular activities). But what about a hybrid job in which you have to commute only two days per week? We can tolerate a longer commute two days per week (especially if we get to choose which days), which means we can expand the geographic area of our job searches. And if you work in a field where your job can be done remotely, you may no longer need to place any geographic limitations on your job search.

And finally, what if someone does have the financial ability to bridge themselves for a few months or a year while they conduct a job search or recharge their batteries? It used to be that such résumé gaps, or career breaks, were frowned upon. But hiring committees have started to learn that taking a break from work in the midst of one's career is okay, and (gasp) perhaps even healthy. Leaders are slowly opening their minds to the reality that stepping away from work for extended periods of time is a good thing and contributes to people's well-being and sustained productivity. We have a long way to go, but one more barrier that holds people back from seriously considering resigning following a jolt—the dreaded résumé gap—is weakening.

For a multitude of reasons, the bar for quitting has been lowered.

This lower bar has a lot of benefits for workers. Those who are in toxic situations are better able to extract themselves, and people are better able to craft careers that fit their needs at different life stages. But alongside those benefits are dangers. Quitting, of course, is risky. For every person who is glad they resigned, there's another who regrets doing so. The availability of alternatives and their ease of access makes it easier to experience a jolt and resign in response to it rather than taking time to consider your options and the short- and long-term consequences of each one. If you want to have a satisfying career, you must be able to recognize when you experience a jolt and then process it in a manner that best serves your long-term well-being (even though it may require short-term sacrifices).

And many of you aren't only workers but also leaders. Failing to recognize when your employees experience jolts, help them make sense of these events, and navigate their effects represents missed opportunities to more deeply engage workers, reduce regrettable turnover, and buffer your business against external events. Employees enter into cycles of job searching more commonly than most managers realize. In any given month, greater than 20 percent of all employed workers actively search for other jobs. While this could be viewed as a threat, the reality is that when employees are in this search process, there's also an opportunity to strengthen their relationships with their current jobs. As we'll discuss, the reason that many people experience regret after they quit is that they misjudge some element as they calculate the trade-offs between their current job and another opportunity (or they skip this calculus altogether). If leaders recognize these crucial moments, they can react in ways that create wins for workers and for the organization. As it stands, all too often, leaders miss or ignore signs that their employees have been jolted and are in the midst of rethinking their relationship with their job. They only learn about the seriousness of the situation in the resignation meeting, at which point it is almost always too late.

For the sake of your own career and those of the people close to you, your ability to respond to jolts in constructive ways is critical. But doing so isn't simple, and in some ways, it's getting tougher. Gone are the days when we spend months, years, and decades in autopilot, dutifully going to work and not questioning our relationship with it or exploring something better. Or go years without experiencing jolts that cause us to rethink our jobs, who we are, and what our priorities in life are. Instead, we're bombarded with events inside and outside of work that have the potential to jolt us.

Push-pull thinking will get you only so far. You have to broaden your mindset to consider the sometimes dramatic effects that jolts can have on our relationships with work. But knowing what jolts are is only the beginning. The next step is getting our arms around *when* life's events jolt us.

CHAPTER TWO

EVERYDAY EVENTS, EXTRAORDINARY EFFECTS

Often, it's the small events in our lives that cause jolts. Learn to recognize these moments and navigate initial reactions to them.

In the middle of the 2023–24 English Premier League season, Liverpool Football Club held the top spot in the standings. The club was helmed by manager Jürgen Klopp, who had spent the prior decade leading Liverpool to win every major trophy in the sport. As a result, he was widely recognized as one of the top managers in the game, a club icon, and an all-time great. With Klopp only fifty-six years old and the team performing as well as ever, Liverpool supporters could rest more soundly than almost any other club, knowing that their team had a proven leader with many years of winning ahead of him.

But what no one knew at the time is that a few months prior, Klopp had experienced a jolt.

On January 26, 2024, the club posted a video in which Klopp announced that the season would be his last. He went on to describe why he decided to resign. The story began at a mundane meeting a few months prior, in which he and other staff members discussed plans for the following season. Groundwork, such as what players to try to acquire in the offseason, has to start being laid almost a year in advance. It was this event—planning for the next season—that triggered a sudden thought to pop into his mind: "I am not sure I am here then anymore."

In the resignation video, Klopp said that he surprised himself with that thought. But critically, he didn't ignore the jolt. Instead, he reflected on it. Later in the interview, he discussed two distinct conclusions from his reflection.

First, he could see that his energy, while still strong, was going to run low in the future. I love how he explained it: *I'm like a proper sports car—not the best one but a pretty good one, can still drive 160, 170, 180 mph but I'm the only one who sees the tank meter is going down. The outside world doesn't see that, that's good, so you go until as long as we have to go, but then you need a break. In this case, you need to go to the petrol station.*

Second, he wanted to try out a different identity, one other than the über-famous leader of one of the biggest sports teams on the planet. He spoke of his need to look for a different purpose and to just be a normal guy. "I don't want to wait until I am too old for having a normal life."

An everyday planning meeting served as a jolt that led to a decision that shocked the football world. Only time will tell if Klopp is ultimately content with his decision, but his ability to recognize the deeper meaning behind a sudden and surprising thought contains lessons for us all about how to identify and respond to jolts.

More Than a Case of the Mondays

Take a moment to think about yesterday as if it was "a continuous series of scenes or episodes in a film." Could you describe each episode, from when you woke up to when you dozed off to sleep? How much time did you spend on each one? Who did you spend it with?

In a 2004 study, Nobel Prize–winning economist Daniel Kahneman and his colleagues asked one thousand working adults to go through this exercise, describing each episode in writing. The resulting data gave the research team a sense of how people tend to spend their time on a given day. The largest chunk of our daily hours is associated with work (6.9 hours). Other activities like eating, commuting, watching television, and spending time on our phone each take up around one to two hours per day. The researchers also examined with whom, if anyone, each episode was spent—family, friends, customers, alone, and so on.

The next part of the study is where things got interesting. They asked participants to then go back through each episode, and report *how they felt* during each one, in terms of positive and negative emotions. That way, the researchers could pinpoint the most and least pleasant aspects of people's daily lives.

The most positive daily activities were intimate relations, socializing, and relaxing, and the most positive interactions with others were with friends and then family. The least positive activities were commuting, working, and doing housework, and the least positive interactions with others were with oneself (being alone), followed by one's boss and then coworkers.

You may not be floored by the results of this study, but for those who work traditional work schedules, these findings explain why so many of us experience the "scaries" on Sunday evenings or "a case of the Mondays" the following morning at work. In general, we like our jobs less than the other parts of our lives. While not shocking, these findings are important, because this relative distaste can create problems when it comes to recognizing and responding to jolts. After all, if our default feeling about our current work is more negative than other activities in our life, we become accustomed to categorizing negative work events, even the jolting ones, as normal. Going back to Klopp, he could have easily chalked up his thoughts of resigning to the usual stress that comes with the grind of a long season. In this way, it becomes easy for us to ignore or not notice jolts at times when they should trigger us to ask deeper questions about work.

Rather than resisting jolts and blocking them out, or reacting to every one of them, our goal should be to acknowledge them, engage with them at an appropriate level, and respond to them in a constructive manner. By appropriate and constructive, I mean in a way that maximizes their positive effects, and minimizes their negative effects, on our well-being. The first step on this journey is simple, but not easy. It's recognizing that we've experienced a jolt. The fact is, dozens of potentially jolting events happen in our lives every day, but only a subset of them force us out of autopilot. By understanding what makes an everyday event turn into a jolt, we put ourselves in a better position to deal with it constructively. Let's dig a little deeper into the distinction between everyday events and jolts.

A Richter Scale for Work and Life Events

When does a potential jolt become an actual one? Perhaps even one that knocks us into a whole new way of thinking about our relationship with work?

Let me level with you here—this isn't an easy question to answer. On any given day, there are hundreds of different factors that affect how we think and feel. The presence or absence of any one of those factors can shape how we respond to the events of our day. Let's take one of those seemingly mundane factors to illustrate why it's so difficult to know just when an event will jolt us: your sleep.

I doubt you need convincing that the quality of your sleep affects you in all sorts of meaningful ways. There is a mountain of evidence that when our sleep quality is low, it harms almost every aspect of our well-being, inside and outside of work. On the flip side, the morning after a good night's sleep, we tend to be in a healthier, higher energy, and more resilient mental space.

So, when a potentially jolting event happens, we're better able to respond to it in a clear-eyed, constructive manner if we're well rested. But here's where it gets tricky. Imagine your boss aims a condescending remark at you in the morning meeting. The positive mental state that proper sleep provides should make you more resilient to the slight—letting it pass in one ear and out the other. Yet equally plausible is that your sharpened mental state could actually give you the clarity to realize that you're not working for the right person, and you need to enact a plan to find a better boss. Complicating matters further, imagine this happened the morning after an awful night's sleep. The bad sleep could make you cranky and particularly prone to react negatively to the rude comment. At the same time, it could make you so mentally foggy that you pay no notice to the remark, not even registering it as negative.

Sleep is but one of the many factors in our lives that has hard-to-predict effects on how we respond to everyday events. Our commute, exercise, diet, relationships, time spent outdoors, and so on, all play similar roles. In addition to these "situational" factors (i.e., the things around us that affect how we feel at any given moment), there is another source of messiness when it comes to how we respond to the events in our lives: our personality.

Each of us is made up of a unique constellation of individual differences. An event that jolts one person may be the same event that causes another person to love their job even more. Think of being in a company-wide meeting where the CEO puts you on the spot and asks for your opinion. For introverts, that could be *the* terrifying experience that makes them realize that they are not a good fit for this organizational culture. For extroverts, the opportunity to share their thoughts in front of the whole firm may be a wonderful experience that deepens their commitment to the company.

The point I'm trying to make is that because of the variety inherent in our daily lives and our individual makeups, I know of no formula, and I don't think there ever could be one, that will tell you *exactly* when a given event will become a jolt. It really does depend on the person and the day. But that doesn't mean we're completely in the dark.

Feeling-Thinking-Acting

Think of the last jolting event that happened to you: something that made you stop and question whether you needed to make some serious changes in your work life.

Can you remember how you responded, both in the immediate aftermath and in the days following?

One of the most useful theories in organizational psychology explains, at a high level, how we respond to events. *Affective events theory* says that we usually have an immediate *emotional* reaction to daily events, that is shaped by our personality. Imagine that a coworker takes credit for a goal that you achieved. A common immediate reaction would be a flash of anger. Such a response would be especially likely if you're an anger-prone person.

Following that initial emotional reaction, the thinking side of our brain kicks in. We have a *cognitive* reaction based on deeper consideration of the situation, along with, again, our personality. That thinking could involve asking ourselves why we're at a job with such awful coworkers, fueling further anger. Or it could involve recalling that the coworker who stole your credit has spent the past year battling health issues and is afraid of being fired. In that case, your anger could very well melt into sympathy, especially if you're an empathetic person.

In terms of jolts, this framework simply tells us that for an event to become a jolt, it must be significant enough to cause a fairly strong emotional reaction that triggers broader reflection on our relationship with work.

After feeling and thinking, we respond *behaviorally* to the event. This could involve doing nothing and simply moving past the incident. Or you may talk to your colleague about how their credit-claiming made you feel. Or you may tell your boss that it's actually you who deserves the credit. Or you may book some anger therapy sessions. In general, when something happens to us, we feel, we think, and then we act, with our personality playing a supporting role along the way.

Of course, some events are more powerful than others, and researchers have pinpointed three factors that, when combined, provide a rough scale we can use to weigh events and see how strong they are. The more these factors are present in a given event, the more likely it is that the event will trigger the whole feeling-thinking-acting process. In other words, they shape whether an event will shake you out of autopilot and compel you to question your relationship with work. When you find yourself in this space, recognizing these factors can help you *identify the event* that triggered this questioning—a critical first step in deciding how to respond to it.

Go back to that last event in your life that was a jolt—that caused you to stop and question your relationship with your work. Let's revisit that event through the lens of these three factors and see if it gives you any insight into why that particular event shook you out of autopilot.

First, was the event that caused your jolt *novel*, that is, something that was different from what you normally experience, or something that hadn't happened to you before? Even if they're small, unusual events catch and hold our attention. Take, for example, the simple act of saying your name. Something you do every time you make an order at a coffee shop or introduce yourself to a new acquaintance. And if you're Oprah Winfrey, it's something you do at the start of every broadcast. By the time she joined the news program *60 Minutes* in 2017, Oprah was one of the biggest stars on the planet, having said her name at the top of thousands of broadcasts. But something unusual happened when she said, "I'm Oprah Winfrey," while recording her first stories for *60 Minutes*. The producers told her that "there's too much emotion in your voice." That seemingly trivial comment was novel; you don't expect people to tell you to tone down how you say your name. And that novelty amplified the strength of that event and its impact for her. In explaining why she walked away from *60 Minutes* after doing only five segments, Oprah pointed to that event.

Next, how *disruptive* was the event? How much did it change your routine and shake up the status quo in your life? Let's consider two equally unfair events. In the first case, you're passed over for a special assignment that you felt you deserved. In the second case, you're told that you need to start coming into the office on Saturday mornings to work a half day. Which event will more likely lead to a jolt? The first scenario is no doubt upsetting and will stir up some negative feelings. But in terms of how disruptive it is to your current life, the impact is fairly low. You'll continue in your current role. The second scenario will likewise generate negative emotions, but working on Saturdays also blows up your weekend. It carries extra disruption to your personal life, so it will be more likely to jolt you out of autopilot and cause you to stop and ask yourself some serious questions about your relationship with work.

Finally, how *critical* was the event to you? Think about times that you've been on a work team that failed or missed a deadline. Did everyone on the team respond in the same way? I'd guess not. The outcome of projects is rarely of equal importance to all team members. It was perhaps more critical to the leader of the team and to new employees than it was to the veteran team members, whose careers are less impacted by a small failure. As another example, think about witnessing a coworker being treated abusively by your boss. This will probably be disturbing in any case. But if the person being abused is a junior colleague who has become your informal mentee, it will feel critical to you, especially compared to a case in which the victim is a high-status employee you don't know very well. It almost goes without saying, but the importance *to you* of a work event and those involved in it will determine its likelihood of becoming a jolt.

Novelty, disruption, and criticality. When you experience an event that could potentially become a jolt, it may just come and go, without causing any reaction. But if the event is novel and/or disruptive and/or critical to you, the odds go up that it will elicit a strong emotional reaction followed by thinking "What happened here?" In other words, the event will make you stop at the thinking phase and try to make sense of the situation. *This is the jolt.* Where, instead of registering the event as something that makes sense in the course of our lives, or something that generates a straightforward behavioral response, we mentally flag it as something that needs our direct attention to figure out.

This "figuring out" process is often referred to as *sensemaking*, a term coined by organizational theorist Karl Weick to explain the process that often unfolds during crises. During impactful events, we try to make sense of the situation, starting by asking ourselves and others, "What the heck is going on?" This questioning happens during the event and then it continues in retrospect. As most of us have experienced firsthand, sensemaking during a crisis is challenging and often leads to poor decision-making. The same applies to the mini crises in our lives that appear as jolts. Jolts often push us into an uncomfortable space where we attempt to sort out what happened and how we feel about it, amid our ongoing personal and professional demands.

Trying to make sense of our relationship with work, in response to a jolt, typically requires time and mental energy. We'll get to that process in the next chapter, but before we do, it's important to note that in some cases, the whole feeling-thinking-acting process happens almost simultaneously. The jolt triggers a seemingly automatic response. Effectively navigating jolts requires understanding these situations and preparing for them.

The Jolts Rapid Response System

In my dissertation research, I heard the story of one worker whose boss, one day, not only insulted the worker but insulted the worker's daughter as well, just out of spite. Immediately, the worker took out his keys, set them on his desk, and walked out for good.

In such cases, a jolt is so egregious that the feeling-thinking-acting process happens all at once and causes immediate quitting. Researchers call this *impulsive quitting* and, in studying why people walk away from their jobs without any future plans, have found that these types of quits are almost always preceded by a singular event that causes a sharp spike in negative emotions. That's because, whether we realize it or not, we have internal thresholds that, if crossed by certain events, trigger immediate action. Thankfully, these aren't limited to highly negative events that spur the "flight" side of our fight-or-flight response. Going back to our old friend the lottery, many of those who play the game have plans in mind for what they would do if they won. These are *if-then* plans. *If* I win the lottery, *then* I'm going to go buy a yacht and sail around the world. If-then planning automates the first step following the event.

It turns out that many of us have at least some if-then plans in our minds when it comes to certain work events. Even if we don't realize it. Lee and Mitchell—the researchers who developed the Unfolding Model of Turnover—proposed that when jolts lead to quitting, they do so by guiding us down one of three paths. We'll focus on the first path here, and come back to the other two at the end of this chapter. In this first path, a jolt occurs—it could be good, bad, or neutral—and employees have a predetermined plan in their mind for what to do next. I think of this as the *prepper* path, named after those who make proactive preparations for different emergencies and disasters. In this case, workers have plans in place for what to do if certain events happen at work (or in their personal lives) and they need or want to bail. You may have some of these plans in your mind right now. If I don't get this promotion, I'm going to apply for a job at a competitor. If we're able to adopt a baby, I'm going to become a stay-at-home parent. If my company's proposed purchase by a private equity firm is approved, I'm going to quit and finally go to art school.

This if-then rapid response to jolts has been represented in various buzzwords over the years. The term *career cushioning* had a moment of virality. Career cushioning refers to "quietly scoping out a plan B"; keeping other potential jobs lined up in case something happens at your current job that makes you want to leave. A coarser phrase is *f-ck you money*.

The idea behind the notion of f-ck you money is that you have a nest egg of funds set aside such that if you ever face a particularly negative event at work, you have the financial ability to leave rather than stay and put up with it. Those who have set aside an expletive-dubbed amount of money are ready for certain jolts. When one occurs, they quit and put their stockpile to use, bridging them until they find another job.

Chances are, the if-then plans that we currently have in mind haven't been carefully considered. They may even surprise us when we activate them, and only in hindsight do we realize that we reacted automatically, without careful thought. But of course, we can also be thoughtful and deliberate in making if-then plans. And doing so can simplify and strengthen our future decision-making in the wake of jolts.

The power of making if-then plans has been most strikingly demonstrated when it comes to staying on track as we pursue goals that we set for ourselves. Every year, as January 1 rolls around, much advice is published about how to stick to common New Year's resolutions, like getting in better physical shape or drinking less. And one of the best pieces of advice they give is to make if-then plans for what you'll do when things inevitably go wrong. If you skip a workout or have a wild night out with friends, how will you get back on track?

Similarly, if your goal is to have a happy and successful career, if-then planning can be a useful tool. Sure, making these plans requires some effort, but as described by cognitive psychologist Annie Duke in her book *Quit*, "exploring other opportunities and at least having a *start* on a backup plan is a cornerstone of making quitting easier." If you take the time now to develop some if-then plans for future jolts in your career, then when you meet that jolt, you'll be ready to respond to it.

Proactively Schedule a Work Relationship Check-In

Jolts trigger us to stop and reevaluate our relationship with work. By definition, this is a reactive process. This reactivity puts us at an immediate disadvantage when trying to deal with jolts in the best possible way. Because jolts are unscheduled, we're often not in the optimal mental state to deal with them. Here, I'd like to suggest a tactic for getting ahead of jolts. My recommendation? Make a regular date night with your job.

I'd better explain what I mean pretty quickly, because that last sentence was weird. Anyone who's been in a long-term relationship has probably heard or read the advice to schedule a regular date night with your partner. The thinking is, committing the time to go on a date amid the hecticness of life can create dedicated space to talk about your relationship and strengthen it, boost your mood as a result of spending time together, and provide opportunities to have new shared experiences and make new memories.

Let's zero in on a date night's communication benefits. When you and your better half dedicate time for each other, it gives you a chance to check in on the health of your relationship and deal with any issues that have arisen, or that may arise. It's the same principle behind regular family meetings—let's strengthen these personal relationships by not letting problems fester and by talking about any upcoming challenges and opportunities.

Similarly, having a regular check-in (let's not actually call it a date night) with your job can hold similar benefits for your relationship with it, especially when it comes to navigating jolts. One side of these benefits comes from it being a *proactive* process, where you have dedicated time to think about the health of your relationship with your work. As opposed to reacting to events as they happen, being proactive at work is associated with higher well-being and career success. If you notice problems in your work relationship, you can deal with them largely decoupled from the feeling-thinking-acting process tied to any one event. The feeling has already come and gone, and you have postponed your thinking and acting until a later date.

Second, and as importantly, when jolts happen, you'll be less disrupted because you'll know that you have a process for dealing with them. The problem with jolts becoming more common than ever is that they can put us in a near-constant state of thinking about our jobs. I'll repeat—such ruminating isn't good for our well-being. A scheduled check-in can help keep this rumination at bay. When a jolt happens, you can note it as something to reflect on at your next check-in and, hopefully, move on. Obviously, this may not work for egregious jolts, but it will keep you from continually dwelling on the health of your relationship with work.

Finally, creating dedicated space to reflect on work events and their meaning will increase the chances that you'll recognize the patterns between, and the problems underlying, different events in your work life and will have epiphanies about how to resolve them. Erik Dane, a researcher who studies epiphanies, argues that we're more likely to experience positive epiphanies when we deliberately put ourselves in a "psychologically ready" state. With regular check-ins, we're proactively moving ourselves out of autopilot and calmly learning to process any new insights pertaining to our relationship with work.

With a romantic partner, date nights should probably be every week or month. Work relationship check-ins needn't be as frequent. I tend to do this every six months—at the start of a new year, and in the summer. Your work anniversary could make a nice annual milestone as well. Much of the time, I feel that the relationship is healthy, so my check-in is pretty brief. But at other times, there's a problem or opportunity I need to consider. When this happens, I usually find myself on one of the other two paths Lee and Mitchell identified.

Hitting the Pause and Ponder Buttons

When you experience a jolt, but you don't have an if-then plan in mind, it can cause you to pause and say, "I *may* need to leave this job." I think of this as the *pauser* path. Here, you don't think about the external job market, only about whether you can stomach continuing to work at your job and institution. This path can lead us to quit with no future plans in mind, driven only by the unhappiness that the jolt uncovered.

And finally there's the *ponderer* path. What's unique about this path is that your decision process following a jolt is slower, because it involves full consideration of "what the heck am I going to do if I quit my job?" Here, you experience a jolt, causing you to weigh the pros and cons of your current work situation *relative to other alternatives available to you*. This path can be a long one; most of us have experienced months or years during which we deliberated the benefits and drawbacks of leaving a current job, after being jolted into that space by a singular event. This is why I'm never surprised by reports that some large percentage of employees are planning to quit their jobs in the next year. At any given moment, a good portion of us are on this pondering path, trying to determine whether staying or going is the right move.

So, what do you do when a jolt turns you into a pauser or ponderer? How do you find your way to the optimal end of these paths, to a correct decision regarding whether to stay or leave? You have to return to the scene of the jolt, and figure out whether it has revealed a problem or opportunity that needs to be acted upon. Entering this space of questioning your relationship with work, between the jolt and your reaction to it, requires zooming out from the events of our daily lives, and thinking more broadly about our pursuit of the good life.

CHAPTER THREE

GETTING TO THE ROOT OF THE JOLT

Putting jolts and your relationship with work in perspective.

Neil Jones, a tiler from north central England, won a £2.4 million lottery jackpot in 2010. His first purchase? A pool table, on which he practiced almost nonstop after retiring early from his tiling career. Fast-forward to 2023, and he was living his dream of captaining the national team at the European Pool Championships in Malta.

A few years before Jones's win, Callie Rogers became the youngest lottery winner in UK history, winning £2 million at the age of sixteen. At the time, she was working at the checkouts of a local supermarket. Like Jones, she quit her job. But then, she proceeded to quickly spend all her winnings, largely on frivolous items (as many of us would have done at that age). After using up the money, she reported that the whole ordeal made her miserable, and she regrets how she handled it.

When the fun question "What would you buy if you won the lottery?" comes up at group gatherings, someone will inevitably chime in with "You know, winning the lottery doesn't actually make people happier." Are these Debbie Downers right? Does hitting the lottery have no effect, or even a negative effect, on winners' happiness? This isn't an easy question to answer, because people who win the jackpot are relatively few in number and often prefer to remain anonymous. They're hard to study. But researchers have made solid efforts despite this difficulty.

The notion that winning the lottery does *not* increase one's happiness is backed by the most frequently cited lottery study. This 1978 study compared twenty-two lottery winners in the US state of Illinois to a matched sample* of twenty-two nonwinners from the same area. Not only were the winners no happier than the nonwinners, but they also appeared to be less able to take pleasure in everyday mundane events. The problem is that forty-four folks in Illinois is a small and geographically limited sample, and statistical tools have improved a bunch since the 1970s. A 2020 study followed a similar approach to the 1978 study but surveyed a whopping 3,362 Swedes who had won at least $100,000 in their country's lottery. Compared with a matched sample of Swedish nonwinners, the researchers again did not find an effect of winning the lottery on daily happiness. But they did find a positive effect of winning on *life satisfaction*. This bump in life satisfaction wasn't driven by winners' higher happiness with their family, friends, or jobs; it came from a rise in their feelings of financial security.

This new evidence suggests that the Debbie Downers are wrong. All else being equal, winning a significant amount of money (not surprisingly) appears to have a positive effect.

But the usefulness of these findings is limited by the reality that the relationship between hitting the lottery and winner well-being *isn't strong or direct*. It *does* harm some winners' lives, like Callie Rogers. While for others, like Neil Jones, it is transformationally positive. What really matters, of course, is what you do (and do not do) in response to the windfall.

There are many different paths people take after experiencing an event like winning the lottery. A study of the career decisions of over one

---

* A matched sample approach involves building a comparison group with characteristics similar to the group that is being studied (in this case, matching lottery winners with similar nonwinners).

hundred small jackpot winners in the US found that while most people (63 percent) kept working at their jobs, many others made big changes, from leaving the workforce altogether to switching to part-time work, to taking a career break and then returning.

The takeaway is that whether winning the lottery would have a positive or negative effect on your life depends not just on the amount of money you win but perhaps more on *how you respond to it*, and how you deal with the opportunities and challenges it presents.

And the same is true for any event that jolts us.

How jolts ultimately affect our relationship with work and our well-being in our career and life depends on how we react, *if* we react at all.

The Post-Jolt Balancing Act

Ideally, our sensemaking in the wake of a jolt would involve a full reflection on our situation—putting the event that jolted us, and our emotional reaction to it, in perspective. Easier said than done.

On the one hand, we have this specific event in some area of our life that jolted us into thinking about our relationship with work. In many cases, this singular event does demand attention and correction. On the other hand, there are a bunch of other parts of our relationship with work that may factor into whether and how we should make a small or big change. Keeping these hands balanced can be challenging. It calls to mind F. Scott Fitzgerald's quote "The test of a first-rate intelligence is the ability to hold two opposed ideas in the mind at the same time, and still retain the ability to function." In this case, it's the test of a first-rate jolt reaction—to hold (1) the immediate effects of the jolt and (2) all other aspects of our relationship with work in our minds at the same time, all the while continuing to function in our jobs and lives.

From what we can glean from Jürgen Klopp's resignation, he achieved this balance. The event of planning for next season jolted him to think about resigning. He then paused and reflected on that surprising thought, and eventually came to two very different realizations. First, his day-to-day energy level had an expiration date. Second, he wanted to explore a different side of himself. Together, these led him to hang up his managerial ball cap at the end of the season.

That Klopp's process was one of careful consideration and balance isn't too surprising, given that he is one of the great strategic thinkers in his sport. But what I have learned from my discussions with people in the midst of this post-jolt sensemaking is that such a balanced approach is the exception. Instead, it's often lopsided and biased.

In terms of being *lopsided*, people spend most of their energy reflecting on only a fraction of the things that make up their overall relationship with work. This is especially true following a jolt. Our mental energy goes toward the source of the jolt, leading us to under-consider the importance of other aspects of our relationship with work. If we were denied a raise, we focus on pay. If we failed at a recent project, we focus on our lack of skills and development. If we just had a health scare, we focus on work-life balance. Of course, these things deserve our attention, but overweighting them and letting them crowd out consideration of the other elements of our jobs and work can lead us to respond to jolts in a way that we ultimately come to regret.

In terms of being *biased*, people often place too much weight on aspects of the relationship that don't actually drive career satisfaction and personal well-being. Pay and status are perhaps the two best examples of this. When thinking about our current job and considering alternatives to it, we tend to direct our attention to pay, benefits, and status (e.g., job title and rank). Let me say this loud and clear—these things are important. If you're struggling to make ends meet financially, or you're focused on retiring early or paying for your kids' college (or both), or you simply have expensive hobbies or tastes, compensation should be a big component when considering the state of your relationship with work. And whether we like it or not, status and prestige are strong desires for many of us, and work is a key area of our lives where these desires can be satisfied. *But* generally speaking, money and status are not the main paths via which work contributes to our overall well-being—to our pursuit of the good life We'll get to those two main paths (happiness and meaning) in a moment. The point here is that biasing our decision-making toward things like pay and status in the wake of a jolt can lead us to respond in ways that do nothing to improve, or may even harm, our relationship with work and its role in our lives.

Returning to Jürgen Klopp one more time provides an example of how to place a jolt in the context of our overall relationship with work—to get a complete sense of what it has revealed about this relationship. This process requires zooming in and out of our personal and professional lives, and surveying the landscape of this relationship as it stands.

By zooming in, we take the temperature of the things that make for a healthy relationship with work *on a day-to-day basis*. This is where Klopp found that his daily energy stores were being depleted more rapidly than he could replenish them, leading him to speculate that his gas tank would run empty after the season's end.

By zooming out, we assess the state of the things that make for a healthy relationship with work *over the long term*. Here, Klopp found that he wanted to explore other sides of himself. He wanted to find another purpose.

Of course, the conclusion from this zooming in and out may be that although we were caught off guard by the jolt, we feel good about our daily work life as well as the broader arc of our personal and professional lives. Our relationship with work is healthy enough. But the post-jolt assessment may also reveal a gap between the ways that work *can* provide us with the good life and the extent to which ours is *actually doing so*. To get a sense of what this gap can look like, it's time to take a deeper dive into what the good life actually is.

Checking Your Compass on the Trail to the Good Life

I grew up in Nebraska, a state situated just above the geographic center of the US. It's not a populous state, and like the rural middle of many countries, it's considered "flyover" territory. But a more accurate term would be *drive-through* territory. That's because while the state has many claims to fame, including being the home of Warren Buffett and the birthplace of Kool-Aid, many folks know it best because they have driven through it along the coast-to-coast highway that spends five hundred miles rolling through Nebraska. Growing up, I was driven, and eventually drove myself, along every one of those miles, many times. As I think back on those journeys, one phrase always springs to mind. That phrase was the state slogan throughout my early life, prominently displayed on many roadside signs. NEBRASKA: THE GOOD LIFE. I never gave it much thought, except maybe to roll my eyes at it while passing by in the windy, frigid dead of winter. But since I moved away, it has held a pleasant nostalgia for me, and when I go home to visit, the phrase often enters my mind when the plane touches down.

What is the good life? What does it mean to live a good life? You may take a moment now to reflect on what, in your mind, makes a life well lived.

Perhaps the most compelling answer, which comes from ancient philosophers and continues to be used by those who study human well-being, is that the good life can be distilled into two halves. First, a good life is a life of *happiness*. Are you content with your day-to-day life? A life of contentment is one where we regularly experience pleasurable emotions. Second, a good life is a life of *meaningfulness*. Does your life have purpose? A life of meaningfulness is one in which we feel we are part of something positive and bigger than ourselves.

These two buckets—contentment and meaningfulness—offer grounding points for assessing the health of our relationship with work in the wake of a jolt. Let's start with happiness. All things considered, how happy are you with your work? For organizational researchers, this is one of the most common variables we measure in workers—job satisfaction. To quantify your own overall job satisfaction right now, rate your agreement with these two statements on a 1–5 scale where 1 = Strongly Disagree and 5 = Strongly Agree.

All in all, I am satisfied with my job.

In general, I like working here.

Average those two numbers, and voila, you've got a snapshot of how much your job is contributing to the happiness half of your pursuit of the good life, right now. Of course, our overall happiness at work is made up of many components—contentment with pay, our boss, our work schedule, our career development—and when deficient, any one of those can loom large and drag down our job satisfaction. And there are points in our career where the day-to-day happiness components of our job are all we care about when it comes to our overall well-being. If we're struggling to make ends meet financially, then satisfaction with our compensation will play an outsize role in our "good life calculus." If we have had the misfortune of working for a horrible boss, then we may give extra weight to finding a job where we have a competent and kind manager. And early in our career, we may give extra priority to figuring out the kind of work that makes us smile when we perform it.

It is worth iterating here that *work can provide happiness in spades.* Good coworkers, a good boss, good pay and benefits, and doing work that fits your skills—that is a recipe for high life contentment through work. When you have these things, on paper, life should be good. And yet, workplaces of all sorts are filled with stories where someone who is genuinely happy with their work walks away from it. This can be baffling to observers and frustrating for managers, who feel that they've done everything possible to create the conditions for a lasting long-term relationship with the employee.

Likewise, there are many cases in which people willingly choose jobs and careers that limit their potential to make as much money as they could. In millions of instances, people freely opt to work in jobs that pay them less or that cause them to work in worse conditions than they could in other attainable jobs. Why do they do it?

It has to do with the other half of the good life: *meaningfulness*. People often stay at jobs that are lacking in what makes them happy because those jobs give them a sense of purpose and fulfillment. And people often leave jobs with which they are content, in search of work that in their eyes is more meaningful.

Like happiness, you can get a rough estimate of the meaningfulness of your job by rating your agreement with the following statements on a 1 (Strongly Disagree) to 5 (Strongly Agree) scale, and averaging them together.

> *The work I do is meaningful to me.*
>
> *The job itself is very significant and important in the broader scheme of things.*

After a jolt, taking a step back and rating your work happiness and meaningfulness can serve as a quick diagnostic check. Your responses may reveal that, despite the jolt, your relationship with work remains strong. Or they may reveal that the meaning or happiness you get from work has changed, or is simply not as strong as you want. Maybe after being passed over for a promotion, you find that your daily happiness at work has dropped precipitously. Or after doing some volunteering while on vacation, you realize that the meaning you get from your hours at work is not nearly as rich as you want it to be.

When we identify such gaps between the good life we want out of work and what we're actually getting, then we have to dig deeper, burrowing further into the different pieces of our jobs that contribute to our overall happiness and sense of meaning at work. A sensible next step is simply to cut the two "good life" halves—happiness and meaningfulness—in half again, based on the two components of a job where most of our well-being lies—the *what* and the *who* of our jobs.

The what of our job is our *work tasks*. Do we find pleasure and/or purpose in the activities that make up the core of our jobs?

The who of our job is our *work community*. Do the people in our work lives make us happy and/or give us a sense of meaning?

Let's spend a moment in each quadrant.

	SOURCE OF HAPPINESS	SOURCE OF MEANING
WORK TASKS	Does this work fit me?	Does my work matter?
WORK COMMUNITY	Do I like these people?	Does this group matter?

Work Tasks and Happiness = Does This Work Fit Me?

In 2013, Chris Holmes's departure from his job as an airport immigration officer made headlines. His resignation letter was not printed on paper or sent electronically but delivered via cake. Holmes explained, in black icing on top of white frosting, "Having recently become a father I now realize how precious life is and how important it is to spend my time doing something that makes me, and other people, happy." Experiencing the positive jolt of the birth of his son, Holmes realized that his work tasks, which he described as "sitting in front of a row of furious passengers who've been waiting for two hours," were not making him happy. He switched to spending half of his weeks as his family's primary caregiver and the other half as an entrepreneur—making and selling cakes.

Our work tasks are what we do every day, most of the day, on the job. As a result, how we feel about them tends to have a massive effect on how we feel about our jobs overall. If you don't like your work duties, you are going to experience that distaste on a daily basis. Naturally, most of us try to find work that's made up of activities we're good at and that we enjoy (or at least don't find frustrating, degrading, or dangerous). When people are happy with the tasks that make up the core of their jobs, they often describe their job as a good *fit*. Researchers use the same term, calling it *person-job fit*. High levels of fit are experienced when you feel that the job is a good match for both your abilities and your desires. As you'd expect, the higher your person-job fit, the more likely you are to be satisfied with your job overall and the less likely you will be to quit.

Particularly after a jolt that involves our work tasks, like failing to meet a deadline despite our best efforts or seeing a coworker leave to pursue their "passion," we will likely reflect on the match (or mismatch) between us and our work tasks. What also comes into play here is the tangible things we receive for completing those tasks, namely pay and benefits.

But instead of taking this into consideration only when the jolt calls it to mind, checking in on the fit between our job tasks and our happiness can be very helpful in the wake of jolts that do *not* call our job tasks to mind. Doing so can provide us with a more complete and balanced perspective on how our work is contributing to our well-being. For example, in the wake of a jolt such as having a coworker steal one of our clients, we may immediately consider quitting because it's clear that our coworkers are harming our well-being. But by considering our work tasks, which we enjoy and for which we are paid well, it can make us realize that while we do need to do something about our toxic coworker, quitting is far too rash.

Work Relationships and Happiness = Do I Like These People?

The human species spent hundreds of thousands of years living in the wilderness. A remnant of all that time in the wild is that *belonging* is one of our fundamental needs. We are not well equipped to survive on our own in the great outdoors—something that was especially true prior to the invention of puffy jackets, waterproof matches, and satellite phones. But when we band together in groups, we can better handle what nature throws at us. And so those of our ancestors who were motivated to connect and get along with others survived and passed along their belonging-oriented genes. Those who were less interested in belonging or who were naturally disagreeable were more likely to find themselves coping with the challenges of survival on their own.

Through that process, over millennia, we developed a pretty strong internal system for sensing our social value in the eyes of others. Psychologist Mark Leary gave a name to this internal system: the *sociometer*. I don't know why, but I like the idea of this little meter inside us that pings up or down as it detects good and bad social signals, spurring us to feel and act in response to it.

Our sociometers are on constant alert, scanning for social signals from others and tagging them as good or bad signs of our value in the eyes of those around us. The sociometer registers a social signal such as being helped by a colleague as a good thing—something worthy of a positive action in response, such as saying thank you or helping in return. But this system also kicks into action when we get a signal that our social value is being questioned or harmed, registering it as a threat to our survival. In response, the sociometer nudges us into social repair mode, perhaps prompting us to apologize when we realize we have offended someone or to confront a person who has questioned our integrity.

When a jolt stems from an event involving close or valuable members of our social network, our sociometer sounds the alarm. Being treated rudely at work, having a colleague quit, or getting into an argument about work with our spouse represent events that the sociometer will detect right away. This is a good thing, as it can nudge us to reflect on our workplace relationships and take action to make sure they're healthy. The problem is that the sociometer can also give us tunnel vision, narrowing our attention to one or two relationships and allowing them to have more influence over our post-jolt sensemaking than they should.

Those one or two relationships are a good starting point, but it is essential to also zoom out from there and take stock of our interpersonal relationships at work more broadly, and assess whether they are contributing to our happiness or detracting from it. Equally important, when an event that has nothing to do with the people side of our work jolts us, our sociometer will not be triggered. In those instances, it's up to us to intentionally reflect on our happiness with those in our work lives as we appraise the overall health of our relationship with work.

Work Tasks and Meaning = Does My Work Matter?

Sometimes, we're good at what we do and we work with good people, but we do not find the work fulfilling. Our job is a good fit and we feel like we belong, which leads us to be content with work on a daily basis. *But*, then there are moments, often triggered by a jolt, when we question whether our work is meaningful. Whether all of these hours at work are well spent in the scheme of our lives.

One of the best business books ever written was penned not by a business leader, management guru, or professor but by an oral historian who also found success as a writer, actor, and broadcaster—Studs Terkel. His book *Working*, published in 1974, is a collection of over 130 interviews with workers, each one of them in a different job. In the book's introduction, Terkel describes how "work is, by its very nature, about violence— to the spirit as well as to the body." Clearly, he recognizes that many jobs do not provide workers with the dignity they deserve. But he then contrasts this violence with what work can be, a source of "daily meaning" and "astonishment."

About the same time that Terkel was conducting his interviews and penning *Working*, two organizational researchers were approaching a similar conclusion from a different angle. Whereas Terkel got his insights from conversations with workers, Richard Hackman and Greg Oldham were testing different theories about meaningful work using surveys and quantitative analyses. These two defined meaningful work as being comprised of *three elements*, all of which are echoed in the testimonies in *Working*.

Reflect for a moment. When you leave work at the end of the day or look back over the past year, can you identify the visible output of your labor? The first key to meaningful work is how much your work tasks produce something *visible*. Terkel interviewed a stonemason named Carl, who stated that he can't imagine a job where you can't see the work you've done. He spoke with pride about how he can go to the small town where he laid the first bricks of his career, four decades prior, and still see them there. Being able to see the work he's done in his career, and knowing that it'll be there long after he is gone, is "immortality" as far as Carl (and other stonemasons) are concerned.

Next, does your job require you to use a range of different skills, or is it the same activity, all day every day? The second key to meaningful work is whether there is *variety* in your job tasks. Eugene Russell, a piano tuner, enthusiastically described to Terkel how much he enjoys his job and how "every day is different." Even within a given day, he may start by tuning a piano for a record company on a tight deadline, then go to a company and tune four pianos at a time, and then tune a couple of harpsichords. It's clear that this variety is part of why he finds his job so meaningful that he says he'll "never retire."

Finally, when you think about the impact of your work, can you think of the ways in which it has a positive effect on others, both inside and outside your company? The last key piece of the meaningful work puzzle is *significance*—the positive impact of your work (if any) on the lives of other people. In talking about being a firefighter, Tom Patrick summed it up for Terkel by stating, "I can look back and say, 'I helped put out a fire. I helped save somebody.'" Truly meaningful work almost always positively impacts others.

When we experience a jolt and find that we're happy with our jobs and coworkers, it can cause a lot of confusion and stress. *What is wrong with me? I'm happy in my job, and lots of people would probably love to be in this position. And yet, it seems like something is missing . . .* In these cases, the issue underlying the jolt may reveal itself in the answers to the questions above—a lack of meaningfulness, in the visibility, variety, or significance of what you do at work. But it also may remain hidden, in which case it's time to move on and examine the meaningfulness of the work *groups* you belong to.

Work Relationships and Meaning = Does This Group Matter?

In getting our heads around the final quadrant of our relationship with work, it helps to map our current situation. Here, I encourage you to grab a writing device and take a moment for a brief and simple exercise, which we'll come back to at multiple points in the book. To begin, list all the roles in your life you can think of in response to the question "Who are you?"

Mother, brother, Hindu, nurse, choir member, golfer, sculptor, chess master, West Ham supporter, godparent, marathon runner, university alumnus. And probably, a member of your work organization, your work group, perhaps your profession.

In almost all cases, these roles involve membership in a group of people bound together by some shared beliefs and/or goals.

Now, for each of these roles in your life, take a moment to reflect on two questions:

How much of my time and energy (i.e., my resources) do I devote to this role?

How important is this role to me?

Importantly, this is about how *you view yourself*, not how others view you. This is about your *identity*, not your image.

It could help to answer these questions with an illustration. Using your writing device, draw a circle. The circle is you (feel free to make it another shape if you'd prefer). Now, within this circle, insert bubbles for each role you listed above, but not randomly.

First, the *size* of the bubbles should equate to the degree to which the role takes up your time and energy. The bigger the demands, the bigger the bubble.

Second, the *placement* of the bubble should equate to the importance of that role to you; the more important it is, the nearer it should be to the center of your circle. It's fine if bubbles overlap.

Now take a step back and look at "yourself." Ideally, the bubbles at the center of your drawing are also your biggest ones. If so, those roles where you spend a lot of time and energy are also those that you feel are the most meaningful. If that's the case, you're likely living a meaningful and purposeful life, because your days are spent in roles that support your values—what you feel is most important.

The bubble representing your job is probably pretty big. A lot of the time and energy we have, we invest in our jobs. And so it tends to be a big part of how we define ourselves. But the question is: How close to the center of your shape did the bubble(s) associated with your work appear?

To the extent that our work roles are near the center of our sense of self, we *identify* with the group associated with that role. To clarify with an example, a barista at the local coffee shop Roasted would have at least two work bubbles—one for profession (I am a barista) and one for organization (I am a Roasted employee). When we identify as a member of a group, we feel we are one with it. When the group succeeds, we feel we succeed. When it fails, we feel that failure like our own. Such identification makes our experience at work more meaningful. We get the sense that this is a role where I, and the people and organization around me, are investing our energy toward something I find valuable.

When you highly identify with the work you're doing (artfully making coffee), with the organization for which you are working (Roasted), and with the work group of which you are a part (the Roasted team), you'll likely experience a high level of meaning in your job.

Correspondingly, when we experience a jolt or do a check-in with our relationship with work, this bubble exercise may show that we highly identify with our work-related groups. We strongly identify with being a barista and a member of Roasted, and so from the perspective of our group memberships, our relationship with work is healthy. Of course, this exercise may reveal a disconnect between the meaning we hope to get from our work and what we're actually experiencing. Imagine Roasted announces that they will no longer pay for employee health care, and the announcement jolts us. Upon reflection in the wake of this jolt, we find that our identification with being a barista is as strong as ever, but that we no longer find much meaning in being a member of Roasted. In this way, the jolt reveals that we no longer (or never did) share the values of our organization and what it is working toward.

At other times in our career, a jolt may open our eyes to a situation in which we have worked our way into a profession we do not find purposeful. Or that our organization, while full of wonderful people, is focused on achieving things that to us are meaningless. In these situations, we have an opportunity to improve our pursuit of the good life by seeking out more purposeful work roles.

Seeing the Effects of Jolts on the Forest and the Trees

Our journey through the four quadrants of "the good life via work" reveals that checking the health of our relationship with work requires zooming in to understand what the jolt reveals about our day-to-day work life, and zooming out to place the jolt in the context of the bigger picture of our work's meaning and purpose. If you don't, you're liable to respond to a jolt in a way that improves one side of your good life but harms the other, leaving you in the same place you started or (often) worse. Such lopsided focus can cause problems that become evident only once we've taken drastic action, like switched jobs. The problem is that each of us tends to gravitate toward thinking big or thinking small. To avoid our inclination toward lopsided thinking, we need to understand where we fall, and counter it.

There is this classic story about US President John F. Kennedy and NASA. The event at the heart of the story occurred in the days following his publicly declared goal of reclaiming the lead in the global space race. Kennedy was touring NASA headquarters after normal working hours, and he came across a custodian mopping the floors. Kennedy asked the worker why he was working late. As the legend goes, the man replied by saying, "I'm not mopping the floors, I'm putting a man on the moon."

This story illustrates that there are different levels at which we think about our jobs, depending on us and the situation. Psychologists call this *construal level*. At low construal levels, we describe our jobs in their most concrete, basic terms. As an author, I type words onto the screen and make sentences. As a custodian, I mop floors. As a temp worker on a food manufacturing line, I drop toys into boxes of cereal. Your current job description on file with HR probably describes your job in these terms.

But we can also think of our jobs at higher levels of construal. Here, think about the bigger picture of what your job accomplishes, and describe it using loftier terms. Here, I am not just typing sentences; I am creating knowledge. I am not mopping floors; I am putting a man on the moon. And I am not just dropping toys into cereal boxes; I am bringing joy to the mornings of children around the world.

It may be tempting to label one level as superior, especially because each of us has a preferred level of construal—how we tend to view our world. You may be one of those big-picture people, always seeing the forest instead of the trees. Always taking a step back and wanting to know how a given situation relates to broader truths in the universe. Conversely, you may be a concrete, detail-oriented thinker. What is a forest if not a collection of interesting, individual trees, each of which deserves attention? To you, the devil is in the details, and you tend to think about situations in terms of the individual components involved.

So, if you're an abstract thinker, are you always in the clouds? And if you're a concrete thinker, are you always on the ground? No. Over our days and weeks, the situations we face in and out of work cause us to switch between levels. For example, the hustle and bustle involved in our day-to-day lives and jobs pull us away from the big picture and toward sweating the small stuff.

Examining our relationship with work through the four quadrants discussed in this chapter can provide a good sense of whether a jolt has revealed a fundamental issue with our relationship with work that needs addressing. But to get the most complete information out of this diagnostic process, you need to make sure you're seeing the molehills *and* the mountains. That you're not only focused on small details but also the big picture. A trick you can use to make sure your assessment is balanced is forcing yourself to think through these dimensions while switching between construal levels, the concrete and the abstract.

This can be difficult, because the situations we face—and of course, the jolts we experience—can push our thinking in the moment toward higher or lower construal. In response, we could try to shift our thinking in the other direction, to force ourselves to reflect on the jolt either more concretely or more holistically. But this can be difficult to do alone. If, up to this point, you've been navigating the jolt on your own, it may be time to find yourself a partner. Ideally, this would be someone a bit removed from the jolt but who knows you well, and who tends to view the world a bit differently from you.

In the book *Ride of a Lifetime*, Disney CEO Bob Iger described a moment early in his career when he experienced the jolt of his employer (the television network ABC) being acquired by a much smaller company with a completely different culture (Capital Cities Communications), resulting in his getting assigned a new boss. In response, he decided to quit and join the flashy talent agency where his fellow jolted ABC executives were bailing out to. When he told the head of HR of his plan to leave, he learned that he was actually in line for a promotion and that he should take twenty-four hours to consider it before officially resigning.

Iger didn't spend those twenty-four hours alone trying to figure out this pivotal career decision. If he had, he very well may have made the wrong one. Instead, he sat down with his wife and engaged in a process that probably sounds familiar after reading this chapter. Together, they discussed the downsides of staying and working for this new boss versus what working at the talent agency would be like. *Does this work fit me?* Then they zoomed out and talked about the value that Iger placed on being a member of his current company versus a member of a new one. *Does this group matter to me?* By using a partner to help him think through the forest and the trees of his relationship with work, he was able to get a clear sense of the right thing to do next.

CHAPTER FOUR

CARRY ON

Sizing up whether to respond to the alarm
that the jolt has sounded or to hit
the snooze button.

In the end, Bob Iger did nothing. He stayed with Cap Cities, which was later bought by Disney, and went on to have an extraordinarily successful run as Disney's CEO. There are a couple of things that I love about this story. First, because staying at your job after a jolt isn't newsworthy, we rarely hear stories of how remaining at a job rather than resigning has fueled someone's career success. Second, it's an example of what a lot of this book is about—how seemingly small events and moments can have outsize effects on our careers and well-being. Or as Iger describes it, "There are moments in our careers, in our lives, that are inflection points, but they're often not the most obvious or dramatic ones." He goes on to say that his decision to take the more boring and safer path of staying put was one of the best career choices he made.

When a jolt reveals a shortcoming in our relationship with work, quitting often springs to mind. It can be hard to resist the temptation to see quitting as the solution to whatever problem(s) you have at work. By our nature, many of us are drawn to new experiences and new beginnings. And on top of that, quitting one's job is often glamorized in broader society.

A classic example comes from a song written by David Allan Coe and sung by Johnny Paycheck that soared to the top of the *Billboard* country music charts when it was released in 1977. While the song's tune is catchy, the reason it was such a hit had more to do with its message about a worker who has worked in the same factory for fifteen years and has a bad boss. But now, his partner just left him, a jolt that took away the only reason he was still working. And so, what does this worker do? He proclaims, "Take this job and shove it. I ain't workin' here no more."

Pop culture is full of stories like Paycheck's. In the hit film *Office Space*, Jennifer Aniston's character, Joanna, abruptly quits after her manager confronts her about not having enough pieces of "flair" on her vest. In the bestselling book *Eat, Pray, Love*, Elizabeth Gilbert responds to her divorce and a failed rebound relationship by quitting her job so she can travel and write. And in Beyoncé's chart-topping single "Break My Soul," she sings about quitting her job in response to the stressors of work.

When it comes to how employees respond to jolts, quitting is the star of the show. It can be cast as a David-versus-Goliath moment, wherein a single employee stands up to an organization and enacts their freedom to walk away. Our appetite for stories about quitting is massive, with tales of resigning commonly racking up views on social media and generating polarizing reactions of support or disapproval. And news headlines often report the results of surveys showing that a large percentage of people intend to quit their job in the next year. But most of these folks won't quit. The correlation between intending to quit and actually quitting is around .45, which provides a rough indication that most people don't turn their intention to quit into reality.

I'm on record saying that the increased focus on quitting by organizations, the press, and those on social media over the past few years is warranted. I don't feel that way simply because I study resignations. I applaud the spotlight on quitting because the decision to leave is often difficult, and exits can be challenging to navigate. People shouldn't have to figure it out in the dark or feel that they're the only ones going through it. Shining a light on employee quitting and how organizations respond to it helps those who are thinking about whether or not they should take the leap. Seeing other people's stories of quitting can serve as a sort of mental dress rehearsal. How did they quit? How did other people respond? What would I do differently?

But the increased focus on quitting also creates some problems. It can make it seem like *everyone* is quitting, which makes people more likely to resign without giving it as much thought as they should. If everyone is doing it, why not? The perception that people are quitting their jobs more than ever, especially among younger workers, is prevalent. This feeds into the notion that worker loyalty is a thing of the past. But this is simply not true. While there have been spikes in quitting over the past hundred years, the job tenure of workers in the US, including those eighteen to thirty-four years old, is no different from what it was over four decades ago, in 1983, when the US Census started tracking it.

An arguably bigger problem is that the focus on quitting is exclusionary and privileged. *Quitting is not a viable option for most workers.* I don't have big data to back up that statement, but in my years of talking about the resignation process, one of the most common questions I get is what to do if you experience a jolt but you're not in a position to quit.

Many people are stuck in their jobs, and for them, catchy though it may be, Johnny Paycheck's advice is a fantasy. For these people, quitting would lead to undesirable or even catastrophic consequences for them, their careers, and their families. And less dramatically, as we'll discuss, it's common for quitting one's job to lead to feelings of regret.

For these reasons, almost every time I talk to a worker who has been jolted and asks me the question "Should I quit my job?" I start with "Probably not." There are of course exceptions, such as when the source of a jolt is causing serious harm to your well-being or when the jolt reveals an amazing, can't-miss opportunity. But in most cases, taking time to weigh the benefits and costs of staying against the corresponding bright and dark sides of whatever alternatives you've got is time well invested. And moreover, there are serious advantages to simply recognizing the jolt but then carrying on as though it hadn't happened.

Keeping Calm and Carrying On

When jolted, the optimal response will often be to do nothing. To understand why, it's worth flipping the ever-popular question of why people quit their jobs and ask: Why do some people *stay* at the same organization for long periods of time? The answer, according to turnover researchers who shifted their focus to this question, is *job embeddedness*. They describe embeddedness as "a net or a web in which an individual can become stuck." That may not make embeddedness sound very positive, but it absolutely can be.

Job embeddedness comes from three places. First, how strong and numerous are the *connections* you have to people and activities, inside *and* outside of your work? If most of your social network is located in close physical proximity to you—coworkers, neighbors, family members—and your cherished activities are connected to the geographic area around you—the gym you love, the church you've attended since childhood, the concert venue where your favorite bands play—then your embeddedness is high.

The second source of this stuckness relates to how much you feel you *fit* with your current life situation. Do you feel that your job and company are a good match for who you are and what you want to achieve? And what about outside of work; is your community a good fit for that as well? Anyone who has traveled even a little bit has realized that there are some locations that "click" with us right away. We feel quickly at ease and could see ourselves living there long-term. Then there are other places where we always feel uncomfortable, and where we don't feel we can ever be ourselves. If you're in a place that fits your personality, your values, and your dreams, then you are embedded.

Lastly, there is *sacrifice*. What would you have to give up if you left your job? Pay, short commute, perks, benefits, coworkers, meaningful work, and so on. These are somewhat straightforward to assess, but it's tougher on the personal side. What will you and your family members have to give up if you quit? Such sacrifices are most easily seen in cases of expatriate work assignments, where companies ask employees to pack up and move abroad for a few years—a process that requires workers to largely sever their connections to the community where they live. The effects of disembedding can be massive, negatively affecting expats' partners' happiness and career progress, and their kids' education and friend groups. This is why workers often decline international assignments and, even when they do accept them, often struggle to perform well.

As you can see, we largely experience the stuckness that comes with being embedded in our jobs as a good thing. You like the people who surround you and the location where you work and live, and you have cherished benefits that you'd have to sacrifice if you left. But this embeddedness can become a curse when a jolt makes us realize that some part of our relationship with work is hopelessly deficient. Here, we want to quit, but if we have high embeddedness in all other areas of our job and personal lives, we're stuck. In this way, embeddedness can sometimes hold us back from seizing career options that will bring us closer to the good life, because we can't bear to free ourselves from its web.

Speaking of other options, this brings up a less positive reason we often stay in a job for a long time—we have no place to go. There is an economic reality at play for most of us that shapes our decision to stay. Are there desirable *alternatives* to your current job? Alternatives that are appealing not just in the what and who of work but that also give us as good if not better pay and benefits? The best alternatives to our current job are commonly similar jobs at other companies. A lot of the time, our expertise, skills, and abilities are most relevant and valuable to our current company, profession, and/or industry. This means that the easiest and most valuable alternatives lie within the same profession and industry. Nowadays, it is easier than in the past to switch careers, thanks to the availability of online ways to learn new knowledge and pick up new skills. In addition, there are more options for side hustles, wherein workers can try out other jobs or professions on a limited basis and can thus expand their alternatives. Nonetheless, the bottom line is that staying put is driven by both positive forces (embeddedness) and less positive realities (limited alternatives).

When a jolt knocks us out of autopilot and motivates us to make a job change, simply assessing our embeddedness and alternatives can be enough to make us realize that we should stay put. At times in our lives when we're highly embedded or do not have good alternatives, quitting is pretty much off the table. If we do have good alternatives, then quitting is certainly an option, but one that is going to cause a pretty painful separation and correspondingly carries a reasonable chance of ending in regret. If we're not embedded but also do not have good alternatives, then leaving isn't difficult. But hopping over to a new job or role that moves us closer to the good life is risky because of how few options we have. Really, it's only when we're not embedded and we have good alternatives that quitting is as appealing as other courses of action.

Reluctantly Sticking Around

Many of us are embedded, either inside or outside of work, or both. And if you're like me, you don't have boatloads of alternative job options. I feel fortunate to have my current job, and job searching isn't something I relish. But being embedded with few alternatives doesn't prevent us from, at times, wanting to explore quitting. After a jolt, we can go through a period of hours, days, weeks, months, or even years in which we're motivated to quit. But when this desire hits the hard reality that we really *shouldn't* quit, we find ourselves members of a group that turnover researchers call *reluctant stayers*. In her memoir, *Becoming*, Michelle Obama described her time as a reluctant stayer, after the dual jolts of the deaths of her father and her close friend made her realize that she wanted "more joy and meaning" from her work life. The problem was, she didn't know what she wanted to do next, and she was embedded—her current job as a high-performing attorney provided her with a lot of lifestyle benefits. So, she reluctantly stayed for months and months, continuing to work hard and trying to find more joy and meaning in her current job, while searching for that elusive perfect next role. Eventually, she found it, in a role in the Chicago mayor's office that paid half as much as her current job but that put her on a much more direct path to her version of the good life.

Like Obama, almost all of us are reluctant stayers for some periods of time in our careers, often in the wake of jolts. The workforce during COVID-19 was as full of reluctant stayers as it's ever been. The pandemic was a massive jolt, but the economy was terrible, and it was scary to consider making a big move due to the uncertainty about the future. The jolt had awoken a desire in millions of people to move to a new chapter in their careers and lives, but the economy and the pandemic had greatly reduced alternatives and increased people's embeddedness. Thanks to the arrival of vaccines, the pandemic eased, job markets perked up, and a dam holding back a sea of reluctant stayers burst open. This was a good thing not only because of the terribleness of the pandemic but because being a reluctant stayer over a long period of time isn't good for your well-being and isn't a sustainable career strategy, at least if you're trying to advance on your path to the good life. So, if you're going to stay put for a while, it helps if you can view your loyalty to your job as something positive, as opposed to something you're forced to do. But if a jolt has turned you into a reluctant stayer, how do you become a more enthusiastic one?

Always Look on the Bright Side of Staying Put

When we assess our relationship with work, we often focus on the problems. This focus isn't a bad thing; fixing problems that arise is part of the maintenance of any relationship over time. But the focus on problems becomes an issue if we don't combine it with appreciation for the bright spots in the relationship. If we overlook these upsides, we risk taking them for granted and assuming that they'll be present in our next chapter, too. That assumption is faulty. There are at least three types of benefits that do not transfer with us if we quit, two of which people commonly under-consider when they think about quitting. As we'll discuss later, it's often not until we're in the next role, and find that those things haven't transferred with us, that we realize we took them for granted. Sometimes, you really don't know what you've got until it's gone. But, hopefully, you can take some time in the wake of a jolt to take stock of what you would miss if you left.

Hard benefits. When thinking about quitting in the wake of a jolt, if we do take time to consider what we will miss if we leave our current job, it's the hard benefits we think about. Our pay, benefits, perks, schedule, commute, vacation, physical workspace, and so on.

Good ol' goodwill. It is absolutely possible that a new opportunity will provide you with upgrades in every "hard good" element of your work. More money, better retirement, bigger office, more flexible schedule, a shorter commute, the ability to bring your pet to work, and so on. Fantastic. But even if that's the case, you'll still typically be starting back at zero when it comes to a valuable yet under-considered resource—the *goodwill* you have at work. Think about the information you know that makes your job easier. The influence you have with some of your colleagues. The amount that people respect and/or like you. This is priceless stuff!

As we work with others over time, we build up goodwill with them. When you have some goodwill with a coworker, it makes work easier and more enjoyable. If you need something from them, you can ask, and based on goodwill, they will provide it. Over time in a given job, you build up a network of this social capital, which makes work even smoother and more enjoyable. You have people you can count on for support, guidance, and favor-doing. Once your network of goodwill is established, it gives you access to information from around the company that helps you stay in the know and anticipate changes in ways that make work more enjoyable. Goodwill gives us the inside scoop about what's going on at work, the resources we need to do our jobs well, and the connection to people who will champion our careers. All of this fosters career success and satisfaction. Whether you only have a little or you have a lot, your current goodwill likely has a meaningful positive effect on your job performance and satisfaction.

It's not easy to quantify goodwill, which makes it easy to miss when considering what to do in the wake of a jolt. And when you're considering other jobs, it's easy to assume that you'll waltz in to a new gig with a certain amount of social capital, and that it will quickly grow to the same or higher level that you currently enjoy. But that isn't a safe assumption. In some cases, such as if you got the job that someone else at the company really wanted, you may (unknowingly) start with a goodwill deficit. And even when you enter with a certain level of goodwill, it is precarious. It's primarily through *repeated* positive dealings with others that high levels of social capital are amassed. But as a new employee, any missteps or bad first impressions can cause your goodwill to quickly dry up, making work less pleasant and more difficult than in your prior role.

Predictability. Finally, there are even less tangible benefits of work than goodwill, and because they're hard to grasp, they can be easily overlooked in the wake of a jolt. These are the positive things that come only from long-term relationships with others. This is most compellingly (and sweetly) shown in studies of couples in old age. These studies reveal that long-term relationships are a source of *calmness* for those involved in them. This calmness stems, in part, simply from having a shared history together. When you are in a relationship with someone for a long time, you become used to the other person, and can *predict their actions and reactions*, and your reactions to them. This isn't always a positive (if your partner is abusive), but there's often a certain comfort and serenity that comes from your longest relationships. As one study participant remarked about being in a long-term partnership, "And you know even when things get difficult or complicated for some reason, we have so much history together and so many wonderful shared experiences that that's what sort of buoys us through the difficult times."

Just like these long-term relationships with other people, organizational researchers have found that one thing we appreciate when we work for a company with a strong organizational culture is that it makes our professional lives more predictable. After you've worked for such a company for a while, you get used to how it operates, and so you know what to expect on a day-to-day basis. Of course, things don't always go to plan—new leaders take over, restructurings happen, buyouts occur. But even then, your day-to-day experience will likely be more predictable at the place where you've worked for years and come to understand the culture than at somewhere new.

And in my experience, some of us are especially drawn to the predictability that comes from long-term employment with one company. Almost every time I teach, I ask students to choose between two different career paths. You can make the same choice right now. Imagine you had to choose between one of two careers. In both cases, your career will plateau twenty years from now in a position on the top executive team of a large corporation. In Case A, the career ladder involves ten internal moves *within the same company.* In Case B, the career ladder involves ten moves but made *across five or so different companies.* Which career path would you choose?

Regardless of the group of students, the show of hands is almost always in the ballpark of fifty-fifty.*

If you raised your hand for Case A, then you may be one of those people who places extra value on the calmness, predictability, and other

---

* In cases where it's not even, it is a sixty-forty split in favor of Case A. I often hear leaders and pundits claim that employees aren't loyal anymore and don't want to work for the same company long-term like they used to. I am skeptical of such claims. As these nonscientific surveys indicate, there is an underrecognized desire to be a long-term member of a single organization among those currently entering the workforce.

benefits that come from being in a long-term relationship with another entity. Which, as we'll discuss next, means you should think especially hard before saying farewell to the shared history you have with your company and coworkers.

Deep Fake It Till You Make It

Imagine that you've had a jolt (or two), carefully considered your relationship with work, and determined that some aspects are faulty to the point that, overall, work is impeding your pursuit of the good life. To be clear, what I am talking about here isn't a toxic, truly awful job, but just one that feels to you that it's taking more than it's giving, in terms of satisfaction and meaning. So, you want to quit. But maybe you're embedded, you don't have great alternatives, or you're simply not ready to give up. What do you do?

Stay loyal. Don't do anything other than give the relationship time to heal. As we just discussed, work situations change over time. The company restructures, our boss gets promoted (or sacked), coworkers leave. Time doesn't heal all wounds, but it does heal some, including in our jobs.

Does this "stay loyal" strategy actually work? The answer, as with many in this book, is *it depends*. Staying loyal to a deficient relationship can be a recipe for burnout, or it can be a gateway to long-term relationship well-being. It partly depends on how you *act*.

At the most basic level, what is your company paying you for? Think about your job and what your company expects in exchange for giving you a paycheck. Some combination of our brains and our brawn, right? Our mental and physical contributions to the company. In her classic book *The Managed Heart: Commercialization of Human Feeling*, Arlie Russell Hochschild observed that in many jobs, what we are "selling" to our company is more than our mind and muscles—it's also our emotions. Many work roles force us to fake our true emotions and portray (i.e., sell) emotions that the company expects. She coined the term *emotional labor* to describe times when we have to manage our feelings, often forcing positive emotions and suppressing negative ones, to create and maintain a smiley outward appearance that is expected of us at work.

Researchers have spent the past few decades examining what happens when we have to act in ways that are different from how we actually feel, at work. This happens a lot when dealing with customers. When faced with a rude client, a customer service worker will experience negative emotions and want to act out on those emotions. But as part of their job, they have to remain pleasant and professional. This is emotional labor.

In studying how emotional labor affects employees, you won't be surprised to learn that much of the time, the effects are negative. Acting like we're happy when we're not is taxing, and it leads us to feel emotionally exhausted at the end of the day. Just think about a time when you had to act interested even though you couldn't care less about what the person was saying. You fake laughed at your boss's joke (a joke that was actually a bit offensive). You had to act excited even though you were bored. You had to act empathetic even though you couldn't relate. Compared with interactions in which we're able to act exactly how we feel (to be ourselves!), the ones filled with emotional labor exhaust us.

Emotional labor and its negative effects suggest that experiencing a jolt, finding a problem with your relationship with work, but staying loyal and acting like everything is fine is a recipe for burnout. That's sometimes true, but I've told you only half of the story about emotional labor at work. Here's the deal: When employees feel they need to fake emotions at work, they often turn to *surface acting*, which is what I've been describing—when we display feelings on the outside that are at odds with how we feel on the inside. And then we feel exhausted, and perhaps more frustrated than ever.

But we can take a different tack. We can go deeper with our acting. Rather than just changing how we appear to feel, we can change how we feel. This is *deep acting*, and there are a couple of components to it.

The first component is changing the way we think about the problem in our relationship with work. Imagine that your boss passed you over for a promotion, a jolt that caused you to realize that your relationship with work needs to change. Being loyal and surface acting would involve faking how you feel toward your boss, coworkers, and job. Acting like everything is wonderful even though you're deeply upset. But the first step of deep acting involves trying to change the way you feel about the problem. This may be as simple as thinking about the times your boss has supported you, and focusing on those times and the positive feelings they engender. Or it could go a bit deeper, putting yourself in your boss's shoes, or in the company's shoes. You adopt their perspective on the situation. Or you reinterpret the situation surrounding your boss's treatment of you. Rather than being upset over not being promoted and having to deal with a boss you don't like, you relabel it as a career challenge that will build your resilience and make you a better future leader.

If that's not enough to do the trick, or it's simply not an option because the situation is so bleak, then you can engage in a second deep-acting tactic—mentally transporting yourself to a happier part of your job. Here, you redirect your attention, away from the negative situation and toward more positive aspects. Recall that after being jolted, you think about the different sources of happiness and meaning in your job. Maybe during this process, you find that you like your job and your coworkers, but you just can't deal with your toxic boss anymore. In deep acting, you decide that you are going to focus on being the best coworker and the best at your craft that you can be. In doing so, when you do interact with your boss, you see it as a necessary task in being a great coworker and craftsperson, both of which bring you closer to the good life.

I'm not going to sit here and tell you that deep acting is a magic work pill. It's sometimes not possible to adopt a positive view of a toxic element of your job or to shift your attention away from it. Especially when you find yourself in a job where most parts of it are awful, or in a case where you work with an abusive coworker, you may quickly find that the *keep calm and carry on* approach just doesn't work. But let me also be clear: Meta-analyses of over a hundred studies that have examined deep acting show that when employees engage in it, they tend to at minimum avoid emotional exhaustion, and they sometimes have very positive experiences.

Responding to a jolt by simply carrying on isn't a passive reaction and it's not simple. It involves recognizing all the benefits of staying engaged in your current situation, and then actively shaping how you feel about work so that the problem the jolt revealed doesn't become a source of exhaustion and burnout. I think of this as *smart resilience*—bouncing back from the event that jolted us by carrying on, but doing so in a way that we retain our strength. And retaining our strength is important, because it's needed to deal with specific types of jolts that require a more active response.

Next, we'll turn to these specific jolts. We now have a broad understanding of the what and when of jolts, how to recognize them, and how to set ourselves up to react to them in ways that support our pursuit of the good life. In reviewing the academic and practical literature related to impactful events at work, big and small, I've found that there are six specific types of jolts we'll meet in our careers. Allow me to introduce you to the first three—direct jolts, collateral jolts, and honeymoon jolts—and explain why responding to them often requires a stronger strategy than carrying on.

PART II
Jolts at Work

CHAPTER FIVE

DIRECT JOLTS

Dissed, dismissed, and mishandled on the job.
The big effects that can stem from the everyday
bumps and bruises at work.

In 2005, Dave Chappelle abruptly walked away from *Chappelle's Show*, his sketch comedy show, at the height of its popularity. Not only did he quit the show, but he hopped on a plane to South Africa and completely retreated from public life for two weeks. In explaining what triggered this abrupt departure, Chappelle described a single workplace incident that made him stop and reflect on what he was doing: During filming of a racially charged sketch, a White crew member laughed. "I know the difference of people laughing with me and people laughing at me—and it was the first time I had ever gotten a laugh that I was uncomfortable with," Chappelle said. That reaction filled Chappelle with anger and shame and made him question the message that his work was sending to his different audiences. He would later explain that the skit "was the last thing I shot before I told myself I gotta take f—— time out after this. Because my head almost exploded."

Direct jolts are negative events that happen *to you* at work that knock you out of autopilot and make you rethink your relationship with work. When we think of prototypical direct jolts that we've experienced or seen, two types often come to mind. The first is failure at work. By their very nature, blunders cause us to reflect on what went wrong so that we can improve and avoid making the same mistake twice. Many contemporary management books talk about the bright side of failure—that it's actually a gift that signals an opportunity for learning. While I agree with this perspective, there's also the reality that in most jobs, failure spurs negative consequences and self-doubt. Reflecting on what went wrong can provide a jolt if we realize that the work failure isn't actually a learning opportunity but a signal that this job isn't for us.

A second common form of direct jolt is overt harassment at work. Experiencing blatant hostility triggers a strong desire to get away. Being the victim of such mistreatment is jolting. Sure, workplaces have become increasingly intolerant of outright abuse and discrimination, but it remains a far too common feature of organizational life. There are usually policies and procedures in place for how to report harassment and how it will be dealt with. And, *if* reported and *if* dealt with properly,* the likelihood of that jolt leading to a major change in one's relationship with work is mitigated to some degree.

While meaningful, the effects of these main two types of direct jolts should be fairly evident and straightforward to deal with. If you repeatedly struggle with the core aspects of your job even with coaching and training, searching for a different role is sensible. The same goes for experiencing harassment; if your organization doesn't deal with it properly, then you're certainly going to want to get away from that company if and when you can.

But beneath these "big two" types of direct jolts, there is a set of workplace events that aren't as clear-cut. They stem from fuzzier sources. When we fail or are harassed, we have some certainty that something wrong has happened. However, in our daily interactions and activities at work, we commonly experience unpleasant events that don't have a clear cause or simple interpretation. These events can trigger confusion

---

* Both of which are big "ifs." Victims often don't feel safe to report harassers, especially if the perpetrator has high power. And organizations continue to routinely mishandle dealing with the aftermath of harassment.

and reflection—and can jolt us just as much as outright failure or overt harassment. These incidents are often small and subtle in nature, such as the inappropriate laugh by Dave Chappelle's coworker. But their effects can be large, causing us to pause and take stock of the health of our relationship with our work (or storm out on it, like Chappelle did).

When a Slight Is Not So Slight

Imagine it's Monday morning after you've had a wonderful, restorative weekend, and you're ready to jump into a productive week of work. You pop down to your home office a half hour earlier than your usual start time and spend the first ninety minutes of the day building out a marketing pitch that was stumping you on Friday but has been solved by some ideas that percolated in the back of your brain during a few days of rest. You then log on to the regular start-of-week call with your fellow team members and boss, still buzzing from your morning burst of creativity and productivity. After some banter about what everyone did over the weekend, your boss leads a quick spin around to hear a progress update from each person on the team. Once it's your turn, you begin to excitedly share your progress on the marketing plan. But you're only a few sentences in when your boss interrupts you to ask you a basic question about the client. You answer it, and then attempt to get back on track. But a colleague interrupts, asking your boss an unrelated question about the client. The two of them then discuss the client a bit, before your boss comes back to you and says, "Thanks for the info," and then moves on to another team member for an update. Your positive energy has vanished.

What just happened? Your boss and colleague's verbal communication wasn't negative in tone. But their behavior was, in a word, rude. Thinking back over the past week or two, I bet you can recall the last time you experienced rudeness in your job. You're not alone. Around half of all workers report experiencing rudeness at work *on a weekly basis*, with some groups experiencing it even more frequently. Turns out, women experience incivility at work more frequently than men (especially if they work in a male-dominated profession), as do members of historically marginalized communities relative to other workers. And those low on the org chart or new to the company? They experience rudeness more frequently than the veterans and those closer to the top.

What distinguishes rudeness from the straight-up harassment we discussed above? Two things.

First, rudeness is fairly low-intensity and is nonphysical. Because rudeness is subtle, leaders and companies often don't think it's worth addressing. In fact, some of you may be reading this right now, rolling your eyes, and thinking, "Rudeness? Who cares? That's just part of being a worker." I'll get to the answer to the "Who cares?" question in a minute. But my point here is that it typically goes unaddressed and therefore unpunished, which can make dealing with rude colleagues particularly difficult.

Second, the intent behind acts of rudeness is *not clear* to the receiver. We aren't totally sure the other person meant to be rude to us. That ambiguity can be particularly frustrating. We wonder whether we were just disrespected or if we're overreacting or misinterpreting the event. And if we mention it to the person who did it, it's easy for them to deny any malicious intent, making us feel even more conflicted about what happened. Sometimes we can go through repeated episodes of rudeness and denial from one person and begin to experience feelings associated with gaslighting, wherein people are made to question whether what they're seeing or experiencing is real. In this way, despite its subtlety, rudeness often jolts into motion a train of thought that makes it a perfect candidate to trigger bigger questions about whether we belong in a given job or social group at work.

Combined, the disrespectful and ambiguous nature of rudeness makes us *feel* crummy and disrupts our *thinking*. Needless to say, neither of these psychological states is conducive to doing good work, which is why being on the receiving end of incivility is linked to lower job performance.

Alongside lower performance, rudeness makes us want to get away, not just from the source of it but often from the setting in which the rudeness took place. *Get me out of this workplace.* This rudeness reaction was demonstrated in a study by management researcher Shannon Taylor and his colleagues. Once a week, for six weeks, they surveyed a group of over a hundred employees. In every survey, they measured how much these workers experienced rudeness, felt burned out, and wanted to quit. Examining changes in these variables across weeks, they found a chain effect—from rudeness in one week to feeling burned out the following week to wanting to quit the week after that. In their words, "changes relative to one's previous experiences of incivility—irrespective of how high or low that incivility might have been—can generate significant changes in burnout and, in turn, thoughts about leaving." In my words, this means that while we may get used to the normal level of rudeness we face at work, when it ticks up, we notice, and it jolts us into thinking about quitting.

As you're reading this, you may be thinking, perhaps it's for the best if these highly sensitive individuals, who feel jolted by mere rudeness, make their way to the exit door. Maybe they're too sensitive and they don't fit in if they can't handle a bit of disrespect every now and then. That line of thought would be a mistake. Taylor and his colleagues found that being on the receiving end of incivility had supersized effects on burnout and intentions to quit in workers who had high levels of the personality trait that most strongly relates to high job performance: conscientiousness. For those low in conscientiousness, being treated rudely barely mattered. Other studies have shown that these extra-strong harmful effects of rudeness also show up in employees who are *most committed* to the organization. The bottom line is that rudeness is most jolting to precisely the employees that firms do not want to lose—the hardest working and most dedicated.

Out in the Cold

I don't need science to tell me that having a group of friends at work increases my overall enjoyment of my job (although science does offer ample evidence of this). Years back in a prior job, I was fortunate to be a part of a group of great peers, whom I enjoyed as colleagues and people. Much of our communication happened in a group chat, where we texted about everything from the latest episodes of TV shows to workplace happenings to questions about career-related topics. One evening during one of our in-person happy hours, I got a bit confused by the conversation, because it was clear that the others had already discussed parts of it earlier in the day. When I couldn't keep up, I said something like "I'm sorry I don't think I caught the backstory here." That's when one of my colleagues explained "Oh, that's right, we were discussing this in the other group chat."

I sat there, thinking about their other group chat, who was on it, and why I wasn't a part of it. I wasn't devastated or anything; it was just an unexpected signal that maybe I wasn't as much a part of this group as I thought. Maybe my connection to these peers wasn't as deep as I had in my head. Years later, I would laugh as one of the main characters on the award-winning comedy *Brooklyn Nine-Nine*—Detective Charles Boyle—experienced a similar situation after finding that the entire office had a web of multiple group chats, none of which included him. Boyle *was* devastated, and for good reason. As humans, we have a handful of fundamental psychological needs, and as we discussed earlier, one of the most basic is our need to belong. And when our need to connect to others is thwarted or threatened, it causes a strong reaction within us. Yes, even a threat as simple as being left out of a group chat.

Being left out involves *inaction* on the part of others—their failure to include you in the group. When asked, most people can quickly recall an experience of being ignored or excluded at work. Because it stems from inaction, being left out at work is subtle and often blameless. It's also not something that most people feel comfortable bringing up or complaining about. "Are you leaving me out of the group?" sounds too juvenile. But despite its place in the undercurrent of the social side of work, its effects are substantial.

A stream of studies has examined being excluded at work under the umbrella of *ostracism*—the experience of being ignored. Despite being more passive, ostracism is similar to rudeness in that it has harmful effects on how workers feel and think. What I found interesting when researching this topic is that ostracism activates the same regions of the brain as physical pain. This is wild, but people tend to feel physically colder when they're ostracized. I don't recall pulling on a scarf after the group chat incident, but maybe my brain has erased the memory of my impulse to do so. Alongside the chills, ostracism has other negative physical effects, like disrupting our sleep. Importantly, these effects don't depend on whether the ostracism was intentional or not. Most of the time, we don't know the thoughts and motives of those who leave us out in the social cold. We're on our own to figure out why the exclusion occurred. And when deducing this on our own, we often come to the negative conclusion that leaving us out was intentional. Which jolts us.

But really, how jolting could being left out of the group at work really be? Ask yourself this question right now: If you had to choose, would you rather experience ostracism, rudeness, or outright harassment at work? My feeling, before digging into the research, was that while I don't love being ignored, I'd rather be ignored than treated rudely. And I'd certainly rather be ignored than be outright harassed. And I wasn't alone in that sentiment. Research led by management professor Jane O'Reilly found that, in general, people *believe* harassment is more harmful. As a result of this belief, ostracism is more tolerated than other negative interpersonal behavior at work. However, in testing whether it actually is less harmful than harassment, O'Reilly found that ostracism is *more damaging* than harassment to people's sense of belonging and their overall well-being. She also looked at the effects of ostracism and harassment on employee turnover. Sure enough, ostracism was more strongly linked to quitting than harassment. Being left out at work sends a clear signal that you don't belong, which instantly reduces our embeddedness and often jolts us, even more than harassment.

The Customer Is Sometimes Very Wrong

In the late nineteenth and early twentieth centuries, giants began to emerge in the service industry, especially in retail and hospitality. Giant department stores and hotel chains, with titans of industry at their helm. Marshall Field, founder of the famous department store that bore his name, revolutionized the retail industry by offering customers perks that many of us take for granted today, such as giving a refund for a purchased product, even if there's nothing wrong with it. At the time, it was common for the burden to be on customers to be wary buyers, with no recourse for a bad purchase or a bad buying experience. Field flipped this mentality on its head, exemplified by his use of the now infamous phrase "The customer is always right."

Versions of this phrase still reign supreme for customer-serving empires around the world. One of the keys to the success of César Ritz's illustrious hotelier career was imprinting a simple belief in the minds of his service employees—*Le client n'a jamais tort*, which translates to "The customer is never wrong." If you're a customer in Germany, you are king (*Der Kunde ist König*), while in Japan, you are a god (*Okyakusama wa kamisama desu*). Amazon's mission statement begins with "We aim to be Earth's most customer-centric company." The message that these quotes and statements send to employees is clear: The customer is the most important person, and your goal is to satisfy them. In terms of who has the power in a service interaction, it is the customer.

As I've discussed rudeness and ostracism, I've kept the focus on when jolts come from fellow organizational members. Our peers. Our bosses. Our employees. Beyond our fellow workers, though, there is another source of direct jolts that most of us face at multiple points in our career, or for our entire working lives. This group of individuals has shown itself very capable of doling out bad behavior, even though many of us are told that it's part of our jobs to put up with it. That wonderful group of folks? It's us. When we're customers.

Much of the time, customers are friendly with their power. But sheesh, over the last decade, there seems to have been a sharp increase in customers who use their power to abuse service workers. In workplaces like call centers, employees may be mistreated by customers up to ten times per day.

Being on the receiving end of customer mistreatment immediately prompts less positive feelings about our job, followed by a desire to retaliate. And these feelings can last. On days when customers mistreated workers, employees dwelled on the experience that night and returned to work in a worse mood the next morning. Overall, after employees are mistreated, they're more likely to engage in deviant behavior (ranging from slacking off to violence) toward customers and the company.

In a study of service workers in the Philippines and Canada, researcher Danielle van Jaarsveld and her team first asked retail workers how often they experienced customer behaviors such as "yelled at you" and "spoke aggressively to you" over the prior month. Then, three months later, they surveyed these workers again and measured their negative emotions, emotional exhaustion, and intentions to quit. Finally, another three months later, they looked at how many of those employees actually left. The results were clear. To the extent that employees experienced customer mistreatment, they experienced more negative emotions and emotional exhaustion, jolting them to consider leaving at the three-month mark and to actually leave by the six-month mark. The research team replicated these findings in a study of call-center workers, showing that the mistreatment was just as damaging over the phone.

The unique combination of the unpleasantness of customer mistreatment and the message that "the customer is always right" plants the seeds for future jolts. In essence, service workers know that one of their primary goals is to generate and maintain customer satisfaction. For many of these workers, their compensation is partly dependent on achieving high customer satisfaction scores. Because of this, customer mistreatment places them between a rock and a hard place. On the one side, facing the unpleasantness of a rude customer triggers our fight-or-flight system. Our instinct is either to fight back, perhaps by telling the customer what a horrible person they are, or to flee, by hanging up the phone or turning around and walking away.

Failure and harassment. Rude colleagues, being ostracized, and jerk customers. Direct jolts happen *to us* and cause us to rethink our relationship with work. Of course those aren't the only jolts that strike in the workplace. The events that happen to those around us can also spill over and jolt us.

CHAPTER SIX

COLLATERAL JOLTS

The jolting effects of having a front-row seat to the twists and turns of our coworkers' lives.

As a management professor, one academic conference looms above all others: the Academy of Management Annual Meeting. For one week every August, around ten thousand of us take over the downtown core of a major city, leaving vacationers wondering why they're surrounded by lanyard-wearing ~~dorks~~ people excitedly discussing work. Talk about a holiday ruiner.

Several years ago, it was tourists in Chicago whose vacations were disrupted by our presence. That year, I didn't have a busy conference schedule and was anticipating my most carefree Academy ever. It turned out to be one of my worst.

AOM is the kickoff of our job market. For grad students on the market, the week is filled with interviews and networking. Those who already have a job but are looking to make a move also use the conference for these job search activities, though in a more clandestine manner.

On my first day in Chicago, I had meetups planned with friends from other schools. At breakfast I met up with a colleague I'll call Jenny. After catching up a bit, Jenny said she felt compelled to share something with me, but I needed to keep it confidential. She informed me that Dale, my coworker and close friend in my department, was interviewing for jobs at other schools. I was shocked. I thought Dale was completely happy and embedded.

Later that day I went for a stroll with Frank, a peer at another university. He said he felt compelled to share some information with me, but I needed to keep it confidential. I sensed he was going to tell me about Dale looking for jobs. Instead, he told me that Nancy, a *different* coworker and close friend in my department, was interviewing for a job at another school. At this point, I started reeling a bit. I loved my department and was under the impression (delusion?) that we all had little or no intentions of leaving.

At a reception that evening, I ran into Chet, another coworker and close friend in my department. I wondered if Chet knew that our hallway mates Dale and Nancy were interviewing for jobs at the conference. But because I gave Jenny and Frank my word, I couldn't ask him outright. So, I asked him some roundabout questions like "Have you heard any good gossip floating around?" and "Does it seem like this AOM has a strange vibe this year?" Based on his shifty responses, I could tell that Chet knew something but was keeping it from me. So, I switched my line of questioning to something more direct, like "What do you know about what's going on with the job market?"

Chet came clean, but not in the way I anticipated. He told me that *he* had selectively applied to some other schools and was interviewing while in Chicago. What!?

Nothing directly harmful happened *to me* that day. But I went back to my hotel room that night feeling jolted nonetheless. At the start of the day, I had no intention of thinking about leaving my job. No job-hunting activities on my radar. But as the long day ended, I had to ponder: If any one of those three folks leave, what does that mean for my happiness and my workload? And if all three of them go, I'd be a fool to not at least think about doing the same, right? To do some career cushioning of my own?

Neither Nancy nor Dale nor Chet ended up taking a job at another school. But one person in our department did leave that year. Me. The events of that day led me to entertain an invitation to interview at another school—an invitation I had previously declined. The jolt of my coworkers' job searches changed my feelings about my relationship with work in a way that led me to dabble in the job market, taking that one interview. Which led to a quick job offer. That I surprised myself by accepting.

Where Do You Think You're Going?

Have you ever been caught off guard by the news that one of your coworkers is job hunting or leaving? If the person leaving is a poor performer or an unpleasant person, you may be (justifiably) thrilled. But often, they have some or many redeeming qualities, personally and/or professionally. In these instances, learning of their job search or their actual departure can come as a jolt, causing you to question your own relationship with work. Turns out, just like the common cold, job searching and quitting are contagious. This contagion stems from several places.

Let's begin with the cases where we have a positive personal connection with the coworker who is edging toward the door. When they leave, our job satisfaction will go down. This is of course especially true when it's your work bestie. One of Gallup's most interesting questions in their engagement scale is "Do you have a best friend at work?" Their research indicates that people who have a good friend at work are more engaged. The flip side of this is that when a good friend at work leaves, a part of your commitment to the organization leaves with them. The departure of our colleague decreases the contentment we feel in our overall job. Our friend is gone. Our workdays become a bit less happy.

Beyond the loss of friendship, a coworker leaving places strain on the rest of us. Sure, the position may be immediately filled with a temporary replacement. But more often than not, remaining coworkers will take on additional work until a permanent replacement is up to speed. Capturing this common scenario, in a study examining the effects of disruptive work events, one participant described how "two coworkers suddenly resigned last week with many critical tasks incomplete. As it was not possible to hire new staff immediately, the incomplete tasks were assigned to me. This resulted in an unplanned significant increase in the amount of work I had to do." Sound familiar? At multiple points in our career, most of us are asked to take on more work due to a coworker's resignation. Usually, this extra workload doesn't come with extra pay, which adds a dash of unfairness to the situation.

Finally, when our coworker leaves, we want to know where they're going. To a competitor? Back to school? Staying home with family? Becoming an entrepreneur? Taking a career break? If they go to another job, we wonder how much of a raise they're getting (they *must* be getting a raise, right?), or what other improvements in their work lives they're netting. Of course, we don't think about these questions very long without also thinking about whether switching jobs could unlock improvements in our own pursuit of the good life. In this way, we're shaken out of autopilot and thrust into comparing our current work situation to possible alternatives.

Combined, these three reasons explain why merely finding out that our coworkers are job seeking often jolts us. Why turnover is contagious. Why, when someone in our work group engages in a job search, it increases the quitting odds of everyone else on the team.

Research has shed some light on *when* the resignation behavior of those around us at work is especially likely to jolt us into thinking about leaving. First, if the departure is *unexpected*, as was the case when I learned of my colleagues' potential departures, it's more likely to be a collateral jolt. Second, to the extent that the departure causes *disruption* to the team, it's more likely to be a collateral jolt. Having the most valuable member of your work group—whether it be the star performer or the social glue of the team—depart will cause more jolts among team members than having someone on the periphery of the work group leave. Finally, the degree to which you *depend on* the potential leaver, personally or professionally, for your own work happiness and productivity, will directly relate to how big a collateral jolt their departure will be.

One instance when all three ingredients for turnover contagion are present is when we find out that a manager we like is leaving or considering doing so. This explains why employees who have strong relationships with their bosses become particularly likely to leave after their manager does. Obviously, this has implications for the leader succession process, with studies showing that the replacement of a leader often spurs turnover within their work group. The same goes for when a mentor leaves, often jolting mentees and triggering their job searching and turnover.

When a Colleague's Departure Is Not Voluntary

The discussion above focused on times when coworkers' job searches and quitting are *voluntary*. Of course, that's not always the case. Involuntary turnover takes two main forms: layoffs and terminations. Layoffs are especially likely to serve as collateral jolts; they contain all the elements of turnover contagion discussed above, but they come with the added disruption caused by significant organizational change and the added negative emotions, such as guilt, associated with surviving the round of layoffs (i.e., survivor guilt). Not surprisingly, the negative effects of layoffs on remaining workers are strongest among survivors who felt connected to those who were let go.

But what about when a coworker is *fired* (or *sacked*, as they say in the UK)? Until recently, it was unclear if and when a worker's termination would jolt coworkers in a way that made them more prone to voluntarily leave in the future. Helpfully, the cumulative effects of firings, layoffs, and voluntary departures on remaining employees were recently quantified in research led by management scholar Sima Sajjadiani. Her research team examined turnover contagion following all types of employee departures across 1,500 stores over two years.

Let's start with terminations. Firings did *not* meaningfully affect subsequent turnover in work groups. Typically, terminations are caused by employee misbehavior or poor performance that occurs repeatedly over time. So rather than serving as jolts, they often come as a relief to the rest of the work group. Of course, that isn't to say that having a colleague fired will never serve as a collateral jolt. It's just to say that even if you're upset that your peer has been fired, those feelings are commonly tempered by the knowledge that they played an active role in the process that led to their being shown the door.

But layoffs are a completely different story. In the two months following layoffs, resignations among workers who remained jumped considerably. Clearly, layoffs are a jolting experience for those who survive them.

And finally, there's voluntary quitting (with no layoffs involved). Interestingly, having a coworker resign didn't spur *immediate* quitting among remaining coworkers. In the month following voluntary turnover, no contagion effects were detected. However, in the months after that, a spike in quitting appeared and continued in the form of a significant and increasing rate of turnover contagion over time. This aligns with my Chicago story from the start of the chapter; I resigned six months after AOM that year.

Sajjadiani's findings also give insight into *whose* departure is most likely to serve as a jolt to you. Firings of high performers did raise subsequent quits among one small, specific group of workers—*fellow high performers*. This similarity effect happened when a low performer was terminated; it related to some contagion quitting, mostly among other low performers. These matching performance-level effects were also found for voluntary turnover. High-performer resignations disproportionately spurred high-performer contagion, and the same went for low and low.

But when it came to layoffs, eliminating a high performer's position led to higher subsequent quitting in *both* high and low performers. The layoff of low performers had a small effect on subsequent turnover of low performers but pretty much no effect on the subsequent turnover of high performers. This challenges the notion that high performers will respond positively to laying off low performers. It's more accurate to say that it has no effect, in turnover at least.

The takeaway here is clear. When people who we feel are "like us" consider resigning or actually do leave (voluntarily or not), it jolts us into reflecting on our own relationship with work, and whether it is giving us our best shot at achieving the good life. These types of collateral jolts are going to strike many times in our career. Because of how disruptive they can be, it is hard to prepare for them. But by simply reminding yourself from time to time (perhaps in your biannual work relationship check-in) that in the near future, good coworkers may leave, you will be less jolted when it does happen. Perhaps more meaningfully, reminding yourself of this reality will spur you to engage in a behavior that has been repeatedly shown to have positive effects on our well-being—savoring. Savor the time you do have with your similar and close colleagues at work; it won't last forever.

Being the Third Party Is Not a Party

In the prior chapter, we talked about direct jolts that stem from experiencing workplace harassment, ostracism, and rudeness, as well as mistreatment by customers. Now, shift your perspective and think of times when you've experienced these events at work *as a bystander.* Such as witnessing one of your colleagues being treated with disrespect. Turns out, merely observing such events carries potential for collateral jolts. At work, toxic conflict and other types of interpersonal strife commonly involve two people but play out in the presence of others. When leaders get involved, they tend to focus on those directly in the fray. That's the right approach, but it stops short of dealing with the full consequences of the spat. Researchers are increasingly finding that being a bystander to disrespect, abuse, and mistreatment can be as impactful as being involved in it. Being a third party to abuse at work is often referred to as *vicarious mistreatment*, because seeing a colleague become the victim of mistreatment can elicit the same jolts as if you experienced it firsthand.

In the immediate aftermath of witnessing a colleague being treated disrespectfully, we often experience elevated anxiety, burnout, and even physical illness. It can be uncomfortable and revolting. Those feelings often jolt us into reflecting on the event and our relationship with work. One of the main causes of mistreatment at work is the presence of a toxic work culture that allows it to go unpunished. So, not surprisingly, as we reflect on witnessing the abuse of others at work, we think about whether we really want to be a part of a place that allows these types of things to happen. And of course, we worry that we could be next. As a result, we begin to feel less committed to our company, more frustrated with our jobs, and less trusting of our managers, triggering lower job engagement and worse job performance. Sounds like a recipe for being on the pondering path to quitting. Sure enough, merely observing abusive behavior at work can lead to a spike in workers' plans to quit.

The above effects describe situations when people witness incivility at work and do nothing about it. As you can imagine, just like turnover contagion, these jolts are strongest if the victim is our friend or if they're similar to us. But, when we see our friends or those similar to us treated poorly, we often don't stand idly by. Instead, we initiate a second potentially jolting event—we intervene by reporting the incident or confronting the perpetrator. Reporting the incident is akin to whistleblowing, wherein those who speak up about abuse can be stigmatized for having done so, thereby making them more likely to quit in the future.

And then there's confronting the perpetrator. Often, those who dole out the abuse do so because they're in a position of power and feel that they can behave badly with no repercussions. You don't need me to cite research to tell you that confronting someone at work who has more power than you do can be a "career-limiting move." Imagine speaking up after witnessing your boss berating your colleague. It's possible that your boss would realize the error of their ways and apologize, but it's just as possible that they would shift the focus of their abuse to you and your career. A politically savvier (albeit potentially less courageous) strategy would be to intervene after the meeting, talking to your boss in private about the inappropriateness of their behavior. This strategy has a higher chance of not backfiring but nonetheless still carries the risk that you make yourself the target for future abuse from your boss.

To be clear, this isn't to say that workers *always* experience coworker abuse negatively. There are circumstances in which we experience positive emotions, or a reduction in negative emotions, when we witness others being abused. This is most common when we have also been victims of the perpetrator. When we're mistreated at work, we often attribute it to *our own* faults and shortcomings. When our boss berates us in that meeting, we sometimes walk back to our desks feeling lousy about ourselves and thinking that we deserve the poor treatment because of our personal failings. But then, when we see our boss treat others the same way, it can come as a relief because we realize that our boss is at fault. *They* are actually a jerk who treats everyone poorly. While this does provide some relief, it may also strengthen the likelihood that the event will jolt us out of default mode and cause us to question our relationship with work.

In this way, jolts that happen to others around us reverberate as collateral jolts. And there's a specific period of time in our work lives when these negative events, direct and collateral, are especially likely to jolt us into taking drastic action.

CHAPTER SEVEN

HONEYMOON JOLTS

Why our first year on a job is all too often our last.

In September 2016, the ride-sharing company Uber made a much-praised executive hire. The company poached Jeff Jones from the retailer Target, where he served as chief marketing officer. Jones had helped transform Target from a brick-and-mortar retailer to a tech-savvy e-commerce powerhouse. And if any company needed a similar transformation at that time, especially of its image, it was Uber. The company's reputation had been tarnished by the behavior of its founder and the culture that he created. These problems were widely reported, so Jones knew what he was getting into.

Just seven months into his tenure, though, Jones announced his resignation. In explaining why he was leaving, he said: "I joined Uber because of its mission, and the challenge to build global capabilities that would help the company mature and thrive long term. It is now clear, however, that the beliefs and approach to leadership that have guided my career are inconsistent with what I saw and experienced at Uber, and I can no longer continue as president of the ride-sharing business."

Jones had experienced a honeymoon jolt, when a negative event in your new job causes you to reassess whether it is the right one for you.

Think back to the last time you started a new job, and your experience during the first week of that new role. Were all of the expectations you had formed during the job search process fulfilled or exceeded? How about after the first thirty days? Ninety? At the one-year mark?

Going back to Jones, it's hard to imagine that he didn't do his homework before making the leap from Target. He likely went through multiple rounds of interviews and sought advice from those close to him and from those who were familiar with Uber's culture and operations. And he likely felt confident in his assessment that there was a fit between his abilities and values and the needs and culture of Uber. And yet, it turned out that when his *expectations met the reality* of the company and the job, his forecast was wrong. That doesn't mean he or Uber is to blame for the bad match. As we'll discuss, the job search and employee recruitment processes have inherent flaws that make jolts during the first 365 days on the job more common than in any other period of employees' careers.

Jeff Jones is in no way alone in going from being an excited new hire to a disillusioned departer in a matter of months. Odds are, you or someone close to you has gone through this same whipsaw. A LinkedIn poll of 56,000 workers indicated that 42 percent of them had quit a new job within a year. Another poll showed that 30 percent of workers had quit a job within the first ninety days. These statistics align with the findings of organizational researchers, who have long found that the *majority* of voluntary turnover "occurs among new hires who face difficulty adjusting to the job." And there's evidence that resignations in the first twelve months on the job—dubbed *quick quitting*—are becoming more common. Data from 2022 showed that quick quitting had increased 10 percent in the prior year alone.

The fact that most turnover happens in employees' first year in a new job surprised me when I first came across it. We're often in an optimistic state of mind when we begin a new job and have hopes that it's the start of a positive long-term relationship. Our energy is high. And companies invest untold resources into recruiting, selection, and onboarding to boost the odds that new employees have successful beginnings. That's why when we imagine a disgruntled employee, we don't typically picture the newbie who started six months ago; we more often think of the grisly veteran with a bad attitude. And yet, the newbie is more likely thinking about leaving.

Moreover, quitting a job that we just started is something that most of us would prefer to avoid. Making the transition between jobs is tough even under ideal circumstances, so having to go through it more than once in a short period of time is especially unpleasant. As humans, we're motivated to maintain consistency between what we say and what we do. This drive for consistency means that considering leaving a company that we only recently committed to causes internal conflict and guilt. And of course, there's the stress associated with knowing that it's broadly frowned upon to resign from a company shortly after joining it. One survey found that having a job with a tenure of less than fifteen months on your résumé can harm your employability.

So, with all the negative emotions and thoughts associated with leaving right after arriving at a job, why is it so common? Because there's another powerful emotion that overrides the others: regret.

Late 2021 and early 2022 represented the peak of post-pandemic quitting. Later in 2022, headlines began appearing with some variation of the following message: The Great Resignation has become the Great Regret. These headlines appeared again in 2024 and continue to this day. The stories under these headlines tell of the many workers who regret their recent job changes. I am glad these examples of regret are being publicized; they serve as a nice counterbalance to all the stories being broadcast of people who quit and went on to live their absolute best lives. "Jump, and the net will appear," these people would say. Unfortunately, in the real world, the net often misses its cue to materialize.

While I like the dose of reality that these "Great Regret" articles provided, I am dismayed that they make it seem like experiencing regret after making a job or career change is a new phenomenon, unique to the post-pandemic job market. High levels of quitting have always been associated with high levels of regret.

Regarding the type of the regret, much of the conversation on this topic seems to jump to the conclusion that job hoppers' regret stems from missing their prior job. It's the "you don't know what you've got until it's gone" phenomenon. I've found in my own research that it's not unusual to experience some regret and nostalgia (alongside the positive feelings of excitement and freedom) almost immediately after resigning. These mixed feelings come from the reality that (as we've discussed) most people who resign don't dislike *every* aspect of their jobs. Instead, they often hold positive feelings toward much of what they're leaving behind. So post-quitting regret arises in part from missing the positive aspects of one's prior job, even if leaving was ultimately the correct decision. It's a little like homesickness.

But in most cases, a bit of homesickness isn't enough to overcome the stigma associated with bailing on your new company just a few months after joining.

Leaving your new job so quickly is often driven by a more potent form of regret. Not the regret that comes from the decision you made to *leave* your prior job but the regret that comes from the decision you made to *take* this new one. This is why, when quick quitters are asked why they quit so quickly, they don't reply by saying that they missed their prior jobs. No, they overwhelmingly point toward two types of jolts that happened in their new jobs. We've already discussed the first one, explaining why Oprah walked away from *60 Minutes* shortly after she started—the direct jolt of being mistreated by one's boss, coworkers, or customers. The second one? A psychological contract breach.

The Other Employment Contract

Years ago, one of my students told the class the story of a job she had just accepted at a prestigious consulting firm. Throughout the recruitment process, the firm touted its work-life friendly benefits, including a generous amount of paid vacation. This student was wowed by the number of paid holidays, and it played into her decision to accept the job, partly because she had planned some trips to visit family and friends in the coming year. As her start date approached, she began connecting with her soon-to-be peers who had worked at the firm for a few years. At one gathering, she shared her holiday plans for the upcoming year. Instead of being met with the usual positivity you get when sharing holiday plans, her future colleagues responded with awkward silence and low enthusiasm. Finally, one of them shared the reason behind their muted reactions. Although they *technically* have that amount of vacation, it's frowned upon to use it in your first year. It sends a bad signal to management about your dedication and work ethic. Her peers advised her to postpone her travel plans so that using her vacation days (which were just sold to her as a perk of the job) didn't derail her career prospects with the company. The student was stunned, and the positive energy she had about working for the company drained away. Here she was, having not yet begun her work with the company, and already feeling betrayed by it.

This type of jolt—the honeymoon jolt—comes from the unpleasant surprise of learning that an expectation you held about some aspect of your new job is at odds with the reality. As my student's experience shows, this disconnect between what was communicated during recruitment and what you actually experience can show up even before day one, during the period after you've accepted a job but before you've officially started.

You may ask yourself, if we have defined jolts as events that shake you out of autopilot mode, how can they happen so soon in a new job? Has autopilot even been established? The answer is yes, and it comes in the form of a psychological contract. For most jobs, there is the actual, written contract you sign. But that contract covers only the basic terms of employment. It does not (and cannot) capture all the eventualities that may occur once you begin working. Your actual contract may give you the flexibility to take an afternoon to attend your child's school play. But it does not stipulate whether your boss will be supportive when you actually attend the play, or if they'll act annoyed and make you feel guilty for taking the time. My student who was discouraged from using her vacation days? That is psychological contract territory. The psychological contract refers to a worker's beliefs about the two-way obligations that exist between themselves and their organization. What do you owe the company, in terms of your time, energy, and effort? And what do they owe you in return, in terms of organizational culture, rewards, working conditions, and so on?

The psychological contract is established during the job search and recruitment processes. You build a set of beliefs about what it will be like to work for the company. You do your research and ask as many questions as you can to determine whether the job will be a good fit for you. As the company provides answers to your questions, the psychological contract crystallizes. And you're learning what and how much the company expects of you in return. Will there be the occasional late night at the office required? Do you need to check your email on weekends? Is there travel involved?

Once you accept the job, you start to see whether your expectations meet reality. The period between when you accept a job and your start date can be telling. Does the company keep in touch and help prepare you for your start? Do your future coworkers reach out and express excitement that you're joining? Or is there silence? Or worse yet, are there signs that the company isn't what you were led to believe it was? Maybe you can't get the answers you need regarding your benefits, or the relocation process isn't as smooth as you were told it would be. Before the actual work even gets a chance to begin, violations of your psychological contract—honeymoon jolts—can start to occur.

Hopefully, you make it to Day 1 with your psychological contract intact, and a lovely honeymoon period can commence. During those early days and weeks on the job, support from the company should be quite strong. After all, most firms dedicate substantial resources to the onboarding process, with the goal of providing you with what you need to learn the job, socially integrate with your coworkers, and understand your role in the company. When onboarding is successful, by the end of the first year, you hopefully identify strongly as a member of the company and you feel good about your decision to join.

But again, this first year is the most common time for voluntary turnover, suggesting that many employees never make it to this strong identification. Jolts, in the form of psychological contract violations, happen in those moments where you discover that some element of your new job falls well short of your expectations. This can feel similar to a breach of trust, because the conditions under which you agreed to accept the job are not met or maintained. This breakdown of trust can derail the onboarding process, causing you to question whether you would have accepted the job had you known that this was the reality. All of a sudden, the honeymoon of your new job feels more like a hangover.

I wish I could take credit for the honeymoon-hangover language in the prior sentence, but it belongs to management professor Wendy Boswell, who provided compelling evidence of this phenomenon. In an initial study, she tracked more than five hundred executives over the years spanning the time before, during, and after they made a job change. Her research team observed that leading up to the job change, there was either a gradual (think push-pull) or sharp (think jolts) drop in their job satisfaction.

After they changed jobs, these execs' satisfaction spiked. The honeymoon period! The promise and excitement of a new job!

But these positive feelings often didn't last. In many cases, they precipitously dropped, below even the executives' happiness level in the prior job (hi there, hangover). Eventually, if they didn't quit, their satisfaction tapered to similar levels as they had in their prior job. That's where regret comes in: *I made this big job change to improve my pursuit of the good life, and I'm right back where I was before!* In a follow-up study examining why such a drop-off in newcomer happiness occurred, these researchers found that broken commitments (in other words, psychological contract violations) had knocked these employees out of the positive mental space in which they began their new jobs.

This honeymoon-hangover effect is also vividly seen in international assignments. When sent to work abroad, expats initially revel in the novelty of living and working in a new culture. But after that initial euphoria wears off, they start to get disillusioned with certain aspects of the new culture. When I moved to the UK, the initial charm of drying our clothes on a drying rack instead of in an electric dryer like we had back home quickly morphed into annoyance. This disillusionment often builds until, one day, an event jolts expats into full-scale culture shock, often resulting in their asking to go back home (in my case, I just bought a dryer). In cases where expats successfully navigate culture shock, they tend to change their mindset to adapt to the new culture. But their satisfaction typically never returns to the level of the initial honeymoon phase.*

More depressingly for new workers, a study of over 2,500 Australian workers challenged Boswell's findings that most workers at least enjoy a bit of a honeymoon period. This study found that on average, job satisfaction tended to drop almost right away in the first year of a new job. During the following years, satisfaction slowly climbed its way back toward a level close to the first day of the new job, but on average, it never made it all the way back up there. Adding to this bleak picture, job changers' positive energy and sense of belonging tended never to return to their Day 1 levels, even up to twelve years on. Similarly, these folks' work-family conflict spiked in years one and two and peaked in year three following a job change, always staying at a higher level than it was on Day 1.

Our expectation that our new job will be better than our last is often at odds with reality. And a single event often signals to us that our psy-

---

* When it goes well, this adjustment to the new culture can be so complete that expats completely adapt to their new culture, causing this jolt to reoccur when they return to their home country, an effect dubbed *reverse culture shock*.

chological contract has been breached, triggering regret and jolting us into immediately starting to look for a way out, or a way back to our former employer.

An Imperfect Process, at Best

The seeds of honeymoon jolts are planted during two intertwined processes: job search and recruitment. The job search is your quest to find a job. Recruitment is a company's quest to build a pool of qualified folks interested in its job opening. To say that it's an imperfect dance would be putting it mildly. Many people's job searches are a bit of a mess. And the way companies recruit workers often creates massive headaches down the line.

As workers, we don't begin job searches as blank slates. Just as in our romantic lives, our prior relationships have an impact on our attitudes and beliefs when we enter into new ones. If a prior partner unexpectedly broke our heart, we may be more cautious when starting a subsequent relationship, be slower to commit to it, and be faster to leave it. The same goes for our relationships with work. This is why employees who have been on the receiving end of a layoff tend to be less trusting of their subsequent employers, and therefore more sensitive to honeymoon jolts and more likely to quit than their colleagues who have never been layoff victims. Researchers have quantified this effect and found that being laid off made employees 65 percent more likely to quit their subsequent jobs than those who were never laid off. Each additional layoff increased a person's likelihood of quitting by almost 40 percent. The key takeaway for leaders is that by enacting layoffs, they are creating a more "quit-friendly" workforce. But the takeaway for you is that how and why you separated from your prior jobs may affect how you approach your job search and your commitment to your future employer. Those of us who have been jilted by former employers are primed to detect and react to honeymoon jolts.

More than what has happened to us in the past, the stakes of the job search for our present lives add to the challenge of navigating it. For most of us, the success of our job search deeply matters for our personal and financial well-being, and for our long-term career success and happiness. Because of these stakes, the job search process, and the twists and turns within it, causes strong emotional reactions in us. Imagine those times when you see the perfect job get posted. So much excitement! Often followed by worries about whether you'll be able to get the company interested in your application and then actually be able to land it. And then you go through the process of applying, and waiting, and maybe getting an interview, and then more waiting. During this process, you may get rejected or ghosted, or you may be treated so amazingly well that you're more excited than ever to become a member of the firm.

As job seekers, we ride more than one of these emotional roller coasters at a time, as new jobs are posted and others are eliminated. Of course, emotions aren't the main focus of our job search; we're trying to determine whether any of these different jobs will give us what we want. Perhaps more opportunities for career advancement, and a shorter commute. A more developmental boss, or of course more money and flexibility. Sizing up all these variables requires time and energy, followed by weighing the pros and cons of all the different things a company offers: retirement, benefits, pay, work setting, work flexibility, coworkers, career development, and on and on. And for those conducting their searches while working, more calculus comes from evaluating these things against those that your current job is providing.

And despite all this information that you have to size up during your search, some of the most critical information is almost always missing. How do they treat their employees? Will my future team members accept me in the group? Will I be able to work my preferred shift schedule as they say I will? Can I use my sick days without being harshly judged for doing so?

Overall, you're navigating a process that simultaneously throws too much and too little information at you. And because of what's riding on the outcome of the process, emotions are high and volatile. And if there's one thing that interferes with our ability to make rational decisions, it's our emotions.

Now, I realize that some of you live for the thrill of the job hunt. That's fantastic for you, but you're in the minority. For most of us, it's a necessary evil, and its unpleasantness partly explains why so many people stay in jobs they don't like. Better the devilish job you know than going through a foggy, rejection-filled process that doesn't have any guarantees of success.

Across the table, although they typically have the more enviable (read: powerful) of the two positions in this dance, companies have their own set of issues that make attracting the right type of workers to their jobs difficult. They sometimes don't know what type of person will be most likely to be happy and perform well in a given role. It's hard to determine what specific skills, traits, and attitudes best predict happiness and performance in a certain job. In other cases, companies may plan to modify the job depending on who they hire, making giving consistent and precise details to job applicants impossible. In addition, hiring processes are largely carried out by humans who do all sorts of unexpected things when they're recruiting potential employees (and at the moment, AI doesn't seem to be doing any better). The biases and idiosyncrasies possessed by the individuals (and algorithms) responsible for hiring add a massive dose of inaccuracy (not to mention prejudice in many cases) to this process.

The Problem with Being on Our Best Behavior

Altogether, because of the imperfections in the job search process, you have to make a high-stakes decision based on some good information, some incorrect information, and a bunch of missing information. This leads to many psychological contracts that aren't aligned with the reality of the job. And these imperfections are compounded by one final source of trouble in the job search and the hiring process. Both sides, to some extent, are onstage. We're all acting, to some degree.

On the job seeker side, don't get me wrong, I am all for being authentic. But when we're interviewing for a job we want, we tend not to show our unfiltered, wholly authentic selves. We're not (typically) dishonest, but we are on our best behavior, just as we are whenever we want to impress someone. The problem for companies is that because I'm only putting my best foot forward, they don't get to see my other foot. That other foot will most definitely accompany me into the workplace if I get hired. And I'm not alone; studies show that most job candidates engage in a bit of acting to present a desired image to those who are recruiting them.

And of course, the company is acting, too. Companies invest untold sums in convincing you that they're a great place to work. More than ever, companies use the same tactics to recruit employees as they do to market their products. It's called *employer branding*. The goal is the same as marketing a product: to create a desirable employer image that will elicit positive feelings and reactions in job seekers. The upsides for organizations are clear. To the extent that a company has a positive brand as an employer, job seekers are more attracted to it, and more likely to accept jobs when they're offered. When a company has a negative employer brand, the implications are also clear; they have trouble recruiting good applicants and have to pay more for them than their competitors. And when they have no brand, job seekers will have a difficult time differentiating them from other employers. But the brand also sets expectations. Through advertising, via word of mouth, and during the recruitment process, companies typically show recruits the very best side of the organization.

Of course, we have all bought something based on marketing and then realized that the product or service didn't live up to our expectations. The difference between the cheeseburger you see in the online ad when you're scrolling through your phone at 10:00 p.m. and the one you unwrap after it's delivered to your door thirty minutes later? They're both cheeseburgers, and all the ingredients are there, but the real thing falls well short of the perfect, glistening burger you saw in the ad.

Again, there isn't outright lying in most recruitment processes, but there is acting. I've seen instances in which disgruntled current employees are conveniently left out of recruitment activities, for fear they'll tell candidates how they feel about the company. I bet you've observed this as well. While these activities aren't fraudulent, they do give job seekers an unbalanced perspective about what it will be like to work at the company. And by not providing the applicant with the fine print on their psychological contract (like letting my student know that taking vacation in Year 1 is frowned upon), companies sow the seeds of future honeymoon jolts.

To be clear, I'm not suggesting that everyone isn't trying their best in the job search and hiring processes. While there are always some bad actors, job seekers and hiring companies alike want to find a match that leads to a positive and long-lasting relationship. What I am trying to convey is that switching jobs, or hiring someone, is made very difficult by flaws inherent in the process. These flaws cause problems that often won't come to light until after you accept or start your job. Within many happy job offer acceptances, unbeknownst to both parties, a ticking time bomb exists. At some point in the next year, that bomb could detonate in the form of a honeymoon jolt, potentially triggering an episode of quick quitting.

But for those of us who find ourselves in this situation, should a speedy exit be the first response to honeymoon jolts, and the direct and collateral jolts we experience in the workplace? Most of the time, it should not. . . .

CHAPTER EIGHT

SPEAK UP

Using your voice is one of the most effective ways to deal with jolts for workers and employers alike. If only both sides didn't botch it so often.

What are your options when you're in a relationship with another entity—another person, a group of friends, your country's government, or your employer—and some part of it is undesirable, or not as good as it could be?

Albert Otto Hirschman knew a thing or two about finding yourself in a bad situation. The man who would become a renowned economist was raised in a Jewish household in 1920s Berlin. An antifascist during a time of growing fascism in the 1930s, Albert voluntarily joined the Spanish Civil War when he was in his early twenties. There, he learned not only how to fight but how to evacuate and rescue people from harm's way, a skill set he put to use in the 1940s. During World War II, Hirschman changed his identity to Albert Hermant, and worked covertly with the Emergency Rescue Committee in Marseilles to help hundreds of people escape Nazi-occupied France to safety.

Decades later, Hirschman returned to the topic of what humans do when they find themselves in bad situations, such as a citizen being oppressed by their government, or a shareholder losing money due to bad management, or a customer receiving bad service. Only this time, he approached it from the safe distance of academic inquiry. The obvious answer, and the one that his fellow economists favored at the time, is to exit. Just leave. The disillusioned citizen can move to another location, the disgruntled shareholder can sell their shares, and the unhappy customer can boycott the business.

But as we've discussed, when it comes to our jobs, leaving is often undesirable or not feasible. Hirschman acknowledged the same thing when it came to oppressed citizens—bailing out isn't always an option. Moreover, choosing to exit does little to help make the situation better. He elaborated on a second common and powerful response. Speak up. He referred to this as *voice*, a term that lodged itself in the academic literature and continues to be used today to describe instances in which people speak out to enact change.

Compared to carrying on in the wake of a jolt, speaking up represents a bold and active response. But in the face of direct, collateral, and honeymoon jolts, it is often more effective and appropriate than simply keeping calm and carrying on.

In terms of *effective*, the jolts that we experience at work are often not easily dismissed. Being ostracized. Losing your closest coworker. Finding out that you were misled in the recruitment process. Time does not heal all wounds, and these jolts can reveal problems with our relationship with work that, unless addressed, will be a permanent barrier to our pursuit of the good life through work.

And in terms of *appropriate*, when a jolt reveals a problem with our relationship with work that is potentially fixable, doing nothing to solve it doesn't harm just your own well-being but that of people around you as well. In many cases, you aren't the only one experiencing a given type of jolt. The rude treatment of a customer. The shock of the sudden departure of a beloved boss. Learning that the company's advertised flexible work policy is as stiff as a board. By surfacing the problem associated with the jolt, you create the opportunity for healthy change in your own and others' work situation.

At the other end of the spectrum, sometimes when we experience a jolt at work, the first thing that comes to mind is writing a resignation email and hitting send. Of course, the problem with hasty quitting is that unless you have a guaranteed better job lined up, you're just swapping out one problem (the one revealed by the jolt) for another (unemployment and a job search).

So, you've tried (or at least considered) carrying on, but it's not (or no longer) working, and quitting is too extreme. The ideal solution, of course, is to see if you can speak up and solve the issue.

You may be thinking, "Well duh, Anthony." But hear me out. There are countless cases where an employee is jolted to quit over an issue that could have been solved had it been surfaced. I'm confident you've seen it happen. Sometimes, the only reason a problem wasn't addressed was because the worker didn't bring it up. Often, we don't bring up problems because we *think* we know what our boss will say. We think there's no way they're going to work with us to find a solution, so what's the point of asking?

For example, maybe a jolt has made you realize that you want to spend more time with your family, but you're pretty confident your work won't let you switch to part time. Or maybe you've been passed over for some development opportunities and your boss hasn't told you why. In these situations, it may be tempting to conclude that your boss is blocking your pursuit of the good life, and you need to leave. This may especially be the case if you've tried to bring up the issue to your boss and haven't made any progress.

But before throwing in the towel, it's worth speaking up to someone in your organization about the issue at the core of the jolt. Doing so allows us to test our assumption that the company won't be open to accommodating us. It's worth talking to your boss about it, and if they are not receptive, to consider surfacing the issue with a mentor, with someone in HR, and/or with your boss's boss. As we'll discuss in a minute, these strategies aren't without risk, but if you're considering leaving anyway, speaking up to multiple people who can potentially help can be well worth it.

Another upside of voice is that if you do end up leaving, you'll do so with the comfort of knowing that you tried everything you could to make it work with your employer. This will reduce the chance that you'll later go into a spiral of *counterfactual thinking*. Which is just a fancy way of describing what happens when we look back and think "What if?" Counterfactual thinking tends to lead to regret and self-blame—mental states most of us would prefer to avoid. If you speak up and still end up leaving, your future self will be less likely to brood over "what might have been" because your current self has determined "what *is*" before leaving.

Finally, voice can help you avoid the awkwardness of planning your resignation, announcing it, and then after you explain why you're quitting, having someone higher up in your company propose an acceptable solution. Sometimes, going through such an ordeal is necessary for you to be taken seriously by your superiors. But the "just kidding" quit-and-then-stay process is disruptive and often torches a good chunk of your goodwill with those around you.

For these reasons, it makes sense to speak up to your coworkers, manager, and/or others about the issue that the jolt has revealed. This is often easier said than done. You may be conflict-avoidant, and the thought of bringing up a problem with your boss causes instant anxiety. You may work in a company or culture where speaking up to higher-ups is frowned upon. Or the issue at the heart of the matter is deeply personal, and you prefer not to share that side of yourself at work. I get it. There are plenty of reasons to skip this step. Speaking up is a bit scary for most of us. And for good reason. It can lead to conflict, being taken advantage of, losing the approval of others, or simply looking foolish. So, let's go in with eyes wide open and discuss the science behind surfacing problems, starting with the ways it can go askew. With that in hand, we can turn the page to the science of successfully speaking up.

The Downsides of Speaking Up

When an employee resigns, managers often bemoan that the person didn't speak up sooner. If only they had known about the problem, they could have fixed it and retained the worker. Why didn't the employee say something instead of looking for another job?

At first glance, voice seems like the obvious first choice when a jolt reveals that some aspect of your relationship with work is deficient. You've located the problem, and it's probably in everyone's best interest that you speak up about it, right? Share the issue with your coworkers, your boss, HR, or whoever, so it can be addressed. Once fixed, your pursuit of the good life will be back on track, and the company will have retained a valuable employee. Moreover, you're probably not the only one feeling the post-jolt way you do, so shining some daylight on the problem allows the company to fix an issue that may increase the engagement and commitment of other workers as well.

So, voice is a win-win, right? In theory, yes. In practice, less so.

At a high level, having employees speak up about problems *is* a win for the organization. In a study of 1,000 employees spread across nearly a hundred bank branches, management professor Jim Detert and his research team found that in locations where workers spoke up to their leader, branch performance was higher. The logic behind this effect is pretty straightforward. Employees see problems and opportunities that managers do not. But managers have greater power to fix problems and capitalize on opportunities. Overall, then, when voice works well, employees elevate problems and opportunities, and managers deal with them. Yay teamwork!

But we often don't voice *upward*, at our managers, right? Often, we direct our talk of problems and opportunities *sideways*, to our coworkers. Unfortunately, they typically don't have the power to solve our problems, so our talking to peers about problems they can't fix just makes things worse. This may seem counterintuitive. After all, shouldn't venting to coworkers about workplace problems make us feel better, or at least that we've been heard? Sometimes, yes, this can be a form of coping that provides us with a temporary feeling of relief, especially if the listener shows us a different, more positive way to think about the problem. But in general, venting tends to leave you feeling angrier and more hopeless than keeping it to yourself, and it spreads those negative vibes around. That's why in the bank branch study mentioned above, voice directed at coworkers actually reduced work-group performance. So, then why do so many people voice sideways instead of upward?

Because bringing up problems to your boss is one of the riskiest "positive" behaviors in the book. Thus far, I've been talking about how events that jolt us can reveal problems with our relationship with work or opportunities to improve it. I've treated these two things—problems and opportunities—pretty much the same. But speaking up about problems versus opportunities for improvement are totally different.

Think back on the last few times you have spoken up about issues at work. You can categorize each incident in one of two ways. Sometimes, voice is *supportive*, in that its content is all about how to *improve* existing processes. At other times, voice is *challenging*, in that it expresses *concern* about ongoing practices. Both types of voice aim to improve some aspect of work, but the supportive approach involves improving what is in place, and the challenging approach involves critiquing the status quo.

Both types of voice are needed for a well-functioning organization. Supportive voice—"Here's how to do things better!"—drives innovation, which leads to higher overall group productivity. Challenging voice—"There's a problem with how we're doing things!"—helps companies avoid errors and pitfalls, such as safety incidents or the unnecessary turnover of good workers.

Which category do you think bringing up a jolt that's causing you to consider leaving your job will fall under? Supportive or challenging?

It's often going to be challenging voice. And this is where the potential downsides of voice start to add up.

In one of the first studies of these two types of voice, management scholar Ethan Burris found that managers viewed employees who used challenging voice as less loyal and as more of a threat than those who spoke up in a supportive manner. These managers also rated employees who used challenging voice as lower performers. Turns out, challenging your boss can be a career-limiting move.

Since this initial study, research has repeatedly shown that supportive voice leads to higher performance ratings from managers, and challenging voice does the opposite.

As someone who has been a manager, I totally get these findings. When an employee vocally supports what you're doing but suggests some tweaks, it not only feels good, but it doesn't add much work (if any) to your plate. Challenging voice, on the other hand, can be one of the necessary evils of being a manager. Yes, it's part of your job to deal with employee problems, but it's a pain. Challenging voice drains managers' energy—a depletion that subsequently harms their performance (supportive voice has the opposite effect on managers' exhaustion and performance; it gives them higher energy and subsequent performance). Compounding the issue, lower- and mid-level leaders often don't have the power to fix the problems their employees raise, which adds extra frustration to the situation. This is why fatigue from dealing with challenging voice is particularly high among supervisors who feel that they don't have much power. These poor managers are getting dumped on by employees, but the company hasn't given them the tools to clean up the mess.

The takeaway is clear. Speaking up with suggestions for how to make the status quo better benefits the employee, the manager, and the company. Speaking up with challenges to the status quo can benefit the company, but the effects on the employee and the manager are often negative.

Many of us recognize that challenging the status quo can be bad for how our boss views us, and by extension, it can be detrimental to our careers. Which is why we avoid it. Studies have shown that we experience two very different emotions when using supportive versus challenging voice. Supportive voice is associated with the feeling of pride. Sounds nice, right? Challenging voice, on the other hand, triggers social anxiety. I don't know about your procrastination habits, but the things I tend to put off doing are those that spur social anxiety within me. No thank you.

There's an old joke by the comedian Jerry Seinfeld based on the oft-quoted finding that people fear public speaking more than they fear death. The punch line is "This means to the average person, if you have to be at a funeral, you would rather be in the casket than doing the eulogy." Extending Seinfeld's observation from public speaking to challenging voice, along with the above research, this helps explain why employees often quit rather than bring up problems to their boss.

The problem is, when you choose not to voice and instead opt for another way of dealing with the jolt, you forgo what is perhaps the most constructive and effective way of improving your work situation. So how do you thread the needle between the downsides of challenging voice and the upsides of speaking up?

Embrace Your Inner Politician

You may not like the advice I'm about to give.

You've been jolted, it has opened your eyes to some deficiency in your relationship with work, and it's something that you believe your company can fix. So now you want to speak up. Can't you just go to your boss and tell them the problem?

No. First, *you* have to do a bit more work to make it more likely that your boss will respond well. I told you that you might not like this, but trust me here.

The risks of challenging voice mean that you need to change how you deliver your message. This may strike you as unfair. Why should you have to put in extra work just because of your boss's resistance to hearing the unvarnished truth? "Spinning" your message may also strike you as political and, by extension, inauthentic (or downright gross). I don't disagree with you. But organizations are political. Being able to persevere through a skosh of unfairness and engaging in some organizational politics is necessary to be happy and successful in most workplaces. Here's how you do it.

Step one, **make sure you have a realistic solution** to the problem. As an employee, one of the most common phrases I hear from bosses is one of my least favorite: *Don't bring me problems, bring me solutions.* I'll discuss the problems with this management-loved phrase for leaders later, but for now, let's deal with what it means for you and your voice. Are leaders more likely to hear you out if there is a solution attached to the problem or opportunity you're surfacing? It turns out, yes. In a series of studies, researchers examined a whole host of factors that could, in theory, increase or decrease managers' likelihood of responding positively to employee voice. They found the strongest evidence for two factors. The first was whether the manager trusted the employee. This is rather obvious, but if your manager doesn't trust you, your voice is likely to go in one of their ears and straight out the other. Keeping in mind that trust takes time to build, those in new relationships with their manager will need to opt for the other factor, which is more insightful, and actionable. When voice *includes a solution* to the issue raised, managers view it, and the person offering it, more positively. And of course, that means that your voice is more likely to be addressed if you embed a solution within it.

Step two, **make sure your solution benefits someone or something other than you**. Your solution of "I need a $10,000 raise" could be totally legitimate. But it's probably not very compelling to your boss. Again, research tells us why that is and how you can make the solution more appealing. When we make suggestions at work, those on the receiving end make assumptions about why we're suggesting them. And there are two broad assumptions they make. They assume we're speaking up either (1) to benefit ourselves or (2) to benefit our company and coworkers.

When our managers feel that the motivation behind our suggestion is driven by concern for our peers and the organization, they're much more likely to adopt it than when it comes across as being motivated by concern for ourselves and no one else. Research by organizational psychologist Adam Grant found that when employees deeply valued benefiting others, their managers sensed this and these employees' voice resulted in higher evaluations from their managers. When managers sensed that workers held low concern for others, this positive effect of voice disappeared. So, when you speak up, the solution to the issue cannot benefit only you. Of course, it almost certainly will benefit you, but you need to frame your voice in how your solution benefits the company, your coworkers, or of course your manager. So, instead of simply arguing that you're underpaid, maybe ask for a raise by highlighting how that added investment in you will pay off for your organization and coworkers, in the form of your current and future contributions.

Third step, be clear and **don't send mixed messages**. In her fantastic book *The Culture Map*, management professor Erin Meyer describes how styles of giving negative feedback differ wildly, depending on the culture you're in. As an example, Americans are used to the "feedback sandwich," where negative feedback is delivered between two or more slices of positive feedback. The Dutch, on the other hand, prefer to deliver and receive negative feedback much more directly, without the sugar (or bread) coating that Americans use. When it comes to delivering voice, though, mixing messages isn't a great strategy, no matter where you are in the world. Especially when your concern is challenging in nature, you may be tempted to sprinkle in some supportive voice as well. But this mixing of issues is less effective than simply delivering the challenging voice (and far less effective than supportive voice alone).

The fourth and final step is only for special cases where you have a dominant boss—someone who clearly likes the power of being in charge and prefers their followers to act subserviently in recognition of that authority. If this describes your manager (unlucky you), then frame your voice in a somewhat submissive tone, perhaps even in the form of a question. **Making your voice more a question** than a demand will increase its odds of being granted. Of course, if you have a less power-hungry leader (lucky you), then you can skip this demeaning step.

Putting in the extra work described above will help you get your challenging voice "right." But whether you actually pull it off ties back to that politician comment I made earlier. Make no mistake, this is a process of persuasion. You are trying to talk your boss into making a change to the status quo that will benefit you (and, hopefully, others and/or the company as well), which may create extra work for them. That means this is an act of office politics. I know, I know, you don't like dealing with workplace politics. Pretty much no one does. But they're everywhere in organizations.

You need to be honest with yourself here about whether you're actually good at politics. Some of us are. Others . . . not so much. Quick four-question quiz:

- Are you good at sensing other people's motives and agendas?
- Is it easy for you to get people to like you?
- Are you good at projecting sincerity when you communicate with others?
- Are you good at using your connections and network to get things done at work?

If you answered a fairly strong yes to these questions, then you've got political skill. If there were some weak yeses or a few no answers in there, be careful. How managers react to risky behaviors like challenging voice can hinge on whether you have high or low political skill. So, if you sense (or know) that you're not good at office politics, you may want to confer with a trusted colleague, friend, mentor, or family member who does possess these skills, and practice how you'll pitch the challenge voice idea to your boss. Doing so will minimize the chances of making missteps as you speak up to power.

If you follow the steps above, you should increase your odds of getting the issue that caused the jolt resolved in a way that strengthens rather than weakens your standing in the eyes of your boss. As a result, done right, speaking up is one of the most powerful ways to deal with jolts that emanate from work. But what about jolts that come from outside our professional lives?

PART III
Jolts Beyond Work

CHAPTER NINE

CROSSOVER JOLTS

Sometimes what happens in the office doesn't stay in the office, and what happens at home makes an appearance at work.

In 2022, Chris Hemsworth—whom millions of us know as Thor, Marvel's God of Thunder—put himself through a series of tests and experiences designed to help him and viewers understand how to live healthier, longer lives, in a series titled *Limitless*. What he may not have realized at the outset of filming is that some of these tests and experiences would be jolts that would change his relationship with his acting career.

In the fifth episode of the season, Hemsworth took a genetic test and discovered that his DNA includes a pair of genes linked to Alzheimer's disease. Although in the episode he describes developing Alzheimer's as his "greatest fear," he later explained that the discovery was a blessing because it gave him time to take steps to counteract it. But that event, along with other moments that came with doing a show on longevity, made him reflect on his relationship with work and how much time he was (or wasn't) spending with his family. In particular, he thought about his kids and it led him to say, "Oh my God, they're getting older, they're growing up and I keep slapping another movie on top of another movie. Before you know it, they're 18 and they've moved out of the house, and I missed the window. It really triggered something in me to want to take some time off." Hemsworth had experienced a jolt that crossed over from his personal to his professional life.

The realization that he was spending more time than he wanted on work, and not enough on family, eventually prompted Hemsworth to make changes. He decided to take some time off from acting once he wrapped up the commitments he'd made. And correspondingly, he decided to be pickier about who he worked with, saying yes only to opportunities to work with directors who were positive and caring.

Crossover jolts are events that happen at the intersection of work and home, and spur realizations that our work is causing harm to or taking too much away from some aspect of our personal lives. Not long ago, the boundaries between our life outside of work and our life on the job were strong, clear, and stable. Think back a few decades, before email and cell phones. At the start of the day, most people would leave home and make a physical commute to the office, giving them a clear transition from their personal life to their professional one. Once at the office, there were no texts from family and friends during the workday. No checking in on the kids (or pets) at day care via an app. No paying bills online while at work. At the end of the day, the commute reversed, and people largely left work behind. No email from the boss at 8:00 p.m. No notifications popping up from coworker text groups gossiping about office drama. Broadly speaking, our personal lives did not creep into work time, and our work did not creep into our personal time.

That scenario above has vanished for many of us. Technology means that work comes home with us, and life comes with us to work. The increasing flexibility of work has also reduced the boundaries and transitions between our work and our home. This is not inherently good or bad. We could list the benefits and drawbacks of this blurring of boundaries between work and life (and the research would back us up). I enjoy being able to keep in touch with family and friends during the workday. And I appreciate the flexibility to answer emails in my evenings if I'd like. At the same time, these lower boundaries create the potential for work to take over life. Crossover jolts are the result of this friction: when events in your professional life disrupt your personal life, or vice versa, causing you to stop and take a hard look at your relationship with work.

Crossover jolts can come from obvious sources, such as when you carry a bad day at the office home with you and create a bad evening for your family. But as with other jolts, there are sneakier ways that work can disrupt our personal lives, leading to an event that jolts us into critically thinking about our jobs. On the flip side, events that happen outside of work can also jolt us when they interfere with our ability to do our jobs, making it evident that we need to stop and rethink the give and take between our work and nonwork lives.

Taking Work Home with You, and Vice Versa

The effects of what happens to us at work often spill over into our personal lives when we get home. Had a stressful day at the office? You're more likely to feel stressed when you get home. And the more work stress you carry home, the more likely you are to behave badly toward your friends and family members.

What this means is that direct jolts at work, like being mistreated, have the potential to jolt you two ways. First there's the immediate impact we've discussed, and then there's the crossover jolt if the event disrupts your personal life. This is readily seen in couples. As one study finds, on days when workers experience mistreatment, they feel more burned out at the end of the workday, and that burnout leads them to express more anger, be more withdrawn, and provide less support toward their partners in the evening. Bad events at work can make us worse family members at home.

But are these jolts? Although the above study did not examine whether such unpleasant evenings affected workers' intentions to quit, there is evidence that this negative work-life crossover can quickly create an unsustainable situation for many families, leading to a crossover jolt.

Studies examining the effects of work-to-family conflict over time have found that such conflict relates to subsequent intentions to quit, even months after the event has occurred. And people changing jobs or careers commonly report that realization of the toll that their prior job was taking on their family life was the jolt that caused them to make a career change.

Crossover jolts can flow in the other direction as well. Researchers sometimes call these *life spillovers*, wherein personally meaningful life experiences in one domain affect how people feel or think, or what they value, in another domain. Often, life spillovers follow a certain chain of events—an event at home causes stress at work that knocks people out of autopilot, causing them to reflect on their overall relationship with work. One study showed that the 2008 financial crisis caused a spike in fear of home foreclosure in some workers. For these workers, the crash of the markets acted like a jolt—fear of home foreclosure not only caused stress at work but also spurred them to launch new job searches.

Of course, crossover jolts that stem from outside of work are often subtler than a financial crash. Studies have shown that on mornings when employees were on the receiving end of rudeness *from their partner* before work, they were more cognitively depleted and in a worse mood at work. Relatedly, my colleagues and I found that anything that disrupts your personal routine in the morning can negatively affect your mood and ability to concentrate when you get to work. In this way, the molehills in our daily personal lives can become mountains when their effects follow us into the workplace.

The Hidden Cost of Being a "Good" Worker

The crossover jolts described above represent a pretty direct cause-and-effect relationship of negative events across work-life boundaries. But there's another type of crossover jolt from work to home that is harder to detect and arrives in the disguise of being a "good worker."

Has an event outside of work ever made you stop and realize that work has taken over more of your life than you realized?

The origins of such jolts come from the tendency of work to slowly expand over time, almost by its very nature. When we begin a new role, we start by mastering the tasks in our job description. As we master them, more tasks and expectations are added, and we take on more responsibilities. The name of this phenomenon is one of my all-time favorites: *job creep*. With job creep, tasks that were once considered above and beyond our job duties slowly and subtly become the norm, and become expected by our boss and coworkers. Imagine working toward the deadline on a big project where, during the final week, we respond to emails at night after the kids have gone to bed (even though we promised ourselves we would never be a person who does that). In doing so, we've sent a signal to our coworkers that we'll respond at night, and so even after the big project is done, we feel the need to occasionally check our email before bed and respond. Without realizing it, our work life has annexed a small part of our personal life, and we did it to ourselves. We have chosen to go beyond our job description on behalf of the company.

When we love our job and are advancing in our careers, job creep isn't bad; it's part of the process by which we develop as employees and climb the organizational ladder. Because it happens gradually, we often don't notice this ballooning until it causes an event that disrupts our well-being or relationships outside of work. At that point, a jolt reveals that our job is coming into conflict with our personal lives and/or we're not being rewarded for bearing the expanding burden of our job duties. Job creep has become a potential barrier to our pursuit of the good life.

The question is, Why do so many of us unwittingly give into job creep? We all want healthy boundaries between the different domains in our lives. Yet when we experience these types of crossover jolts, we realize that the boundaries have failed to protect our personal lives from our work encroaching on them. The reason is simple. Companies reward this behavior.

To truly understand the roots of crossover jolts, we need to take a journey into our motivation at work, and examine the good, the bad, and the ugly of being seen as a good "organizational citizen."

Think for a moment about what being a good citizen in society means to you. You'll probably imagine someone who helps neighbors in need. Picks up trash on the sidewalk. Attends community meetings. Similarly, acts of citizenship at work refer to the positive things you do, often of your own accord, that are *above and beyond* your job description. Helping a struggling coworker. Attending nonmandatory meetings. Arriving early and staying late. Responding to emails on the weekends.

You can add to that list by thinking about your job right now. What are the extra things you do beyond the limits of your formal job description?

When managed well, citizenship behaviors can be part of a healthy cycle between you and your company. Let's spend a minute talking about this cycle, because one of the neatest discoveries ever made in organizational psychology had to do with it, citizenship, and our relationship with work. It began with a big question:

Are happy employees more productive than unhappy employees?

For a long time, researchers tried to find a clear answer to this question. The importance of the answer is, hopefully, obvious. If employee satisfaction leads to higher performance, companies would be wise to spend big to make and keep employees happy, thereby driving higher performance. Win-win! To many of us, it makes intuitive sense that satisfied employees would perform better at their jobs than disgruntled ones.

The only problem? The relationship between worker happiness and worker performance was hard to find. It's not that happiness lowered productivity; it was just that in a lot of jobs, how happy employees were at work had no relationship with their job performance. This led some to conclude that how employees feel at work doesn't matter, leaving leaders to question how important it was to invest in employee satisfaction. For context, this was back in the late '70s and early '80s, an era that gave us the start of mass corporate layoffs and the phrase "greed is good."

It was during this time that an organizational researcher named Dennis Organ made an astute observation: *In many jobs, employees don't have much influence over their job performance.* Think of an assembly line. Whether a worker is happy or not about their work probably has minimal bearing on how the line runs on an average day. When they're dissatisfied, they really can't slow down much, and when they're feeling great about their job, it's not like they can speed up the line. The same goes for a car salesperson. Much of their performance is determined by how many customers show up, not how chipper they feel that day.

When you look at the core of many jobs, you see that a good chunk of worker performance is determined by things outside the worker's direct control. As a result, whether workers are happy or dissatisfied often has little effect on their output.

So, does that mean that worker satisfaction doesn't matter to the bottom line? Here's where Organ made his brilliant prediction.

Workers' happiness may have limited effect on performance in the core aspects of their jobs. But whether workers are satisfied at work should predict whether they engage in good deeds at work BEYOND their required duties.

Per Organ's reasoning, when workers are happy at work, they will be more likely to help coworkers who need a hand, to stay late and arrive early if needed, to go to optional meetings and stay informed about the company's business, to proactively spot and address problems, to say nice things about the company when others trash it, and on and on. Workers have control over whether they engage in these extra behaviors. All these things, which he labeled *organizational citizenship behaviors*, should contribute to higher company performance. In essence, Organ predicted that companies that invest in their employees' happiness will perform better than those that do not, because making employees happy will lead to increased citizenship, which will provide competitive advantage.

Research has gone on to support Organ's prediction. When employees have positive job attitudes or when the company invests in them, they become more likely to engage in citizenship. And as you would guess, having employees who regularly perform acts of organizational citizenship can drive higher firm performance. Moreover, when employees are good citizens, it can boost their career success, as they get promoted and receive raises at higher rates than their colleagues who don't go above and beyond. That is the virtuous cycle I mentioned above. When a company generously invests in employees, it makes their workers happy and willing to reciprocate by engaging in citizenship behaviors, and then they are rewarded for doing so.* That's a happy story, right?

Yes, but that's not the end of the story.

Citizenship behaviors are a double-edged sword for employees. Sure, they can be a ticket to career satisfaction and success. But they also have a darker side and can be a source of harm. By definition, citizenship behaviors involve employees spending energy *above and beyond* that required by their normal tasks. In many cases, that extra effort leaves people depleted when they get home from work. That may seem painfully obvious, and you may say that being tired at the end of the day is a part of work. You're right, but what I'm saying is that the depleting effects of citizenship tend to sneak up on us. Over the course of weeks, you don't notice how putting in a little extra effort at work is depleting you outside of work, especially when you're getting positive feedback from your boss and peers.

The evidence is clear that if left unchecked, being a good citizen at work can lead to being a bad citizen at home (even as you are praised for it at work). Remember those lower boundaries between work and life?

---

* The reverse is also true. When employees are highly dissatisfied, they engage in more negative behaviors beyond their job description, which ultimately harm the organization.

Those give you even more opportunities to be a good citizen for your company. Think about checking your emails outside of work, even on vacations. Or arriving early and staying late from time to time. Or adjusting your personal plans to accommodate some work demands. These are all linked with being a good citizen and succeeding at work. But research shows that they're also linked with being a worse citizen at home. These behaviors all lead to higher incidences of fights with family members.* The same goes for engaging in too much of "the extra" inside of work. Employees who go above and beyond by helping coworkers are more likely to report events in which work interfered with their engagement in family activities. The evidence is clear; going above and beyond at work quietly lays the groundwork for crossover jolts at home.

Use Your Commute to Build a Better Wall Around Your Work Life

For most of us, an opportunity to reduce crossover jolts resides in keeping work from entering our minds and actions during our personal time. And one of the strongest conduits between our thinking about work at work and our thinking about work at home turns out to be something that we justifiably love to hate: the commute.

Commuting is a fairly new phenomenon. Prior to the Industrial Revolution in the late 1700s and early 1800s, most people lived and worked in pretty much the same place. And up until World War II, commutes were typically only two to three miles. But the last seventy years have seen the bloating of commute distances and times. By 2020, we had reached a point where nearly all workers had a significant commute.

Then, the pandemic happened. And although hybrid and remote work existed long before, it wasn't until this event that these types of flexible work were present in a sizable proportion of the world's jobs. For example, in the US, as of August 2025, 27 percent of employees now

---

* This relationship is particularly strong for female workers.

work in a hybrid arrangement, and 13 percent are in a fully remote arrangement. The number of days that the average employee in the US works from home is almost four times higher than what it was in 2019. The benefits and drawbacks of these forms of flexible work differ depending on the person and the job, but one upside that seems fairly universal is that they reduce or eliminate the dreaded commute. Economists who studied working from home and commute times globally found that, using data from workers across twenty-seven countries, the average person will save seventy-two minutes of time *per day* by eliminating their commute.

Gaining an hour and twelve minutes per day sounds pretty wonderful. And beyond the time and cost savings, other compelling benefits of not commuting include avoiding the frustration of traffic or crowded public transportation and the unexpected delays that can occur as you make your way to and from work. And for those of us who are tree huggers, the positive environmental impact of not commuting is significant. Just to throw one more stick on the commuting dumpster fire; it's dangerous, especially in a motor vehicle. And the evening trip home becomes more dangerous on bad workdays; your likelihood of getting into an auto accident increases dramatically when you're behind the wheel after a particularly taxing or frustrating day at work.

There's plenty of research to back up the downsides of commuting and the upsides of eliminating it. Broadly speaking, commute length relates to lower job satisfaction and performance, and when your commute involves stressors (whose doesn't?), those relationships get more negative.[*]

If you can reduce your commute or make it less stressful, you should.

But this book exists in the real world, and the reality is that most of us have traditional commutes, and that is not going to change. And while

---

[*] An exception here is for those who walk or bike or otherwise exercise their way to work; commuting via our own power tends to have positive effects on our work and our physical health. Moreover, flexible work arrangements dampen the negative effects of commuting, ostensibly because you have more discretion to choose when you commute, and you can therefore commute at off-peak times or at times that are most convenient to you.

that may make the above discussion extra depressing, there's a silver lining for those of us who can't eliminate or reduce our commute. Pioneering research is showing that when we're able to mentally detach and reattach on our commutes, our travel to and from work shifts from a stressor to a powerful barrier that can protect our personal lives from the jolts that can stem from coming home with work on our minds.

Let's first focus on the commute home. Take a moment now to reflect on your typical commute at the end of your workday. What do you do on the commute? What do you think about? In general, there are three main tactics we use during our commutes to try to recover from the demands of work. We can relax, we can mentally detach our brains from work, or we can try to learn new things (aka "mastery"). In a study of Dutch workers, researchers found that on days in which workers were able to *relax* on their evening commute, they felt greater serenity and less anxiety at home. *Mentally detaching from work* on the commute had a more nuanced effect; its positive effects on serenity and anxiety appeared only on days in which workers had faced high demands. No effect was found for doing learning activities on the commute home (sorry, fellow Wordlers). The takeaways are clear. After normal days at work, try to relax on your commute home. After tough days at work, make a deliberate point of mentally putting the workday behind you on your way home. Even something as simple as acknowledging the tough day and then telling yourself that it's over and it's time to forget about it and focus on the family until tomorrow can be enough to do the trick. Use the commute as a vehicle to psychologically detach from work.

Now, what about the trip *into work*? A team of researchers ran a clever intervention study wherein they sent workers a daily text message before their commute to work. Each worker got the same text message every day, depending on which of the four conditions they were randomly assigned to. After two weeks, participants completed a final survey measuring their job satisfaction.

Here were the four text messages:

- Use your commuting time to make a plan for your upcoming workday/workweek.
- Use your commuting time to do something enjoyable and relaxing.
- Use your commuting time to make a plan for work *and* also do something relaxing or enjoyable.
- Do what you normally do during your commute.

Of these four, which would you guess had the most positive effect on people's job satisfaction later in the day?

Turns out, using the commute to gear up for work made work more enjoyable. The effect of commuting time on job satisfaction was positive for those who used their commute to plan for their work. The effect of commuting time on job satisfaction was *negative* for those who used their morning commute for relaxation and enjoyment. There was no effect for the other two conditions.

Detach and reattach. When a crossover jolt reveals that work is hijacking your home life, try to reduce your commute. If you can't, shut down your work brain on your commute home, and fire it back up on the way in.

CHAPTER TEN

REMOTE JOLTS

How events in faraway places can send
tremors through your relationship with work.

The Butterfly Effect, Work Edition

As far as jobs go, being a starter in the National Football League is a pretty desirable one. NFL stars are typically paid huge amounts of money and enjoy the adulation of millions of fans, all while playing a sport they enjoy. Back in 2000, Patrick Tillman was one of those stars, starting as safety for the Arizona Cardinals and being recognized as one of the top players in the league. The next year, just before the start of the season, the September 11 attacks happened. There is no indication that the attacks directly harmed Tillman or anyone he knew. He'd spent his life and career in California and Arizona, about as far away from New York City as you can get in the continental US.

Despite not being directly affected, 9/11 caused Tillman to stop and reflect on life, and work. On September 12, he told a reporter, "At times like this you stop and think about just how good we have it, what kind of system we live in, and the freedoms we are allowed. A lot of my family has gone and fought in wars and I really haven't done a damn thing." Looking back, it was clear that 9/11 had jolted Tillman.

He was contracted to play that season, and he did. But when it ended, he informed the Cardinals that he was pressing pause on his NFL career to join the army. In doing so, he walked away from a contract worth almost $4 million per year. "Sports embodied many of the qualities I deem meaningful," he said in 2002. "However, these last few years, and especially after recent events, I've come to appreciate just how shallow and insignificant my role is . . . It's no longer important."

The butterfly effect is a famous theory developed by meteorologist Edward Lorenz. The gist of it is that an event in one place can have big effects in a distant location. Lorenz, of course, was referring to weather. The most well-known prediction he made from his theory was that a single flap of a butterfly's wings in Brazil could generate a tornado in Texas. His job being to explain the weather, he stopped there. But as Tillman's story illustrates, the effects of human events can also extend far beyond the immediate area and affect those who hear about it in faraway places.

Remote jolts spring from negative events that happen beyond our immediate context. Events that don't have a direct or instant impact on our lives but are often extraordinary. At any given time, the news alerts on our phones notify us of potential remote jolts—disturbing events from around the globe. Wars, weather disasters, mass shootings, financial meltdowns—you name it.

At minimum, these types of jolts can be a distraction that affects our work performance. A study of news consumption during the pandemic found that the more news people consumed, the more uncertainty they felt (side advice: watch less news). And at work, feelings of uncertainty from the news consumption hampered people's progress toward their work goals and their creativity at work. As this research shows, consuming information about the events that happen in other people's lives can affect how we think and perform at work. But they can also jolt us, shifting our perspective about our work and making us take a step back. Sometimes learning about distant, negative events can even cause us to reconsider what we're doing with our lives, and our jobs.

To understand why, think about what the notifications on our phones often bring us news of: threats to people's lives. It turns out that some unique psychology unfolds when the thought of death enters our minds, psychology that explains when a news alert can become a remote jolt. I feel compelled to offer a bit of a disclaimer here. By bringing up this topic—death awareness—I may be inducing in you the effects that I describe below. As a preview, while sometimes unpleasant, the effects of thinking about our own mortality can be quite positive. Of course, if you're not in the mood for thinking about death, I wouldn't fault you one bit for skipping this next section.

Health Reminders of Our Mortality

Remember what jolted Chris Hemsworth (aka Thor) into taking time away from acting? It was a discovery about his personal health. Research on the link between health threats and personal reevaluation helps explain why faraway events can jolt us. In one study, researchers looked at why people decided to retire early, before they had originally planned to do so. One of the themes that emerged across multiple interviews related to "health scares or deaths of loved ones." One informant reported:

> [After the death of three family members] my husband and I were having great, deep discussions about life and the pursuit of happiness and value and meaning and all these wonderful philosophical things. . . . I said, "Oh, my God. If that's true, I've got 20 years left with you." And that is not very much time after I've worked 42. "Why are we doing this? You know, it's more money and it's more stability, maybe, for the future. But what if we're not even around to enjoy it?" . . . And I went in and gave six months' notice the next morning . . . that was exactly the impetus.

Based on multiple accounts like this one, the researchers concluded that when mortality was brought to the forefront of folks' minds, the importance of their jobs was diminished, triggering the realization that it was time to walk away from their work, ahead of when they had originally planned to leave.

In his Pulitzer Prize–winning book, *The Denial of Death*, anthropologist Ernest Becker explained how the fear of death affects humans. He proposed that one consequence of humans' advanced mental capabilities compared to other animals is that we know we will die. According to Becker, although it's not often in the *front* of our minds, the reality that we will die dominates the *back* of our minds. And from that back seat it shapes our thinking and behavior. To cope with the disturbing knowledge that one day we will cease to exist, he proposed that we cling to *eternal things* that will outlast us and that we seek to view ourselves positively in relation to these things.

Eternal things are anything that will let us "live on" past death, either symbolically or literally.

Symbolically, it could be the artwork we created, the impact of the good deeds we did for others, the contributions we made to an organization, or the memories and associated mementos that our family keeps over generations.

The ability to *literally* live on past death is at the core of many religions. These faiths provide members with an avenue to an afterlife (by being a good member of that religion), thereby giving believers literal immortality.

To put this theory in motion a bit, if you're a family-oriented person (which you are if your bubbles associated with your family were big and center in the identity exercise we did earlier), thinking about death could trigger you to reflect on the importance of your family and focus on how you're an upstanding member of that group. If you are not as good a family member as you would like to be, this process may motivate you to think about how you can do even better. In this way, you deal with the thought of your someday demise by reminding yourself that your family-based belief system is meaningful and valid and that even when you do die, you will live on through your family.

Becker's work inspired researchers to examine the extent to which his ideas about death were valid and useful for understanding how we live. These scholars went on to develop *terror management theory*, so named because it describes how we manage the primal scariness of the finiteness of our time on earth. At a fundamental level, terror management theory proposes that each of us develops and maintains worldviews that make us a part of *something* meaningful, that will last beyond death. In order to cheat death and achieve immortality, then, we're motivated to view ourselves positively when judged by the standards of that *something*.

When we're good family members, positive memories of us will live on in our future generations. When we're good religion members, we will live forever, in an afterlife. And when we're good citizens, we will live on in the ways that our positive deeds enhanced the lives of others and society.

But wait, it's not like death is on our minds all the time, right? Many of us report that we rarely think about death and don't experience anxiety when we do. That's because terror management primarily operates in the background of our consciousness. In moments of *mortality salience*—times when we're reminded of death—our brains immediately initiate defenses to keep us from dwelling on it. We tell ourselves that we're not vulnerable and we try to suppress further thoughts of death. It's following this initial defense that the core predictions of terror management theory come to life. And sure enough, studies show that once we move past those initial moments following mortality salience, a second set of defenses kicks in. Here, we double down on the way we view the world and confirm that we are *in good standing* with the standards of that worldview.

So what does all this have to do with jolts and our relationship with our jobs? Well, when we're doing work that we find satisfying and meaningful—work that aids in our quest for the good life—not a whole lot. If we generally feel good about our jobs and the work we do, work can actually help us manage any terror related to death. When death scares us, we can point to what we do and/or what our company is doing and what it stands for, and say to ourselves, "I will live on through my work!" When we're doing meaningful work, moments of mortality salience may even spur us to be even better contributors. Imagine working for a nonprofit that secures grants for entrepreneurs in developing economies. Maybe over the past year, you've become complacent and beaten down by bureaucracy and aren't as engaged as you once were. A news story about a deadly flood in a developing nation could trigger a moment of mortality salience that reminds you of the importance of your work and thus reawakens your desire to push through challenges and strive forward in your important tasks.

But as we've discussed, many jobs don't provide workers with such a pathway to immortality. While some jobs are truly terrible, many are just . . . meh. Or going back to Patrick Tillman, they may be fine for some people but simply not meaningful to you. When working in a job we don't find meaningful, being reminded of death forces us to look elsewhere for immortality, to other aspects of our life that *do* provide us with worldviews that give us a sense of purpose. Studies indicate that a fairly common response to mortality salience is to back away from our work, suggesting that thoughts of death cause people to redirect their attention to other parts of their lives.

But equally likely is that when we search for a source of immortality in the wake of a remote jolt, and do not find it in our jobs, it will prompt us to question why we're working there at all. Why am I spending so much of my finite time on this planet doing *this*?

Alongside terror management theory are perspectives that highlight how death awareness not only triggers attachment to one's worldviews but also triggers positive reflection and reappraisal. This perspective has been around for centuries. The founder of the Jesuit order of Roman Catholics—Ignatius of Loyola—advocated regularly meditating on one's death. He suggested imagining yourself on your deathbed and reflecting on your life and what you would have done differently. Relatedly, researchers have observed that as people get older, think about death more often, and come to see death as a natural part of their lives, they become more focused on others' well-being. This is the *generativity perspective*, which argues that thinking about death can make us more generous, causing us to grow and enrich our lives. Overall, thoughts about dying can make us reflect on life, and look at our lives through the lens of others' eyes. It can make us think about our legacy.

The link between external events that cause us to reflect on death and people experiencing a jolt was one of the main reasons I predicted the Great Resignation. In some ways, COVID-19 was the terror management event of the century. Although it was not just a remote jolt (it impacted everyone directly), the awareness of death that it caused affected people at work, illustrating how mortality salience stemming from outside of work can affect us on the job. In two studies conducted with workers from Canada and the UK, researchers found that to the degree that people were exposed to information about COVID-19 through social media and traditional media, they experienced increased levels of both stressful and generative reflections about death. Not surprisingly, but meaningfully, they found that stressful thoughts about death led employees to disengage from work, whereas generative reflections led employees to engage in more helping at work.

In another study, researchers examined people's death anxiety stemming from COVID-19 and their intentions to quit their jobs. Across four studies, using samples of workers in China and the US, they found that increases in death anxiety from the pandemic corresponded with an increase in people's desire for meaning in their work, which subsequently related to higher intentions to quit their jobs.

In a non-pandemic example, researchers weren't even intending to study jolts when they set out to study the careers of a classic set of traditional employees—bus drivers. Their initial plan was to survey the drivers, measuring predictors of quitting as well as these workers' intentions to quit. Then, two years later, they would look at how many of them actually left. They expected to find the usual positive relationship between intentions to quit and subsequent actual turnover. So they conducted the first survey, and then they waited. One year after the survey, the region in New Zealand where the study was taking place was hit by a large earthquake. A year after that, they peered into the turnover data and found that 26 percent of those in the sample had voluntarily quit. That struck them as a high number, given that there weren't many alternative jobs for bus drivers in the region. Then they looked at the relationship between intentions to quit two years earlier and actual quitting. There was no significant relationship. The correlation was almost zero.

When researchers fail to find a significant effect that they expect to be there, it's hard to figure out why it's not there. It may be missing for all sorts of reasons. So, it's dangerous to conjecture too much from a "null finding." But the absence of *any* relationship between intention to quit and actual quitting is unusual compared to what most studies have found, and it led the research team to surmise that the earthquake must have jolted some employees who had no intentions of leaving into leaving, and it probably jolted others who had intended to leave into staying.

As suggested earlier, our mortality is made more salient for us now than perhaps in any other era. Some use terms like *permacrisis* to describe the times in which we are living. Of course, there have certainly been prior times, whether it be as hunter-gatherers or during medieval times or times of war, where awareness of the threat of death was constant. But while hunter-gatherers may have been in much more immediate danger, their sense of danger was limited to a few sources in their immediate surroundings. Today, our phones tell us of dangers near and far, some that threaten us but also many that threaten others. We're in a time of heightened death awareness, and as a result, we experience the effects of such awareness more frequently than most prior generations.

Above, I've focused on remote jolts that stem from negative events that happen to others with whom we don't necessarily share any connection. But sometimes, these faraway events happen to people with whom we *do* have something in common. And emerging research is showing us that the potential for remote jolts goes up in these instances.

Harm to a Social Group We Identify With

The 2019 attack on two mosques in Christchurch, New Zealand, may have registered as a general terror management event to anyone who heard about it, but for members of the Muslim faith, it was likely something more.

The 2023 earthquakes in central Europe were a reminder of mortality salience for all of us, but for Turkish and Syrian people around the world, the effects were likely stronger.

When a gunman killed forty-nine people at the Pulse nightclub in Orlando in 2016, the world was stunned, but it was likely especially harrowing to members of the LGBTQIA+ community.

Researchers have only begun to understand the consequences of these events—those which involve harm to members of a group we identify with—for workers. But the initial research is eye-opening. Management professors Angelica Leigh and Shimul Melwani study *mega-threats*, which they define as "negative, large-scale, diversity-related episodes that receive significant media attention." Their work explains that even though mega-threat events don't affect most people directly, they nonetheless cause a unique kind of harm to those *who share an identity with the victims.*

Remember our identity exercise earlier, and keep in mind all of your different identities, because they're relevant here. Here are how mega-threats work: You learn of a negative event somewhere that happened to a person or group who shares an identity with you, and you perceive that the cause of the negative event is tied to that identity. You then experience feelings of threat due to your possession of that identity. Then you go to work (or you're at work when you learn about the negative event). Here, although you feel threatened, you typically cannot talk about these feelings or their cause. Suppressing these thoughts and feelings of threat while at work is uncomfortable, which causes you to pull away from your work tasks and social interactions. Through this process, events far removed from your workplace have jolting effects on your relationship with work.

Leigh and Melwani tested this theory in a set of studies. First, they recruited a sample of Asian Americans and White Americans and had them (individually) watch news coverage of the Atlanta spa shootings in which a gunman killed eight people, six of whom were Asian women. After viewing the video, participants completed a survey about their emotions and their behavior at work. They found that the Asian participants (compared to White participants) experienced higher levels of threat and subsequently higher work withdrawal and lower social engagement.

They then tested their theory with a different, very clever type of study. First, they waited for a slow news week, and then they launched their study and collected baseline data from a large sample of workers who belonged to a few different identity groups. They asked these workers how much threat they felt, how much they suppressed feelings of threat at work, and how much they were engaged at work. Then they waited for a news week in which events occurred that would cause a threat to an identity held by some, but not all, of their participants. A few months later, there was widespread coverage of two different police shootings of unarmed Black civilians. The week following this news coverage, the researchers launched another survey to their participants, asking an equal number of Black and White participants about their levels of threat suppression and engagement at work.

That was supposed to be the end of the study. But several months later, George Floyd was murdered in Minneapolis, a tragedy widely covered by the media. The researchers launched another survey, identical to the prior one.

They then compared how much, on average, the Black participants in their study felt threat, suppressed these feelings of threat at work, and disengaged at work, relative to the White participants, in the wake of these two rounds of mega-threats. Both sets of results showed that in the week following these events, Black workers had withdrawn more from their work than their White counterparts, directly due to experiencing heightened feelings of threat stemming from the external event and then suppressing these threat feelings at work. Clearly, while death/mortality salience cues can serve as jolts for anyone, they are especially jolting for those who identify with the given group.

Research on mega-threats is in its nascency, and studies have not yet shown whether the suppression and withdrawal that these events cause relate to workers thinking about quitting or actually doing so. However, multiple anecdotal accounts of Black people resigning or making major life decisions as a result of the murder of George Floyd suggest this is the case. And such a response to a remote jolt should be especially likely in workplaces where you cannot speak up about the threat that the event spurred within you. Leigh and Melwani's studies provided indirect evidence of this. In studying the link between employees' experience of threat based on their identity and these workers' subsequent suppression of threat feelings at work, they also measured whether workers felt safe to discuss identity threats in their workplace. When workers had a sense that it was acceptable to discuss such issues at work, they did not suppress their thoughts and feelings as much, and did not withdraw from work.

Overall, despite their geographic distance, negative events that don't directly affect us or those close to us can nonetheless stop us in our tracks and make us reflect on the work we're doing, consider whether it is meaningful, and initiate change if not (or increase our commitment if so). Because we are made aware of remote threats more than ever, keeping ourselves from constantly being jolted by them requires some effort. In this case, that effort can involve shifting mindsets.

Be Aware of the Pain Spiral

Do you believe in the saying "Bad news comes in threes"? If so, after two negative events happen to or around you, you likely become extra cautious, looking out for that final negative event to happen. While I don't necessarily buy into that saying, I certainly have experienced a run of bad luck over a few days or weeks, causing me to be extra cautious to avoid any further harm. This is a healthy and common response. But the frequency of remote jolts in our lives today can cause us to be in this vigilant mindset almost constantly, always waiting for the next dangerous shoe to drop. As a result, when we experience a true jolt, we enter into the feeling-thinking-acting process with an overly negative and cautious mindset, leaving us prone to making biased decisions about how to deal with the jolt. We need a more open-minded approach, and to achieve this requires forcing yourself to switch between this mindset and a more positive one.

The events that happen to and around us on a daily basis affect our overall mindset about whether our future is full of danger versus whether good things are just around the corner. The theory that explains why this is so goes by the boring name *regulatory focus theory*. Despite the yawn-inducing name, its predictions are simple. The basic notion is that in life, we seek to increase the amount of happiness and minimize the amount of pain that we experience. Increasing pleasure and reducing pain are not two sides of the same coin. They represent two different goals, accomplished by different types of action: pursuing pleasure and avoiding pain. Here's the interesting twist; at any given moment, our brains are more focused on one of these goals than the other.

Important to our understanding of jolts is what causes us to flip between happiness-seeking and pain-avoiding modes. Some of it simply comes from who we are. Each of us tends to have an innate tendency to be either more focused on making gains or more focused on avoiding losses. But regardless of personality, the situations that we face cause us to shift into one mode or the other. Receiving harsh feedback from a supervisor can push us into pain-avoiding mode. Unexpectedly receiving praise from a coworker can lift us into a happiness-seeking mode.

Here's the thing, though: Whether you're wearing pain-avoiding or happiness-seeking glasses affects not only how you view the world but also how you behave. Importantly, the happiness mindset isn't always better. It does tend to lead to higher productivity and achievement, but it can also lead to disasters due to overlooking potential pitfalls such as safety concerns. On the flip side, always being vigilant of losses tends to harm our productivity, but it also keeps us safe.

When people are in a pain-avoiding mindset, instead of focusing on the good aspects of their current situation and the positive possibilities that could happen in the future, they fixate on the negative and try to avoid it. This can be tiring and is associated with emotional exhaustion at work, which makes good decision-making even more challenging. In the world today, people are likely spending more time in this state where, instead of thinking about a brighter future, we are simply bracing for the next impact. What calamity will happen next? And getting out of this mindset can be a quagmire because negative events plus the pain-avoiding mindset can have a spiraling or cascading effect, creating a negative cycle in which more negative events occur. In one study, management researchers found that on days in which workers experienced an unfair event, they subsequently experienced negative emotions that made them more likely to enact their own bad behavior at work later in the day. Of course, this bad behavior leads to being treated unfairly and being ostracized, so the cycle of negativity continues and builds.

This pain-avoiding focus can be contrasted with what happens when we experience good events—they put us in a happiness-seeking mindset in which we focus on the positive possibilities that could occur in the future.

A best practice when reflecting on what to do in the wake of a remote jolt, then, is to force ourselves to shift back and forth between pain-avoiding and happiness-seeking. When thinking about the jolt, a pain-avoiding mindset can make us overestimate the risk of the negative event happening again, while at the same time making us overemphasize the risks associated with changing our situation to address it (e.g., switching jobs). On the flip side, happiness-seeking can make us gloss over the ways in which our current situation is holding us back, and make the grass surrounding other opportunities look greener than it is. Thus, when jolted, spend time thinking deeply about *both* gains and losses. Catch yourself in a moment of positivity, and think about the silver lining of the jolt, or what good can come of it. And then at some other time, channel your inner skeptic, and think of all the potential losses that the jolt has revealed, both now and in the future. After that, you can take a step back and look at the lists of potential gains and losses that surround your decision. This may not give you clarity, but it will give you a broader understanding of what the remote jolt has revealed about your relationship with work than staying in one mindset.

Although here I've focused on how remote jolts can cause prevention focus, it is possible for the opposite to happen, where jolts cause a happier mindset. At last, it's time for positive jolts.

CHAPTER ELEVEN

POSITIVE JOLTS

Birthdays, job offers, and vacations—jolts from the bright side of life.

If you wrote a book based on your life story, what would it include? Think back, over the past twenty, forty, sixty years. What would make the cut?

Obviously, there would be a lot of variety across what each of us would highlight in our autobiography. But there would be commonalities as well. I can make this statement confidently, not because I'm an avid reader of life stories but because some researchers who have examined hundreds of them, like Dan McAdams, have found common threads. According to McAdams, one thing that most life stories share is the presence of multiple *nuclear events*. I really like how he defines that term: Nuclear events are "particular scenes that **stand out in bold print**" in our lives. McAdams goes on to talk about the transformative power of nuclear events. He includes positive occurrences like lucky breaks, and negative occurrences like falls from grace. But he observed that as people looked back and placed these events within the arc of their life stories, they experienced the events as moments of revelation in "which the me experienced a rather sudden or decided transformation." These events are "aha moments" that change us and help explain why we are the way we are today. And in many cases, these life-changing jolts stem from positive events.

We've spent most of our time together talking about negative jolts. Of the six types of jolts you'll encounter in your career, five stem from negative events. You may be thinking, "Jeez, Anthony, you do know good things happen in and out of work as well, right?" I do. But when it comes to causing jolts, positive events are simply less relevant, for two reasons.

First, broadly speaking, positive events tend to bring relationships closer, so they're less likely to make us question our bond with our work. This is something that the aforementioned researcher Albert Shapero observed about the events that jolted people into entrepreneurship. He found that 65 percent of the time, people could point to a negative event that had triggered the move into self-employment. On the bright side, he also found that 28 percent of the time, a positive event was the cause of the career change. The remaining 7 percent attributed their move into entrepreneurship to a transitory moment in their lives, such as at the end of school or military service.

The second reason for the heavy emphasis on negative events is because we humans are drawn to darkness. Negative events are more noticeable and we devote more resources to dealing with them than we do to the positive things that happen to us and around us. Sad, right? This is known as the *bad is stronger than good* phenomenon (or more dryly as the positive-negative asymmetry effect). We direct our attention to negative events much more than we do to positive events, leading to stronger psychological reactions to bad versus good. This goes for small everyday occurrences as well; they affect us more deeply when they're negative. If your barista smiles and hands you your morning cup of coffee, you pay it little heed. But if they scowl and set the cup on the counter and then turn away, you'll likely notice, and your emotional reaction to it will linger. The same holds true for when we're on the job; negative events at work cause stronger reactions than experiences that are equally positive. And finally, upon experiencing a negative event, we tend to overestimate how long it will make us feel bad afterward. So don't blame me for the seeming obsession with negative events; blame our minds!

But just because our minds seem to love negativity doesn't mean that positive events don't hold the potential to jolt us. It's just that these more pleasant shocks affect us in different ways. How? A lot of it has to do with the potential of positive events to spur *epiphanies*. In a nutshell, positive events *open* our minds, whereas negative events tend to narrow our focus. As we discussed in the last chapter, think about your mindset after something bad happens, like pulling a back muscle while getting the laundry out of the dryer one morning (purely hypothetical example). Until it heals, your thinking is often narrowly focused on, and hypersensitive to, your physical movements—minimizing movements that cause pain or risk reinjury.

Now think about your mindset after something positive happens, like getting a great performance evaluation at work, running a race at a personal best time, or having one of your children tell you what a great parent you are. Events such as these elicit emotions like love, joy, pride, curiosity, and happiness. As we experience these emotions, we gain an increased capacity and willingness to consider new thoughts and actions to further improve our well-being and our lives. I've studied this on a small scale in my own research, in studies that examine how office workers respond to encountering nature during their workdays. It's well established that in general, coming into contact with (nonthreatening) forms of nature makes us feel good. In one paper, we found that when employees encountered nature during their workdays, it broadened their thinking, leading to higher creativity for the rest of the day. Although these effects were somewhat modest in size, they show how, on a small scale, little positive events in your workday can make you feel good and open your mind. You can therefore imagine what more nuclear-size positive events must do to our thinking.

And open-minded thinking often begets more positive events. Can you recall a time in your life when you have been "on a roll"? A time in which two or three positive things happened in succession, and you got that feeling that anything is possible? That's part of the magic of good things happening to us; they unleash emotions that facilitate even more positive events, sometimes creating a positive spiral.

The open-mindedness that positive events generate provides fertile ground for considering new possibilities in our lives, making positive events good candidates for jolting us and causing us to think about our relationship with work in a new light. This is why, when management professor Erik Dane studied people's career epiphanies, he found that one common element was the presence of positive emotions. After interviewing dozens of professionals who had experienced a career epiphany, he learned that a prerequisite for having such an "aha moment" was *being open* to the revelation that a professional change was needed. Those he interviewed talked about how, at more closed-minded points in their lives, they likely missed moments of insight that would have launched their life pivot sooner. But being open to possibilities allowed them to see a way of working and/or living that they hadn't recognized before. Typically, the new life path they discovered resolved some long-standing tension they'd been grappling with, such as how to balance work and life, how to square their personal values with their company's values, or simply how to find a better fit between their interests and their job tasks. In short, positive events can open our minds to new possibilities, helping us find ways to resolve long-standing tensions in our lives.

Circling back to our life stories, we find that positive change in our lives often happens following positive events. Positive jolts can lead us to think about our relationship with work in new ways, ways that sometimes spur changes in our jobs and careers, including the pursuit of new ones. Although less common than those stemming from negative events, positive jolts reside in all the same places.

Positive Direct Jolts

As research on epiphanies indicates, jolts can stem from positive events that happen directly to us at work. To illustrate, let's take one of the quintessential positive events that happens in our careers: being promoted.

Think about the last time you were promoted. Earning a step up on the career ladder typically makes us happy and more committed to our organization. But at the same time, getting a promotion can also spur positive reflection on your career—where you've been and where you're going. And this reflection takes place when you're perhaps more marketable than you've ever been in your career. After all, you just added a new, higher status line to your résumé. Not surprisingly, then, rather than becoming more committed to their company, employees sometimes become more likely to leave after they've been promoted. Are they ungrateful traitors? No, of course not. But thinking about our careers with a broad, positive mindset can open our thinking to alternatives to our current job. Researchers call this phenomenon, wherein being promoted can make some people more likely to leave the company, the *employability paradox*.

Strategy scholar Daniel Sands found evidence of the employability paradox among chefs in fine dining restaurants, after they receive what many would view as the most positive jolt in the industry—earning a Michelin star.* Funnily enough, restaurants that earned their first star when the prestigious *Michelin Guide* expanded to NYC for the first time in 2005 were more likely to shut down in the following decade than those that did not. Counterintuitive, right? Looking into the reasons, Sands found business became more difficult post–Michelin star in part because many of the chefs, who had gained an immediate status bump

---

* A Michelin star is a prestigious mark of culinary excellence, awarded annually by the Michelin Guides.

from the recognition, became more demanding (e.g., expecting higher wages) and were more likely to quit.*

I want to be clear here. The relationship between promotions and higher employee commitment is positive. The same goes for employee recognition and commitment. Thus, leaders should develop and promote internal candidates and reward them as much as possible. But what the research shows us is that in some cases, the positive events that happen to us at work, like promotions, paradoxically jolt us into reconsidering our relationship with work.

Positive Collateral Jolts

Of course, we don't only experience positive emotions in response to the good things that happen *to us* at work; we're excited and happy when good things happen to our coworkers, too. Well, I should say that we're *sometimes* excited and happy. Let's be honest. It depends on the coworker, right? When it's someone we don't particularly like, we might feel jealous or annoyed. But when something great happens to a work friend, we *do* like it when they share their good news. Research tells us that when someone shares their good news with people they're close to, they not only feel even better, but the people they share the news with also get a bump of good feelings. Win-win!

Concerning jolts, when we're happy for our friend, we may bask a bit in the reflected glow of their greatness. And in this happy state, we're in a prime mental space to consider new possibilities for ourselves. So, when close coworkers' happy news involves their careers, it creates a situation in which we feel positive emotions with them but are also prompted to

---

* Other reasons that the Michelin star made it more difficult for some restaurants was that those who supplied the restaurant with ingredients and supplies increased their prices. In addition, landlords often raised building rents, and there is evidence that Michelin stars increase the rents in the entire neighborhood. Finally, customer expectations increased in response to the Michelin recognition.

reflect on our own careers. This combination of positive emotions and reflection can be a perfect recipe for spurring career changes of our own.

Positive Crossover Jolts

It stands to reason that the big positive events that happen in our lives should give us moments of pure happiness. Getting the big promotion. Having your first child. Graduating from school. And yet, this is not always the case.

Have you ever had something good happen to you, and those around you celebrated it and told you how you must be so happy, but inside, you actually didn't feel as happy as everyone said you should be?

In 1963, Betty Friedan coined the phrase "the problem that has no name" to describe a phenomenon she observed in American housewives in that era. These women, who were largely middle- and upper-class, were told by society that they "had it all" and as such, that they *ought to* be fulfilled. And yet, Friedan found that many felt the opposite of fulfilled, even depressed, as they experienced positive events that society told them should have made them happy. Organizational researchers have observed that this effect continues today, but of course it's not limited to housewives; these *work-family ought events* are common across workers. Such events occur when something good happens to us at work or at home—something that we're expected to want and to celebrate—but instead of experiencing only positive feelings, we feel a mix of more negative feelings, too. This tension often stems from disconnects between what we *ought to* want at work and what we *actually desire* out of life. Imagine spending years earning your master's degree, toiling away in your evenings working on school rather than spending time with your family, so you can get a better job when you graduate. As graduation nears, you earn that better job, one that comes with more money, more responsibility, and more challenging work. At your graduation party, while everyone celebrates your accomplishment, you find yourself wondering, *Is this really what I worked so hard for? For a job that will require me to spend more time away from my family?*

As the above example illustrates, positive events in either our personal or professional life can reveal a gap between how happy society tells us we should be and how we actually feel. We say to ourselves, "I know I *ought to* want this, but I'm not sure if I do. I'm not sure if that's who I am." The discovery of this tension, revealed by the positive event, can come as a jolt. It can trigger the process of re-evaluating the boundaries between work and life, similar to the process negative crossover jolts trigger.

Birthdays and holidays. There are also epiphanies that stem from our personal lives but seem to come more out of thin air than from a specific positive event. Much of the time, the ingredients that create such epiphanies are there; they're just subtler. They come from situations in which we find ourselves in a *liminal space*. A liminal space simply means that we are in between two things in our life. This most commonly happens in transit. Have you ever walked through a bus depot, train station, or airport terminal and gotten the sense of being a bit anonymous? Like, you're traveling between two well-known places in your life, but while between them, your mindset changes a bit, and you don't feel quite yourself? This is what "the experience of being betwixt and between identities, social roles, and physical spaces" can do to us. Traversing liminal spaces can make us think a bit differently, and often more freely. In this way, events that place us in liminal spaces in our personal lives can provide fertile ground for spurring us to rethink our relationship with work.

Let me explain what I mean with two examples: milestone birthdays, which occur between date-defined chapters of our lives, and vacations, which represent pauses in our work lives.

When the actor Portia de Rossi explained why she abruptly quit acting and became an entrepreneur, she pointed to the approach of her forty-fifth birthday. Why would nearing a big birthday cause such a jolt? I first came across the answer in Shapero and Sokol's research about why people become entrepreneurs. As they described it, "One recurring precipitator of entrepreneurial activity can best be referred to as *traumatic birthdays* or *magic numbers*." They quoted an entrepreneur who remarked, "I realized I was going to be forty years old within three months. It was now or never."

You may question my listing getting older as a positive (especially when researchers have called these traumatic birthdays), but given that birthdays are generally a cause for celebration, I feel justified in categorizing it as such. Fascinatingly, as people approach a new decade of their lives, they become especially likely to make big life decisions. And when we reach ages that end in nine, and become *9-enders*, we become particularly likely to engage in a life review. In general, people become more evaluative when thinking about their life satisfaction during a milestone age year. Researchers have gone on to show that this aging-spurred questioning of life's meaning may lead to major actions, both positive and negative. Sadly, 9-enders are disproportionately represented in suicide rates and in extramarital relationships. Less depressingly, they're especially prone to launching new goals, such as running a marathon or starting a new career, and to pursuing them in the time periods around "temporal landmarks" in their lives.

So being in a temporal "in-between" space in our lives can jolt us out of autopilot, broadly speaking. The same goes for being in a physical in-between space. We enter one of the ultimate feel-good liminal spaces in our lives when we go away on vacation. It provides us with a temporary escape from work and from the routines of our daily lives, and that escape tends to feel quite nice. While on vacation, we experience a spike in positive emotions and life satisfaction, and these good vibes tend to continue when we return. But they don't last. Over the course of a few weeks, they fade. It's this boomerang in our well-being that makes vacations potentially jolting. We get this big dose of positive emotions while we're in a new space, on a break from our normal lives. This makes a perfect setting for epiphanies, including when we return and find that the satisfaction we gained on our vacation fades away.

Don't get me wrong; vacations are a good thing for employee well-being. The few studies that have examined employees' intentions to quit pre- and post-vacation have shown that going on vacation slightly *reduces* employees' likelihood of leaving. But at the same time, researchers have found that reflecting on work during vacation, either positively or negatively, is common. When the reflections are positive, we return to work in a more engaged state; when we have negative thoughts about our job while away, we return to work more disengaged than when we left on holiday. Although research has yet to examine the link between vacations and epiphanies, this evidence about reflection suggests that they're positive events with ample potential for jolts.

Positive Remote Jolts

When discussing remote jolts, I brought up the negative news alerts that ping our phones, and how even though they don't directly affect us, the events they report can jolt us out of default mode. Although less powerful and less commonly reported in the news, faraway positive events can have the same jolting effect as their negative counterparts. The most compelling evidence of this comes from stories of how major positive events have served as epiphanies for people who aren't sure what careers they want to pursue. Positive events that make the news are often "firsts," such as the first human in space. Such events can make the impossible seem possible, opening our minds to new possibilities for what we can achieve in our lives. This is especially the case when the "first" is accomplished by someone who shares our identity or background. It's the opposite of a mega-threat; it's like a mega-thrill. The story of Sandra Day O'Connor, the first woman to serve on the US Supreme Court, is uplifting regardless of her background. However, as is clear by the number of women she inspired to pursue law, she was more than just a role model. O'Connor becoming the first woman (and wife and mother) to serve in the highest court in the US had a positive jolting effect on many women. When we see people like us accomplishing great things, it can jolt us into dreaming about what we might accomplish as well and, in some cases, making life changes to pursue that dream.

Positive Honeymoon Jolts

Prior to returning to school to pursue my PhD, I spent three years as an entrepreneur. I was a minority owner in a car repair business with my good friend, taking what I had learned while working in a big company and trying to use it to help a small one grow. The main shop was (and still is) a big operation, with a rental car company's branch office housed within it. I typically worked in the office, so I interacted with the rental car employees on a regular basis. Most of their job entailed trying to keep three different parties happy: the customer, us, and the insurance company that was paying for the repairs. And on top of that, they also had to clean the cars upon return, to get them ready for the next customers. It's not an easy job, and being early in their careers, many of these employees struggled. But others excelled. And these high performers caught my attention, because the skills that made for a successful rental car representative were the same as those that made for a successful "estimator"—the primary and critical office job in our business.

We were always on the lookout for people who would make good estimators, and after working with a star rental car employee for a while, we would sometimes ask the person if they had any interest in working for us. Often the answer was no. But every once in a while, we'd get a yes. Regardless of the response, it always was received as a pleasant surprise. In most cases, you could see the boost it gave them after we made the pitch. Looking back now, I can see that we were doling out positive jolts to these folks, which sometimes resulted in career changes.

Years later, I came across this tactic in research articles that described the *unsolicited job offer* and measured these offers' effects on employees' decisions to quit. The researchers argued that unsolicited job offers represent an underrecognized reason that people abruptly quit their jobs. It's a classic jolt. One day, you're cruising along, happy in your job, when out of the blue, someone offers you a new job. These offers often come from those who are outside your organization but who are familiar with your work performance. Like a former colleague who has gone to work for a competitor or a customer or supplier who works closely with you.

Outside job offers tend to be quite effective at triggering turnover, even though they usually target workers who are satisfied with their current jobs. I know I share this sentiment with many HR professionals and managers out there; the ideal candidate is not someone who is disgruntled in their current job but a person who likes their company and their colleagues. This higher happiness makes it more difficult to dislodge workers from their current jobs. But interestingly, researchers have shown that employee satisfaction plays a smaller than usual role in the decision to quit when the decision has been prompted by an unexpected offer. It's like these offers have a special gravitational pull that works as a positive jolt on even satisfied workers.

The point is that unsolicited job offers are positive events that have high potential to be a jolt, even to workers who are new to their roles. Due to the positive nature of these job offers, they open our minds. And due to their being directly focused on an alternative to our current job, it makes us think about the possibility of taking on a new job and leaving our current one.

Crossover jolts, remote jolts, and most positive jolts emanate from our lives outside of work. Because of that, the first two responses to jolts that we've discussed—carrying on and speaking up—may not be effective. While they should still be your go-to first and second responses to consider for all jolts, nonwork jolts sometimes signal that some aspect of the boundary between your work and your life needs to change. As we will discuss when we get to the final part of the book, such changes can sometimes be made in partnership with your manager and company. But I also want to be realistic here. The return-to-office mandates of the few years post-pandemic have shown us that in many cases, your organization won't be receptive to ideas for how to redraw the boundaries between your work and your life. In these situations, we need to take matters into our own hands and quietly make changes to our relationship with work, in order to make it sustainable for us.

CHAPTER TWELVE

LEAN BACK

How and why taking a step back in your work can be a step forward in the health of your relationship with it.

In my mind, the best kind of research question is one that is simple but practically important and relatable to almost everyone. In the early 1980s, social scientist Caryl Rusbult asked such a question: How do people respond to being in a dissatisfying romantic relationship?

If you're going to study bad romances, what better place to start than the love lives of college students? Rusbult's research team began by asking undergraduates to write about a time in their life when they became dissatisfied with a romantic relationship, and what they did in response to that dissatisfaction. The responses identified a decade earlier by Albert Hirschman showed up clearly and distinctively in the responses. For *exit*, one respondent stated, "I told him I couldn't take it anymore, and that it was over." For *voice*, there was ample evidence of respondents taking action to improve the situation, such as "I tried my hardest to make things better." And then there was *loyalty*,* sweetly portrayed by quotes such as "I supported him, even when my friends criticized him."

---

* Hirschman recognized that people differ in how quick they are to enact voice and/or exit when they find themselves in a tough spot. Some of us are speedy to speak out when things don't go as we would like, or quick to peace out if we don't like the situation in which we find ourselves. Then there are those of us who are more patient, content to wait it out even when things are not going our way, perhaps only speaking up or walking out if things get horribly bad, or even staying put and silent until the very end. Hirschman dubbed this force—which causes some people to move quickly to voice and exit, and leads others to

But that wasn't the end of the story. Their findings indicated that at least one more response was common among college students. And when they ran a similar study with a group of older professionals, Hirschman's three categories plus the fourth one showed up again. That final type of response? *Neglect*. This response was typified by quitting the relationship without actually ending it. Quitting without leaving. As described by one study participant: "I guess I just kind of quit—I didn't try to salvage it—I just didn't know what to do."

The Loudness of Quiet Quitting

During the Great Resignation, executives would sometimes point out to me that while employees currently had the upper hand due to the strong job market, that market wouldn't last forever. Once the economy slowed and the job market weakened, they told me, the balance of power would shift away from employees and back to companies. At that point, employees would no longer have as much freedom to quit. They were right. Starting with Russia's invasion of Ukraine, economic storm clouds began to signal that the economy was going to slip, a lot or a little. Moreover, many organizations were making positive changes to work, like better pay and more flexible schedules. Combined, the slowing economy and improvements to work curbed resignations over the course of 2023 and beyond.

Putting aside the fact that, economically speaking, these executives were spot-on, there was something I found odd about these discussions. Some of these leaders seemed to be rooting for an economic downturn in order to regain the upper hand in the job market. They were focused on

---

stand pat—*loyalty*. We discussed loyalty as the most basic response to a jolt: carrying on. It describes situations in which you remain an active and obedient participant in an organization or relationship, even in difficult circumstances. Although Hirschman viewed loyalty as a delayer of voice and exit, as opposed to a separate response to undesirable situations, researchers have increasingly viewed it as an independent action. Thus, people tend to respond to being in a bad relationship in three ways: exit, voice, and loyalty (which happens to be the title of Hirschman's book on the subject).

how to stop employees from quitting, and they were waiting and hoping for a lazy solution to their turnover problems—a sluggish economy that would reduce workers' alternatives so that most couldn't leave their jobs, even if they wanted to.

What this signaled to me was that these executives lacked an understanding of the psychology associated with workers being trapped in a job by a slow economy and a poor job market.

By this point of the book, you know where I'm going. The jolts associated with the pandemic caused many employees to want to leave their jobs. Many did, and because turnover is often disruptive, that's a headache for leaders. I get it.

But critically, a reduction in employees' ability to quit, caused by the job market, doesn't solve the headache for companies. It just shifts it elsewhere. Instead of having high levels of resignations, you have a high number of employees *who want to leave but can't*.

The question I began to ask these leaders is, Which of the two would you rather have, a large group of employees who want to leave *and do so*, or a large group of employees who want to leave *but stay*? It would take only a moment of thought for most to realize that instead of having a turnover problem, a bad job market could leave them with a disengagement problem. A workforce full of reluctant stayers.*

---

* It's worth noting here that voluntary turnover, albeit disruptive, isn't uniformly bad for companies. The ideal amount of turnover is not zero. A study across over 5,000 retail outlets across almost forty countries showed that the relationship between voluntary turnover and store performance was actually positive, as long as such turnover was relatively low. This is often referred to as *functional turnover*. But as turnover increases, there is a tipping point at which the relationship begins to turn negative. Turns out that turnover can be good for business, until there is too much of it.

Why does some degree of turnover help companies function well? First, companies need new perspectives and ideas in order to innovate and grow, and so some level of turnover facilitates that process. But more importantly, employees who want to quit but cannot can hinder an organization's performance. In many cases, it creates a situation in which the employee is unhappy but still doing a good enough job not to get fired. As a result, not only is the employee dissatisfied, they're also not contributing as much as they could to the company. Thus, when the economy is bad, the lack of job alternatives stymies healthy turnover and bottles up unhappiness within organizations, creating a lose-lose situation for companies and workers.

As I was having these discussions with leaders, a buzzword blasted onto the scene that captured the point I was trying to make (and captured the attention of seemingly the entire internet). Of all the buzzwords that emerged in the late- and post-pandemic world of work, it was the most polarizing: *quiet quitting*. At first glance, quiet quitting sounds like neglect or disengagement—doing the bare minimum at work. As a result, many pundits expressed negativity toward it and at workers who would engage in this behavior.

But these pundits were misunderstanding quiet quitting. Part of this misunderstanding stemmed from the fact that quiet quitting emerged from TikTok as opposed to a thought leader, think tank, consulting firm, or academic. But putting that aside, the way quiet quitting was described on TikTok was, in my mind, as clear and nuanced as anything produced by those other sources of knowledge. It was *not* defined as doing the bare minimum (as many people interpreted it) but as simply not doing anything *extra*, above and beyond one's job description. In the words of the viral TikTok that defined it, quiet quitting is "not quitting your job but quitting the idea of going above and beyond at work" and happens when you're "still performing your duties but you're no longer subscribing to the hustle culture mentality that work has to be your life."

I came to view quiet quitting as a different, healthier, form of what academics and consultants have long studied under the umbrellas of terms like *withdrawal, disengagement,* and *neglect*. Quiet quitting involves placing strong boundaries around your work—boundaries in accordance with your job description. In the parlance of buzzwords at the time, quiet quitting is akin to "acting your wage." It isn't disengaging from the core of your job but leaning back from engaging in everything above and beyond that core—all those citizenship behaviors that, as we discussed earlier, can be harmful to your well-being.

Quiet quitting points us toward a third jolt response, especially if carrying on and speaking up do not yield results in improving our relationship with work—*leaning back*. This tactic doesn't focus on resolving the problem that the jolt revealed. Instead, it deals with reducing how much of ourselves we invest in work while still maintaining acceptable performance levels in the core aspects of our jobs. In this way, it is both an act of self-help and a push of the reset button. By reducing how much unpaid time and effort we invest in a job that isn't contributing as much as it should to our pursuit of the good life, we can reallocate our most precious resources to better endeavors. We may find that in rebalancing how much of our energy goes toward work, our work becomes more satisfying. You know how when companies do layoffs, they sometimes call it rightsizing? In theory, *rightsizing* refers to reducing head count to bring it back into alignment with the size of the business. Leaning back is similar; you're correcting the size of work in your life, based on what it contributes back to you.

How to effectively lean back from work hasn't been the subject of a great deal of research. However, there are at least two boundaries between your work and nonwork life where there's room to quietly make adjustments that will ease you away from engaging in, and thinking about, all the extra "stuff" that creeps up around the core of your job over time.

Get Crafty with Your Extra Job Tasks

A primary strategy for leaning back is to do some landscaping of your job. Rather than cutting back the hedges and pulling the weeds that are slowly encroaching on your garden, you trim the extra work that has accumulated around your core job tasks. Perhaps the best process for doing this goes by the name *job crafting*, developed by management scholars Amy Wrzesniewski and Jane Dutton. They bill job crafting as an exercise that can help you turn the *job you have* into the *job you want*. Here is how it works under normal circumstances: You inventory your job tasks, your relationships with others at work, and how much of your mental well-being is being taken up by work. Then you question the extent that these work tasks, relationships, and thoughts contribute to your happiness and sense of meaning at work. When you identify tasks, people, and patterns of thinking that are derailing your progress and well-being, you brainstorm ways to change your job such that you spend more time on the tasks you like and with the people who bring out the best in you, and less on the ones that you feel the opposite about.

Sound simple? It can be. And it often works. Research has shown that job crafting relates to higher satisfaction and performance.

You can engage in the same process to deal with the weedy job creep that has sprouted up in the landscape of your job over the prior weeks, months, and years. But here, you target your craftiness toward all the ways you spend your time and energy at work *beyond your core job description*—your citizenship behaviors. While you may enjoy some of these extra tasks, others, such as attending happy hours, responding to email after hours, or being the notetaker at all your meetings, may deplete your resources but give nothing back. You would be happier if they were gone. These are the tasks you should craft out of your work life. Think of it as the opposite of job creep. Slowly, without calling anyone's attention to it, dial back on attending nonmandatory meetings. Instead of arriving earlier than you need to, spend those extra minutes with your family, corresponding with your friends, or simply relaxing. Rather than answering emails after the kids go to bed, go for an evening stroll around your neighborhood. Lean back. Quietly quit the extra. Shrink your job.

The benefit of this *citizenship crafting* process is that you're still delivering to the company what you owe it. There is no psychological contract breach. You're just silently taking back the extra you were giving them, to create the proper balance in your relationship with work.

As you plan your citizenship crafting, you may realize that enacting it could come as a surprise to those around you at work. If job creep in your work life has created the expectation that you will respond to emails at night, stopping that without telling anyone could cause red flags in the minds of your colleagues. Did they do something to upset you? Are you becoming disengaged and entering the ranks of a reluctant stayer? Ideally, citizenship crafting isn't a solitary process. I get that it's not always possible to craft your citizenship in collaboration with your boss and colleagues, but if you can, it will greatly increase the likelihood of its being successful.

Really Use Your Work Breaks

Leaning back from our jobs also involves making the most of the moments during the workday when we're granted reprieve from our work tasks—during our work breaks. Thinking back over the past week, what activities do you tend to do during the scheduled and unscheduled breaks in your work? Turns out, whether these breaks are actually benefiting us, and how much, depends on how we use them. Let's break better, shall we?

First, think of your scheduled breaks. Nearly all of us check social media during work breaks. The findings on this are mixed, with some showing that it contributes to emotional exhaustion during the workday and some showing it may help maintain a healthy balance between work and life. These mixed findings can be contrasted with break activities that have *universally positive effects* on our well-being. Number one on that list? Exercise. Physical activity during work breaks has myriad benefits for our mental and physical health. Beyond exercise, taking a short nap, spending time in nature, and simply finding the space to relax without any distractions all have clearly positive effects on our well-being.

What about another ubiquitous break activity—socializing with your coworkers? This is where an interesting caveat comes in. The prior paragraph assumed that we all have the freedom to do whatever we want on our work breaks. Some of you may have read that section and thought, "Klotz, dude, I work in a warehouse or cubicle farm in an industrial park with no sidewalks. Where am I going to take a nap? Or exercise? Or see some nature?" What researchers have discovered is that many of the benefits of work breaks are contingent on *work break autonomy,* which refers to how much freedom you have to do what you want on your breaks. This is where the double-edged sword of socializing with coworkers comes into play.

In a research paper that has one of my all-time favorite titles, "Lunch Breaks Unpacked," researchers had employees report what they did on their lunch breaks every day—how much they relaxed, did some work, or socialized. They also measured how much independence these workers exerted over their lunch break that day, asking workers to report their agreement or disagreement with statements like "On my lunch break today, I did exactly what I wanted to do." At the end of each workday, they measured employees' fatigue levels.

The first few findings aren't surprising. Relaxing during lunch breaks leads to lower end-of-day fatigue, and working during breaks has the opposite effect. If you're doing work on your breaks, one of the simplest and most effective ways to lean back would involve swapping out working for relaxing during your breaks. Reclaim your work breaks!

The effect of socializing is more surprising. Chatting it up with colleagues actually leads people to feel *more fatigued* at the end of the day. BUT, when the researchers accounted for workers' lunch break freedom, things got really interesting. For workers who exercised high lunch-break freedom, the effects of socializing during breaks on their end-of-day fatigue flipped, and became positive.

Simply put, if the decision to socialize at lunch was yours, it's a boon to your well-being; if you had no choice but to make small talk with a coworker you barely know, it's likely sucking the life out of you.

The effects of work break freedom extended to other lunch activities. When people freely chose to work while they ate, the negative effects of working during breaks went away (although it still isn't good for you). And when people felt forced to relax during lunch, the break's positive effects on end-of-day fatigue vanished.

To maximize the benefits of work breaks, you need to take whatever control you can over them. For some, that simply means shaking yourself out of the rut of your current routine of scrolling social media or listening to your extroverted coworker blab over everyone for your entire lunch. Put your phone in your pocket, stroll outside, and eat there. Maybe invite your favorite coworker to go with you. Maybe bring a book, or some knitting, or a pen and paper to do some journaling. In some cases, you will feel pressure to do breaks the same way as everyone else. Break those norms, if you can. Blaze your own lunchtime path.

Finally, and regardless of how much freedom you have during your scheduled breaks, consider your ability to take another form of break. Teensy, tiny unscheduled ones.

In many jobs, the number of breaks you take is seemingly out of your control. You get, say, fifteen minutes in the morning and afternoon, and thirty at lunch. End of story. But if you look closely, you get more breaks than that, and those breaks matter. Just ask LeBron.

LeBron James has accomplished more in his basketball career than almost any other player. More points than any other player, more assists than almost any other player, and more championships than most people who have played the game.

You know what else James does more than almost every other high-performing player in the league? Walks during games. I'm not talking about traveling penalties. He literally walks instead of runs more than any other player in the league. Based on his accomplishments and his well-documented work ethic, you certainly couldn't make the case that he walks because he's lazy. A more sensible and research-backed explanation is that he does it because he's smart. He's resting when he can, within his "workday," so that he has energy later in the game if it's needed. He refers to this as saving "pockets of energy."

The tactic that James is using to squirrel away pockets of energy is what researchers refer to as *microbreaks*. The more of these breaks you take, the less fatigue you will experience, giving you more vigor to pursue the good life in your personal time when the workday ends. Look for the little pockets in your day—as you switch between tasks or as you head to a meeting across the hall or across town—and use them to relax and recover a bit.

When jolts occur at the intersection of our personal and professional lives, they may reveal that a rebalancing between these two domains is in order. At the touchpoints between our work and home lives, there's room to quietly lean back and rebalance things. In doing so, we can correct imbalances in our relationship with work that a jolt has revealed. Especially when we find ourselves as a reluctant stayer, in a bad job that we cannot quit and cannot change, these boundary management strategies can be critical for keeping our pursuit of the good life on the rails. For maximizing our well-being outside of work, until our situation at work improves or we're able to quit. Speaking of quitting . . .

PART IV

Walking Away

When a jolt has revealed that something needs to change with your relationship with work, the three responses of carrying on, speaking up, and leaning back are all worth considering and attempting. But there are cases where they just won't do. To address the issue that the jolt has revealed, and to place yourself on your optimal path to the good life, you need to separate yourself from your employer.* If you've reached this point in your post-jolt journey, you have likely done so with a lot of thought and care. You may be a bit tired of the whole process and just want to get this final step over with. But as I'll explain, how you resign has lasting effects on your career success. And so you gotta dig deep and muster the strength and stamina to resign thoughtfully.

I present resignation as the final response to jolts for a few reasons. First, as we discussed earlier, it's not accessible to all of us. At different points of our careers, we're stuck. Walking away from the job we've got isn't an option. Second, quitting comes with fairly high risk (honeymoon jolts may await us on the other side) and it is often irreversible. Finally, the resignation process is arguably the most difficult of all jolt

---

* Full disclosure, there is a fifth option for how to respond to a bad relationship. Sabotage. Actively destroying it. We will touch on destructive behavior a bit later when we discuss the "bridge burning" resigning style. The reason I don't give it much airtime is that while it certainly does happen, sabotage isn't recommended under pretty much any circumstance in the work domain. The relationship between engaging in bad deeds at work like sabotage and negative outcomes for oneself is strong. While this isn't true in every domain of life, in the workplace, you would almost always be better off continually trying carrying on, speaking up, and leaning back (and quitting, if it's an option) rather than lashing out at your company and coworkers.

responses to navigate. People struggle to figure out the best way to go about announcing their resignation and engineering their exit. It turns out, breaking up (with your company) is hard to do.

Before jumping into the resignation process, a couple of heads-ups. First, we're skipping over the topic of what you're going to do after you resign. In many cases, when we quit our job, we move to another, similar job at another firm. But at other points in our lives, a jolt can lead us to quit to go back to school, start a new business venture, stay at home with family, take a career break, switch to part-time work, move to a different industry, expatriate, become a digital nomad, and on and on. Deciding what to do next is beyond the scope of this book, but, thankfully, it has been within the scope of many other great books.

Second, resignations are a specific area of expertise and excitement for me. As I shared earlier, I have been on the giving and receiving end of them many times, they were the topic of my dissertation, and I've studied them for over a decade. As a result of my familiarity with, and passion for, resignations, you may notice my tone shift a bit in this part of the book. If you do detect an uptick in enthusiasm and forwardness, know that this is still *your* post-jolt journey and you should take or leave these insights as you see fit.

CHAPTER THIRTEEN

PREPARING TO EXIT

While the resignation announcement gets all the fanfare, what you do in the period before may be even more important for your transition and career.

Entering the Space In-Between

I enjoy studying resignations because they're common, they're impactful for individuals and organizations, and they're often confusing and difficult to navigate. One of the main reasons that quitting can be confusing and difficult is that it involves the start of a transition from who you were, professionally speaking, to who you're going to be in your next professional chapter. It's a change in *who* you are. Think back to the identity bubbles in chapter 3 that represent the different roles in our lives; resigning from a job will almost always cause changes in our identity. In a big career move we may change our company, our profession, and our location at the same time. Such transitions are certainly exciting, but they are also filled with the unknown. Successfully navigating them requires moving into these murky, liminal career spaces thoughtfully and with eyes wide open.

Your resignation process kicks off with the *pre-resignation period*. This is the time between when you decide to quit and when you actually resign. I've found that on average, there are six weeks between the time people decide to leave and when they actually give their notice. But that average is a bit misleading; many spend less than a week in the pre-resignation period whereas others are there for many months, even years.

Preparing to leave and planning how to do it can be tough. We only do it a handful of times in our lives, and each time—in terms of the reasons for quitting and the people and processes involved—it's different. Also, because this period typically takes place in secret, we can't observe others going through it and learn from their best practices and mistakes. There is no "how to" manual with a single set of rules for how to leave any job. The answers to questions such as how to communicate your decision to leave and how much notice to give can be hard to find. This is, of course, why it can be a good idea to confide in others during the pre-resignation period. Confidants outside of work can provide a sounding board and give experienced advice about how to resign in the best way possible.

Whether people choose to confide in others about their resignation plans, and if they do, who they confide in, varies depending on the person and the situation. But I've found that around four out of five people tell *someone* about their plans prior to actually quitting. Commonly, people confide in family and friends. Occasionally, people share the news with one or more coworkers. In rare cases (which we will discuss), people bring their boss into their confidence before they're ready to formally announce their plans. But in general, the pre-resignation period is a time of relative secrecy, when you figure out how to make the transition to the next chapter of your career, whatever that is.

Through conversations with confidants, planning the resignation in their mind, and researching it online, people tend to figure out how they will resign. They settle on the reason for quitting they will give their company. They decide how they'll communicate their decision. And they decide how much notice they'll give. Let's unpack each of these elements.

The why. Sometimes, the reason you'll provide for why you are leaving is blissfully easy to figure out, especially in cases when the cause of quitting is an external pull factor that is out of your control. If your spouse's relocation is the cause of your need to quit, then it's as simple as explaining that. But most of the time, it's not so straightforward. As we've discussed, there's often not one single reason that we quit. Even though a jolt may have triggered the reflection on your relationship with work that has led to quitting, your final decision to leave typically involves multiple push and pull factors. And moreover, even if you can pinpoint one or two things that have driven you to leave, that doesn't necessarily mean you should broadcast them as the causes of your departure. Imagine you're leaving because you dislike your boss, or you disagree with the company's values. Airing these displeasures during your resignation can damage how you're seen by those you leave behind, while providing you with little benefit in return.

Because of the limited upside to sharing any negative reasons for quitting, people often decide not to disclose the real reason. Instead, they may provide an honest but generic answer, such as pursuing a "can't miss" opportunity. Or they provide a specific but "not the whole truth" answer, such as saying that the job is in a better area of town for their kid's school. That may be true, but it's not the real reason for the move. A study of 300 workers who had resigned in the prior year found that around 30 percent of them did not tell the truth when telling their employer the reason they left their job. The main reasons for these leavers not telling the truth were because they didn't want to risk losing a positive reference, they didn't want to upset management or have a confrontation, or they simply found it unnecessary to disclose that information. All sensible reasons.

These reasons for not being fully transparent when resigning can provide good guardrails for how best to deliver your message of resignation. Sure, in life, honesty is the best policy. That applies to quitting as well. Under few circumstances would I recommend being dishonest. However, because there are typically multiple factors driving your decision to quit, picking the one that's least likely to cause damage to your reputation or that of others is a good idea. Ask yourself, which reason carries the least risk of harming your image in the eyes of those you're leaving? Which minimizes any potential conflict with your soon-to-be former boss and coworkers and avoids casting them in a harsh light? And which may actually be useful to your soon-to-be former firm, in potentially triggering positive change in response to your departure?

The how. Once you know "the why," you need to figure out how you'll communicate it to your organization. In the next chapter, we'll discuss the seven primary ways that people resign, and as you'll see, there are different approaches for deciding who to tell first, how to tell them, and what to say. But as you figure out the how of your resignation, this should be your starting point: resigning to your boss, in a private, face-to-face (in person or via live video), brief, and positive-toned meeting.

From this starting point, you can customize the delivery of your resignation based on your situation, desires, and goals. For instance, you likely have colleagues you would like to tell first, before they hear it from someone else. So, you could plan to ask the first person you tell (often your boss) if they would honor your wish to have the rest of the day (or a reasonable time period) to share the news firsthand with others. If you don't think your boss will honor that, you may consider sharing it with your close colleagues first, asking them to keep it quiet until you tell your boss. Here, you'd weigh the risks of this approach. It's never good when your boss realizes that they were one of the last to know about your decision to quit—that other members of their team have known about it for days, weeks, or months. I'm not saying that their feelings in this matter are your problem. But if your goal is to leave on a good note, such a scenario will stand in the way of you achieving that. Overall, to figure out how you are going to resign, you think through the trade-offs of different ways to deliver the news of your departure, and make the best plan for your situation.

The when. Throughout all your planning, a major consideration is how much notice you'll give, and whether you'll continue to be available after you leave. In a study where I asked individuals who had recently quit their jobs what factored into their decisions to give the amount of notice they did, they gave five reasons. Their main consideration was courtesy and respect toward their employer. Next, they accounted for the time it would take to find or train a replacement for them. They then thought about themselves and how much notice would allow them to maintain a positive image in the eyes of their boss. Another important consideration was any company policies and norms around leaving (however, they often found that company handbooks did not provide helpful guidance). Finally, when thinking about how much notice to give, they reflected on any poor treatment they had received from their boss or the company, and adjusted their notice downward accordingly.

These five considerations strike me as great guideposts, but I would add one more. How much of a break would you like, if any, between jobs (or between your current job and whatever comes next)? I realize this comes with some privilege; many of us cannot afford to take a break between career chapters. But I strongly encourage you to ask yourself if you can create some personal time in the space between walking out of your company for the last time and walking into your next role. If you can, it can make for a healthier transition between the two, helping you achieve closure on your prior role and being fully prepared for your new one. It's just like the healthy commute practices we discussed in chapter 9, but now it's for career changes.

The who. A final element worth considering during the pre-resignation period involves preparing for how people will react to your announcement of departure. Quitting isn't just about you; when others hear about it, it is an event in *their* lives, sometimes one that will trigger a collateral jolt. But beyond jolting others, there's one person in particular who may react unexpectedly and strongly to news of you quitting: your boss. In a study where I asked recently resigned MBA students to describe their boss's reactions to the news that they were quitting to go back to school, I found that 40 percent of the time, their bosses responded negatively, with disappointment, irritation, and in a couple of cases, even tears. Bosses reacted positively in 30 percent of cases, neutrally in 20 percent of cases (typified by expressions of understanding and nothing more), and around 10 percent of the time, they reacted with outright shock. And keep in mind that these reactions were in response to workers who were not going to work for a competitor but were simply going back to school. Although you may think you have a pretty good idea of how your boss will respond, take the time to prepare for unexpected reactions. The reality is that you don't know everything that is going on in the lives of those who will be affected by your resignation. Mentally prepare for all possible reactions from your boss, coworkers, and others.

There is one more critical element of planning for others' reactions to your resignation during the pre-resignation phase. What if you get a counteroffer? Given how common they are, there's surprisingly little research on the dynamics of counteroffers and the consequences of halting your resignation to accept one. In many instances, when you turn in your resignation notice, you will be asked the question "Is there anything we can do to change your mind?" How will you respond to that question? If you have gone through the "speak up" actions described earlier in the book, you may have already voiced the concern or opportunity, giving your organization a chance to respond to it. But of course, resigning takes things to a new level of seriousness, and it may give you bargaining power that you didn't previously have. Deeply think through how you will respond to this question. Imagine yourself being given a counteroffer that solves your primary reason(s) for leaving. Would that change everything? Or have you fully made the decision to move on?

Leaving on Your Mind, and in Your Actions

You might think that if either (1) you don't tell anyone that you are leaving or (2) those you do tell don't disclose it, your quitting plans will come together in secret, with no one the wiser. But as it turns out, that's not always the case. Our behavior during the pre-resignation phase sometimes betrays us. One time when I resigned from a job, I told my closest friend in the department, then immediately informed my department manager, and then immediately told another close colleague. The first two were shocked; neither of them saw it coming. But my third colleague surprised me. As soon as I started our conversation with "I need to share some news," she immediately replied, "You're leaving, aren't you?"

What? How did she know?

This person has really good instincts and is an expert in human resources and organizational psychology, but I was still surprised that she saw it coming. She explained that over the past month or two, especially in department meetings, she noticed that I had been unusually quiet. That silence was enough to tip her off that I was possibly backing away from my job and inching toward the door.

Research has provided evidence of my colleague's sixth sense. Our thoughts about leaving that we intend to keep locked in our minds often leak out and show up in our behavior. In a study entitled "Quitting Before Leaving," researchers made the sensible case that often once we decide to leave, we typically don't quit right away, but instead we slowly psychologically detach from the company as we plan to depart. They found that one hallmark of this detachment process is . . . *silence*. Not silence in general but silence related to speaking up to suggest ways to improve work (i.e., supportive voice). This article came out in 2008, over a decade before the term *quiet quitting* entered our lexicon, but it does a pretty good job of describing the phenomenon.

More directly, another team of researchers asked large samples of workers to reflect on the most recent time they resigned, and to report any behaviors they engaged in that might have tipped off their managers that they were going to quit. They also asked managers to think about the two most recent episodes of their employees quitting, and whether there were any signs that the workers were going to leave before they did so. This process resulted in *fifty-four different* pre-quitting actions!

What are some of the things we do as we prepare to quit? We update our LinkedIn profile. We block our computer screen from onlookers. We take longer lunch breaks than usual. I'm sure you could add to this list. But interestingly, these little "tells" didn't relate to subsequent quitting. The pre-quitting signals that most strongly related to subsequent leaving were subtler and more mundane. Not committing to long-term deadlines. Putting less effort into work. Not trying as hard to please your manager. And voicing dissatisfaction more than usual. In other words, the reactions to jolts that we've already discussed are of course visible to others. And if those others are astute and paying attention, they might correctly read them as signs that you're working through a process that may culminate in resignation.

Let me repeat: The entire jolts-response process that we've discussed does not happen in secret. The whole way through, you're sending clues to any attentive observers that you are starting to move toward the door. This isn't a good or a bad thing; it is just a subtle reminder to be aware of your behavior and to be prepared for someone asking you if you're thinking about quitting as you process a jolt.

The "Thinking About Quitting" Power Surge

A final pre-resignation heads-up. Once you've made the decision to quit, and as you plan for how you are going to do it, you may feel a surge of *power*. Deciding to quit is one of the most empowering decisions you'll make in your career.

When it comes to the power balance between you and your employer, who has the upper hand? For most of us, most of the time, our company has the power. We *need* the job to pay our bills, and/or we *want* to keep our jobs because of all the other good things that work can provide for us. On the flip side, most of us are fairly replaceable. I'm under no illusion that my university would cease to keep humming along just fine if

I quit tomorrow. I need them more than they need me. I feel a relative lack of power when I think about it.

But as soon as I start to think about quitting and start planning for what I would do if and when I quit, things change. The power balance begins to tip toward me. And once I make the decision to quit, it really swings in my favor. I'm no longer dependent on my employer. I've got plans for a new life without them.

And although your leaving won't sink the company, it will cause some disruption and cost. It would be best for them if you kept working rather than leaving. Suddenly, you have the upper hand. You have the *power*.

And this raises the question: What are you going to do with this power?

The answer is relevant for how you enact your resignation. You could use your newfound power to strengthen your relationship with the organization as you leave. Of course, it may also be tempting to use your power to get even with the organization, especially if a negative event related to work has jolted you to this point.

This power shift, which occurs once an employee decides to quit, was identified in a cleverly conducted set of studies by management scholar Ben Tepper. His research team argued that employees who have strong intentions to quit their jobs will be more likely than other workers to push back when they're treated poorly. So, they examined how employees with high intentions to quit responded to abusive leader behavior (relative to those with low or no intentions to quit). Across samples of fast-food workers, hospital staff members, and law enforcement officers, their findings were consistent. When workers are mentally prepared to quit, it empowers them to defend themselves. In response to experiencing abuse, those who had high quit intentions pushed back against the company and their supervisor, compared to those who were abused but had low intentions to leave.

Once we're ready to quit, we feel freer to act in whatever way we want.

We are unconstrained. Of course, this doesn't mean that we're going to use this power for bad. You know the maxim "power corrupts"? As it turns out, research doesn't support it. It's more accurate to say that power *reveals*. Power frees us from having to exercise self-control and liberates us to act on our impulses. If we're a genuinely kind person, power frees us to engage in whatever good deeds we choose. On the flip side, if deep down we're more of a jerk, power liberates us to be bad. The power surge that comes from making the decision to leave can lead us to act on how we really feel about our organization. And this power comes at the end of our time with the company. It presents itself as a final chance to get even. So how will you enact that power as you leave?

CHAPTER FOURTEEN

TURNING YOUR RESIGNATION INTENTIONS INTO REALITY

Maximizing the odds that your future self will thank your current self for the way you resigned.

In 2012, Greg Smith quit his job as a vice president at Goldman Sachs, after over a decade of working for the firm. In enacting his resignation, he published an opinion article in *The New York Times*, in which he slammed Goldman's culture and the company's treatment of customers. The piece went viral and was heavily discussed on social media and by traditional news outlets. Much of the discussion centered on Smith's criticisms of his former company, arguably harming Goldman's reputation as an employer and financial service provider. It also forced the firm to dedicate time and energy to damage control.

Fast-forward to today, and "public" resignations such as Smith's are commonplace. Though they don't appear in the op-ed section of newspapers and they often don't involve the vitriol that Smith directed at Goldman. Instead, they appear on social media. And instead of being focused outward, on the company and its reputation, they focus on the resigning employee and their experience as they deliver the news. But similar to Smith's farewell, they often go viral, eliciting thousands of positive and negative reactions.

While you may not opt for such a spotlight, these stories and videos highlight how emotional and difficult it can be to deliver your resignation news. And whether you broadcast your resignation on social media or do it privately, the reality is that thanks to today's communication technologies, news of your decision will spread faster and wider than in previous work generations. To the extent that you can, then, it's critical to take time to craft a resignation approach that sends a precise message. Your message may be fairly direct and simple, or your circumstances and preferences may lead you to consider a more complex approach. Either way, the way you enact your resignation will have immediate consequences for your remaining time at the company and lasting effects on your reputation.

Seven Ways to Leave Your Employer

Once again, take a moment to think back on times you have quit a job. How did you do it? How did it go? What would you do differently, if anything, if you could do it again?

In studying the quitting stories of hundreds of workers, I have learned that there are seven general ways people quit their jobs. Reflecting on your own resignations, and those you have witnessed, you can probably classify them as one of these seven styles (or in some cases, a combination of two).

The most common style of quitting, used around one third of the time, is the *by-the-book* resignation. By-the-book resignations have three hallmarks. First, departing employees inform their manager *in person* (which could mean via a video chat) of their intention to leave. Second, in that conversation, they tell their manager *why* they're resigning and *what* they're going to do after they leave. Finally, employees who use by-the-book resignations give an appropriate amount of notice—not more or less. The "Goldilocks" length of notice depends on the company, industry, and job title. In some countries and companies, it's dictated by your contract, but in most places, it's not. As a result, people sometimes default to the two-week notice period. But two weeks isn't a good rule of thumb. In some jobs, that would be too long. In others (including academia), it would be woefully short. As we discussed, a key consideration in the pre-resignation is to determine what the "right" amount of notice is, given your work setting.

Closely related to by-the-book resignations, and nearly as common, are *perfunctory* resignations. Perfunctory resignations also involve giving in-person notice to one's boss and providing an appropriate amount of notice. What distinguishes this style from by-the-book quitting is that in perfunctory quitting, you don't explain why you're leaving or what you're going to do next. You keep that to yourself. The resignation announcement is kept short and sweet. "I'm leaving. Here is my notice." While not disclosing these details may seem like a small decision, as we'll see, it can have big implications for how the company reacts to the news of your departure.

Beyond by-the-book and perfunctory quits, the remaining one-third or so of resignations are more specialized in nature and have clearer positive or negative effects on the organization you're leaving behind.

Let's start with the most positive of resignation styles: *grateful goodbye*. The grateful goodbye is characterized by two distinct positive actions by the departing employee. The first is that they give more notice than would be expected or is necessary. For example, if three weeks is stated in the company policy, a grateful goodbye could involve giving multiple months' notice. This way, the departing employee has time to wrap up as many outstanding projects as possible, and the company is able to find a replacement and take other steps to minimize the impact of the departure. In some cases, employees who resign via grateful goodbye go further and offer to keep helping after their last official day at the organization. The second characteristic of grateful goodbye resignations is that the departing employee not only tells their manager in person and provides the reason they are leaving, but they also express and show gratitude to the organization for what it has done for them. In short, extra notice and displays of appreciation are what set the grateful goodbye apart.

The opposite of the grateful goodbye is *bridge burning*. Greg Smith's resignation from Goldman Sachs would fall under this style. Another example comes from Joey DeFrancesco. He quit his hotel job by handing his manager a resignation letter while having friends from his brass band burst in and loudly play a celebratory song, all of which he filmed and posted on YouTube. These types of departures are characterized by one thing: intentional harm to one's manager, work group, or organization. Bridge-burning resignations often involve the departing employee's disparaging their manager or the company. In doing so, leavers do reputational damage to the people and company they leave behind, potentially causing collateral jolts and making the departure extra disruptive to the ongoing management of the business. Bridge-burning resignations can go beyond the verbal and include physical harm to the company's property or its members. A simple way this can manifest is through theft, with employees taking company property (which can include the firm's customers) with them when they leave. Of course, in rare cases, it can involve extreme acts of violence that cause physical harm to other employees.

Let's move back to the positive side of leaving. An *in-the-loop* resignation occurs when employees don't wait until they've fully made their decision to leave before informing their boss of their intentions to do so. Instead, during the pre-resignation phase, as they consider leaving, they bring their manager "in the loop" and let them know that they are considering leaving. This way, the manager can provide counsel to the employee and can prepare for a potential disruption to the work group. It's worth noting here that this can be a high-risk strategy for the departing employee, who may not have fully decided to leave yet. Your manager may feel compelled to share your news with HR or with their boss. As such, in-the-loop resignations are typically enacted only when employees deeply trust their manager, and/or when the reason behind the departure is something out of the employees' control (e.g., a partner's relocation).

Next comes a style of resigning that has become increasingly common, and is the hardest to classify as positive or negative. Here's a question for you:

Is it acceptable to resign via email or text message?

Every time I ask this question to a group of students, workers, or leaders, I tend to get an equal amount of strong yeses and nos. When resignations are delivered via written communication, they turn into an *avoidant* resignation style. This written communication is often via email but increasingly also via the many other messaging platforms we use at work. The upside of avoidant resignations for employees is clear; you can say exactly what you want to say—no more, no less. But the downside is equally clear. I spoke with one employee who quit by leaving their written resignation letter on the boss's desk after the boss had gone home on Friday. You can imagine how that boss's Monday morning started off!

Here's another question:

Is it acceptable to deliver your official resignation announcement to someone *other than your direct manager*?

Again, this question tends to elicit a lot of passionate yeses and nos. Avoidant resignations also occur when employees cut their direct manager out of their resignation communication process. The most common non-boss paths that employees take are by resigning to their HR representative or to their boss's boss. We'll discuss the implications of this style shortly, but I think you can accurately predict how managers tend to respond to being left out of their direct report's resignation communication.

Finally, there's the resignation style that is akin to a mic drop. When Jack Paar, the host of the *Tonight Show* in 1960, announced his departure, he did it live, on-air, with no notice. The day after NBC censored one of his jokes, three minutes into the ninety-minute broadcast, Paar said, "There's gotta be a better way to make a living," and walked off the set. In doing so, he enacted the final resignation style, one that we discussed earlier: *impulsive quitting*. This style is unique among other resignation styles because there's no notice provided. Employees simply walk off the job. In recent years, this style has been extended to include "ghosting," in which employees simply don't show up for work one day, and do not respond to any company communication.

At the Bridge, Lighter in Hand

Does it really matter how you quit? You're leaving, so if the company has trouble adapting, that's not really your problem, right?

Yes, of course it matters. I'm sure you can easily glean how some resignation styles (like grateful goodbye and in the loop) boost your professional reputation, while others (like burning bridges and perfunctory) harm it. Before studying these questions, I thought I could line them up in order of the relationship damage they'd cause between the quitting employee and their manager, from lowest to highest: grateful goodbye, in the loop, by the book, perfunctory, avoidant, impulsive quitting, and bridge burning.

I was mostly right, but not completely. My research revealed that the resignation style that elicits the lowest level of negativity from one's boss is in-the-loop resignations. If you have a close relationship with your manager, and you inform them of your quitting intentions during the pre-resignation phase, it's received quite well. Keep in mind, though, this strategy tends to be risky, and is mainly used when the reason for quitting is benign (e.g., spousal relocation, going back to school).

By-the-book and grateful goodbye resignations also elicit very little negativity. But what surprised me is that how managers respond to by-the-book resignations is very similar to how they respond to the much more effortful grateful goodbye resignation. While giving greater notice might earn you a few bonus points, it often won't make a huge difference to your manager.

Significantly more negativity is generated by perfunctory and avoidant resignation styles. It's somewhat striking to me that despite by-the-book and perfunctory resignation styles being identical except for one thing—whether or not the reason for departure is provided—managers respond much more negatively to the perfunctory approach. Their reactions to avoidant resignations make more sense to me. It doesn't feel good to be avoided (recall our discussion of ostracism). In addition, avoidant resignations can open managers' eyes to the possibility that it was their treatment of the departing employee that played a role in that person's decision to leave.

Least surprising was that bridge burning and impulsive quitting cause the most negative managerial reactions of all resignation styles. These styles are not only disruptive, but they also cast an unfavorable light on the managers of employees who use them.

So what does all this mean for your enacting your resignation in the wake of a jolt? First, if you're not sure about the best way to resign, then defaulting to the classic face-to-face meeting, with a reasonable amount of notice for your role, company, and industry, and sharing at least part of the reason for your departure, is a good approach. If you have an exceptionally close and positive relationship with your manager, then you could "upgrade" to an in-the-loop resignation. If you want to leave on a really good note, and you have the bandwidth to extend your notice period, then a grateful goodbye should help you achieve that goal.

Given that perfunctory and avoidant resignations aren't very well received, they should be used only if necessary. This is easier said than done, because these are the two easiest, and therefore most tempting, styles to use. One situation where it might make sense to use them would be if you're going to work for a competitor. In general, if you're going to work for a direct competitor, be prepared for your employer to not allow you to go back to your desk and to have you escorted off the property.* If you anticipate such a reaction, then being avoidant or perfunctory is a somewhat sensible tack. Of course, this indirectness will likely only postpone your company's finding out where you're going, and not disclosing

---

* Unlikely as it may be, you should prepare yourself for this possible reaction anytime you resign, regardless of how positively you expect it to go.

that information up front could unnecessarily damage your reputation with the company as you leave.

Finally, you might expect that I would suggest never using bridge burning and impulsive quitting. Generally speaking, you'd be right. In almost every case, resigning in these ways damages your reputation and doesn't create any wins for you or the organization. They are lose-lose propositions. But there are a few possible exceptions to this rule.

Why would people burn bridges or impulsively quit their jobs? Is it because of who they are (i.e., a bad worker/person) or because of what has happened to them (i.e., a bad situation) or both? I've tested both hypotheses and found much stronger evidence for the latter. People don't resign in negative ways because they are bad people. They do it because of their situation.

In particular, two aspects of our relationship with work influence whether we'll resign in negative or positive ways. The first is *toxic management*. If we feel that our supervisor is abusive, we become significantly more likely to resign in negative ways. The second is *unfair treatment*. When we feel we've been treated unfairly by our company, we become more likely to view our resignation as *the last* opportunity to get even.

If you're working for a toxic manager, there may come a point when you need to immediately separate yourself from them to protect your own well-being. To impulsively quit. *But what about your colleagues whom you leave behind, stuck working for that jerk?* This is where bridge burning comes in. I have heard from employees who, as part of their resignation, criticized their manager to their organization's leaders and to HR. They did so to call the company's attention to the problematic manager and possibly help the colleagues they left behind. Sacrificing your own reputation and causing organizational disruption to spur change that will improve the work lives of your former coworkers is courageous, but hopefully it's something that most of us can avoid during our resignations.

Don't Forget to Manage Your Notice Period

It is common to feel a bit (or a lot!) of guilt when resigning. One time earlier in my career when I quit, to deal with the guilt I felt (the company had been very good to me), I gave well over two months' notice. This was far more than what was required. My manager was appreciative, but it quickly became clear that it was too long. After a few weeks of goodbyes and wrapping things up, everyone around me moved on and adjusted to life without Anthony. At that point, the goodbyes switched to "You're still here? I thought you'd left." I felt a bit foolish, but it wasn't my fault. Again, there is no guidebook for how to resign. And the mentors who I would have normally asked for advice worked for the company I was leaving, so I hadn't discussed it with them.

The notice period begins immediately after you deliver your resignation news. Once you've decided to resign and enacted it, then all that stands between you and your next chapter is navigating the notice period, if you have one. I say "if" because sometimes, even if you give notice, the company will pay you for the time and ask you to no longer come in rather than have you serve it out.

This period often begins with a lot of emotion and a bit of confusion. The minutes, hours, and days after resigning can come with a whirlwind of feelings. It may not surprise you that the most common emotions people experience after resigning are positive ones, like relief, happiness, and excitement. In about a quarter of cases, though, people experience sadness, nostalgia, and guilt. These more negative emotions occur alongside the positive ones. Excited but guilty. Relieved yet nostalgic. Happy and nervous.

So don't be surprised if you have unexpected feelings or some emotional conflict after you resign. As we've discussed throughout this book, our relationship with our work is multifaceted. Even if you dislike most of those facets, much of that dislike will melt away once you take the final step to free yourself from it. And at the same time, there are those aspects of our job that we do like and we will miss. Combined with the trepidation that often comes with embarking on a new chapter in our careers and lives, you may experience all sorts of mixed emotions, including even regret. That is not unusual. You are not alone.

Beyond managing how we feel during the notice period, we also have to manage how we *act*. Our actions during the notice period can leave an impression on our former coworkers and boss that lasts a long time, perhaps forever. Given those stakes, it's worthwhile to make a plan and set expectations with your boss and others for what you can accomplish during your notice period. It's like a short-term psychological contract. It's critical to be realistic here. Often, we have too many unfinished projects to complete during this limited time. Focus more on smoothly transitioning most of them to others, or simply shutting some down. Especially when we want to leave on a positive note, we can easily overcommit to getting them all done. This is the path to a stressful and disappointing notice period, which can spoil the start of your career transition.

In addition to planning for how you're going to wrap up your work, it's useful to set expectations regarding whether you'll continue to attend team meetings and, if so, how much you'll contribute to them. Meetings can be tricky to navigate because they often involve solving current problems and making plans for the future. If everyone in the room knows you're leaving, they may suspect that your motivation to find the root causes of current problems is low. Moreover, you won't be around to see how decisions about the future play out. My advice would be to make yourself available to attend meetings (in other words, stay engaged), but speak in them only if you have something truly value-added to say or if you're asked to contribute. You're still being paid, and so you need to provide as much effort as you can; but at the same time, your work group is transitioning as well, to a future without you. So you also need to do what you can to facilitate that.

Finally, the notice period is a time of ending some relationships and trying to ensure that others live on. It's absolutely worth investing the time and energy in planning for *whom* you would like to say goodbye to, one-on-one, and with whom you would like to build a bridge to keep the relationship going after you depart. When you resign, you'll have some coworkers asking if you can grab a coffee, a drink, or a bite with them before you leave, or after you do so. That's nice, but your effort is best spent on the people you want to keep in touch with long-term. So, create a list of people that you want to connect with before you leave, think about what you want to convey to them, and prioritize accomplishing those farewells.

Because once you walk out those doors or close that laptop for the last time, those people are no longer your peers; they're your former coworkers. And you're no longer a member of that organization; you are an alum. Your jolt process has reached its most extreme conclusion.

But what about the jolts happening to those around us?

PART V

Helping Others Navigate Jolts

If you won the lottery, would you tell anyone? Of all the news stories I came across in researching this book, perhaps my favorite was one entitled "10 Ways to Know If Your Partner Has Won the Lottery and Is Keeping It a Secret." Now, it makes sense to me that many lottery winners would prefer to remain anonymous to the general public, and perhaps even to some of their extended family. But can you imagine not telling your partner that you'd won more than a million dollars? It turns out, quite a few of you can. One survey revealed that one in four people wouldn't share their winnings with their partner. And from China to England, there are stories of millionaire winners who didn't tell their partners or share the riches with them.

Now, I certainly wouldn't be laughing if I found out my partner had struck it rich and kept it a secret from me. But I find the general notion of hitting a big jackpot and acting as though nothing happened pretty funny. It would make for a great sitcom or dark comedy. But beneath the laughs, this story points to an insight about jolts: that people often traverse the jolt-based process alone, without disclosing it to those around them.

People certainly have the right to navigate jolts solo. But keep in mind that we don't always realize we've been jolted, and when we do, we often steer through what comes next in ways that harm our well-being and career success. All of us, at times, could use a sounding board, a copilot, or a coach to help us deal with jolts. But we may not realize we need it or may not feel comfortable asking for help. Being reluctant to ask for and accept assistance is especially common in our professional lives; seeking help at work can be difficult, and it comes with the risk of looking needy in the eyes of others (not an ideal look for many work situations).

This tension—between the difficulties of navigating jolts well and the lonely way that people often cope with them—creates an opportunity to improve the lives of those around us by helping them deal with jolts. But because people struggle to ask for help, we have to be on the lookout for the signs. Without being told or witnessing it, we may sense that something has changed in someone close to us. As significant others, we might trigger a crossover jolt when we confront our partner about bringing their work home with them. As coworkers, when we experience a collateral jolt, there's a good chance that our colleague who has been directly jolted is going through a similar process. As friends, we may sense the change in our friend's demeanor after hearing about an act of injustice against a social group to which they belong. As coworkers, friends, family members, and partners, we are the ones who are confided in when a jolt happens to those around us, and we sometimes see a jolt coming even if they don't.

Note that I haven't mentioned bosses yet. But they're arguably the most important of all. Baked into the managerial role is influence over the employees who report to you. You have some say over certain aspects of their jobs—the feedback they receive on their work performance, the ways they're rewarded (or not) for their effort, and the speed at which their job changes over time. This power puts managers in a more critical position than family, friends, coworkers, and others when it comes to jolts. Managers often make decisions that have the potential to jolt employees. Managers are tasked with maintaining and (ideally) improving their employees' well-being at work. When practiced well, managers are the ones whom employees speak to when problems in their work and even nonwork lives arise. And finally, managers are in the best position to help employees enact changes in response to jolts. In short, because of the control our managers have over our work, they can and often do play a deciding role in when jolts happen to us, and whether a jolt is ultimately a positive, neutral, or negative force in our lives.

In recognition of this managerial influence, you'll detect another tone shift in this final section. *It will feel aimed squarely at managers in some places.* However, the insights are relevant for all of us. We all have more ability than we probably realize to shape the causes and effects of jolts on those around us—our family, friends, coworkers, and even acquaintances and strangers.

CHAPTER FIFTEEN

RECOGNIZE YOUR ROLE IN OTHERS' FUTURE JOLTS

Recognizing your hidden ability to detect jolts before they happen, and how you can reduce their negative impacts on others.

Organizational Changes = Employee Jolts

My Great Resignation prediction was based on something that was already happening (the pandemic) and decades of study on why people quit their jobs. It would have been much more impressive (and useful) if I had seen the pandemic coming and predicted the wave of resignations back then. But I'm not psychic and don't have a crystal ball, so my ability to *predict* a pandemic, or the next war, or your next jolt, is limited.

But our ability to predict the jolts of those close to us is less limited. If I know my colleague is up for a promotion, then I also know that being turned down for it will be a direct jolt for him, while earning it might be a positive crossover jolt in his life. I can see my sister about to have a milestone birthday, and anticipate the positive jolt it may cause. My well-liked boss is nearing retirement, and I can foresee the collateral jolts that her departure will cause in my work group. Take a moment now and think about the upcoming weeks and months. Can you see some potential jolts on the horizon for the people closest to you? I bet you can.

For managers, foresight of their employees' futures at work is often even clearer.* One of the four classic fundamentals of management is *planning* (along with organizing, leading, and controlling). Leaders spend much of their time making future plans for their company and the teams and people within it. At some point, these future plans will be implemented, thereby becoming a current reality for workers. Simply put, *leaders' plans become employees' events, and jolts.*

A plan to expand the business into new markets will create opportunities for some employees to work abroad but will require others to change their work schedules to service customers in distant time zones. A plan to redesign the office to foster more collaboration will energize some workers but leave others pining for the quiet and privacy of their old cubicle. A plan to sell a stake in the firm to external investors will be celebrated by some employees but unsettle those who are distrustful of handing control to outsiders.

As these examples illustrate, the plans and decisions that leaders make are often the cause of future jolts. This is why organizational changes of every shape and size tend to trigger turnover. And sometimes, the quitting that stems from those jolts takes place in droves, in a process called *collective turnover.*

In 2023, Sam Altman was abruptly removed from his CEO position by OpenAI's board. Within one week, over 700 of the company's employees had signed a petition vowing to quit if he wasn't reinstated. As this vividly shows, when organizational changes are made, workers don't make sense of them alone, in a vacuum. The process takes place in groups—at the water cooler, in group texts, and in those informal chats that fill the room before and after meetings. Research has shown that pretty much all significant organizational changes, including leadership changes, mergers, or rounds of layoffs, trigger an initial period in which remaining employees talk among themselves and try to collectively make sense of what the heck is going on.

---

* I use the terms *managers* and *leaders* (and *bosses* and other similar terms) interchangeably.

If together, people can make sense of the change, such as when it was planned or expected, there won't be much subsequent turnover within the group. But when organizational changes are unexpected, the group will struggle to make sense of it, leading to collective uncertainty that simultaneously jolts individuals across the work group to reflect on the current state of their relationship with their jobs.

There are a few lessons here for all of us who want to help others navigate jolts well. First, many jolts are predictable. Second, if people can make sense of a potentially jolting event, they're in a better position to deal with it constructively. That may strike you as common sense, but then why isn't it more common for managers and companies to help employees make sense of organizational changes? Going back to the OpenAI example, companies routinely make changes ranging from small role reassignments to mass layoffs, yet put little effort into helping employees make sense of those disruptions.

In other cases, firms take extra care to try to cover up these types of collateral jolts, but that just makes it more difficult for employees to understand what's going on. *Silent layoffs* have become common at large firms, wherein remaining employees are kept in the dark regarding why some colleagues have been let go. When PwC initiated a round of these silent layoffs, certain employees were offered a package to leave immediately. Once these folks accepted the severance, they had to commit to leave silently and follow company-provided scripts if asked about their departure by their former colleagues. The result, of course, is that remaining employees are left to figure out among themselves what happened. In the absence of an honest and thorough explanation from their employer (and no assurance that they're not the next to be let go), remaining workers often reach the conclusion that the change is unfair. Now, as a leader, you may feel that it's your right to make changes in your life or in your company without having to explain why. That may be your right, but as I'll explain next, that's the recipe for brewing an unnecessarily big batch of jolts among those around you.

Necessary Evils May Be Necessary, but Unfairness Usually Isn't

If you were to read all the literature on organizational behavior published in the last fifty years, one of the main takeaways would be that few things consistently cause strong negative reactions in employees like being treated unfairly. But this research has also shown us that how strongly we react to injustice at work—whether it jolts us—depends on our access to one piece of information about the event or decision: *why* it occurred.

Imagine you're in a meeting with your boss and peers, discussing plans to hire temporary workers for the upcoming busy season. Every year, someone on your team has to shoulder the extra lift of coordinating with the staffing company and making sure it supplies the proper number of workers with the proper qualifications for the different jobs that require extra staffing. You know what a big pain it is, because you did it last year and it took so much extra time that your spouse said he hopes you never do it again. As the discussion wraps up, your boss says to you, "Since you did such a great job last year, I'd like you to take it on again this year." Your peers quickly chime in with expressions of appreciation (and relief on their faces) and then the meeting wraps. You think about how your spouse will react to the news, and feel the pangs of a crossover jolt forming, stemming from this seemingly unfair decision.

When a decision is made at work, how do employees decide if it's fair or unfair?

It's a two-level process. First, there's the recognition that something unfair appears to have happened. In the case above, the meeting ended with you getting more work piled onto your plate while your peers waltzed away with no extra assignments. Plus, your boss didn't mention any compensation associated with the extra work, whether it be in the form of some extra pay, the ability to flex the extra hours you'll have to work at some point in the future, or the removal of some other tasks from your plate. In short, your workload just went up relative to that of your peers, but what you get out of the job stayed the same. Unfairness seems to have occurred.

But there's a second set of fairness calculations that happen alongside or follow this initial assessment. Here, you consider whether the *procedures* by which the decision was made were fair. So, you might reflect either briefly or deeply on why your manager would saddle you with this extra work. Either by pondering a bit or by talking to your boss, you may realize or learn that there's a justifiable reason. Perhaps in your performance appraisal meeting the prior month, your boss told you that if you take on a few extra assignments, it will give you an inside track to a lucrative promotion that is opening soon. If that's the case, you may quickly switch your perspective and be grateful for this opportunity to boost your career (although explaining that to your spouse is another story). In this way, considering the whole situation overrules your initial conclusion that you've been treated unfairly.

Of course, imagine a different case, where you can't figure out why your boss assigned that project to you, so you ask her, and her response is "Because I'm the boss, and that's what I decided." In this case, you have zero insight into the reason the decision was made, which will strengthen your initial conclusion that you're on the receiving end of unfairness.

Given the importance of explaining the procedures underlying unpopular decisions, you would think that leaders would always invest the bit of extra effort to unpack their reasoning behind potentially unpopular decisions. And yet, they often don't.

Take what happened in late 2022 and early 2023 when there was a series of layoffs in the tech industry. The differences in how those layoffs were communicated were staggering. The CEO of better.com fired 900 workers over Zoom, displaying no emotion as he did so and calling the workers who were affected "unlucky." In contrast, when Microsoft laid off thousands of workers, the company's CEO explained, "We will treat our people with dignity and respect, and act transparently," going on to say, "These decisions are difficult, but necessary. They are especially difficult because they impact people and people's lives—our colleagues and friends." He also went into detail to describe the business conditions that led to these layoffs.

Now look, I'm not a fan of layoffs. Full stop. They're often not necessary or result from bad leadership. But part of the mantle of leadership is that you sometimes have to engage in necessary evils, wherein you cause harm for the good of the person (e.g., a tough performance review) or for the organization as a whole (e.g., temporary pay cuts). Doctors and veterinarians perform these all the time. But it's critical that those affected know *why* the evil is necessary, so that they can make sense of the pain.

Explaining the procedures behind decisions isn't just the right thing to do; it's also good for the bottom line. When we, as humans, conclude that we've been treated unfairly for no good reason, we become strongly motivated to get even. And in the workplace, getting even can be quite costly to organizations.

A cleverly designed study from several decades ago highlighted the consequences of poor leader communication following unfairness in stark terms. In this study, the researcher became aware of a company with three similar manufacturing plants that was instituting temporary pay cuts of 15 percent for the next ten weeks. Somehow, he convinced the company to let him run an experiment to study fairness by tweaking aspects of the pay cuts at the three factories.

In one factory, the pay cuts would be announced with basically no explanation of what caused the cuts.

In another plant, the communication accompanying the pay cuts would not only explain *why* the cuts were happening but go on to explain that every possible alternative had been examined and that the leadership would also be taking the same 15 percent pay cut.

In the third plant, no pay cuts happened; it was the control group.

Ten weeks later, the researcher examined the rate of employee theft at the three plants before, during, and after the pay cuts. Before the pay cuts, theft rates were similar across the three plants. Once the pay cuts were instituted, the rate of theft at the third plant, where pay was untouched, remained level. In the second plant, where the *why* behind the pay cut was thoroughly explained, theft increased by about 50 percent. In the first plant, where the pay cut came with only the briefest of explanations (i.e., no *why*), *theft shot up 167 percent.*

What's more, during the pay cut period, no one quit their jobs at the third plant and only one person quit their job at the second plant. What about turnover at the first plant, the one with the perfunctory explanation? There, 27 percent of workers quit their jobs during the ten-week pay cut period.

I can't stress this enough—while potentially unfair events are a part of life, the harm they cause hinges on whether (1) those affected are informed of the procedures via which the potentially unfair decision was made, and (2) whether the affected employees view that explanation as fair. When people get an outcome they don't want, but it's from a fair process, it's painful but comprehensible. When a bad outcome stems from an opaque process, it elicits a strong "get even" response from us, including through theft or quitting.

As a manager, if you make a decision that could jolt some of your workers, and you don't explain the reasoning behind the decision, you'll create bigger and more jolts. And this goes for all us. If you can give others a heads-up when you see potential jolts coming and help them make sense of the reasons behind them, then you'll be doing your part to make harmful jolts less disruptive. It's simple *courtesy*, which turns out to be the right thing to do from a human and a bottom-line perspective—taking action to prevent problems that would unnecessarily harm other people. A quintessential form of courtesy in the workplace involves simply informing others of changes that could negatively affect them and, when reasonable, taking any available steps to prevent future problems.

Often, companies know that difficult change is coming, but rather than helping employees understand the change and preparing them for it, they keep it secret until the last possible moment and then unleash it all at once. Doing so is the opposite of courtesy, so why does it happen? It happens because of the faulty assumption that the bad news will cause the same amount of disruption whether it's delivered early or late, so may as well leave it until the end. But what actually happens is that the negative information is much more jolting when it comes with the realization that others around us have known for months but didn't tell us. At work, this breach of trust makes it far more likely that employees will see the bad news as a reason to decommit from the organization, rather than stay loyal through the changes.

Courtesy can feel vulnerable—letting people know about problems and challenges that haven't yet happened. But while preemptively delivering future bad news may cause some immediate discomfort, it strengthens relationships between the jolters and the jolted overall.

Be Real with Your Recruits

As I've described, job seekers and companies alike engage in some acting during the job search and recruitment processes. I feel that the responsible thing for me to do here is to recommend that both sides cut back on such behavior. But that may not be realistic. Of course, you should always be honest when job searching or recruiting, or else you're asking for serious problems down the line. Companies that overstate how flexible they are (i.e., flex-washing) are going to wind up with a high level of quick quitters. And job seekers who overstate their skills often don't just "fake it until they make it." They often fake it, don't make it, and are exposed as fraudsters.

But even the most honest companies have realized that by its very nature, recruitment often places expectations in applicants' minds that aren't always met when those applicants begin at the company, resulting in honeymoon jolts and quick quitting. So, they came up with a solution: the *realistic job preview*. Especially in high-turnover industries like telemarketing, companies can use these previews to lower quick quitting.

Here's how it works: At the end of the recruitment and selection process, ideally before anyone has been offered the job, companies give job seekers an unvarnished preview of what working at the company *is really like*. Here, the recruiters reiterate the great things about working for the firm, but then it's time for some real talk. Company reps share the negative side of working at the company. Perhaps they share the results of their recent employee surveys, showing places where leadership is falling short. Perhaps they allow job seekers to hear from a panel of current employees about what the workers like least about their jobs and the company. Increasingly, companies from Waste Management to Netflix are using their corporate YouTube channels and podcasts to give prospective employees an unvarnished inside look at a day in the life of an employee. Whatever the method, the goal of the realistic job preview is the same—to set realistic expectations about working for the company, thereby scaring away any job seekers who are turned off by the imperfections (or glaring problems) that they'll encounter when they join.

Although the evidence is a bit mixed, most research shows that realistic job previews are effective in reducing honeymoon jolts and associated turnover. If that was the end of the story, I would be advocating for everyone to use them. But here's the deal: In some cases, these previews scare off the employees most likely to become high performers. Think about it. The very best job candidates are the ones who likely have the most choices in the job market. So, imagine these stars are juggling multiple offers, and you're the lone company using realistic job previews. True, you may earn the respect of these stars, but you'll also look worse compared to their other options. Contrast that with job seekers who have fewer alternatives. Regardless of the negative information they hear in a realistic preview, they will likely still take the job. But they'll start their new role with a lowered set of expectations, which means that when they experience some psychological contract breaches, it won't come as a jolt.

There hasn't been as much research done on the flip side—what happens when *job seekers* give employers a realistic job preview of themselves—but I imagine the effects will hold in this direction. If a hiring company is desperate to fill jobs, it may not be scared away by your sharing that you go for jogs at lunchtime and sometimes are sweaty all afternoon back in the office. However, for the very best jobs and companies, which have far more applicants than posts to fill, sharing your complete, whole, true self in that way may make you less hirable than those who don't disclose such potentially unpleasant information. So, what I am suggesting is that honesty is the best policy, but *oversharing* negative information may not be a part of that policy.

What is more realistic is that each side *lowers their expectations* a bit. In one study, researchers simply told new hires that, in general, people often have unrealistic expectations when they start a new job and that these expectations can cause "reality shock" when they are eventually unmet. They went on to encourage these new hires to consider whether any of their expectations are too high. In tracking the subsequent turnover, they found that these simple directions were as effective as realistic job previews at reducing quick quitting.

Anyone who takes part in company recruitment has the potential to foresee future honeymoon jolts and to reduce them. Of course, many jolts come from unexpected events, and are unforeseeable, so the best we can do is to spot them when they appear.

CHAPTER SIXTEEN

SURFACE JOLTS AS THEY HAPPEN

Creating a vantage point so you can see jolts
when those around you experience them.

The Sound of Not Listening

My first significant management role began six months after college. I was in a leadership development program at a plant in Albuquerque, New Mexico. The plant was the youngest in the company, and it was designed as a high-performance work system, meaning that the workers (or *technicians*, the more accurate term we used) were highly skilled and were given substantial discretion and ownership over their work. Although I didn't know it at the time, I now know from research that these work design elements relate to higher employee engagement and performance than the command-and-control systems or low-employee-investment systems of the past.

It turns out that wasn't the only thing I didn't know about engaging and motivating employees back then. I was given leadership over one of the teams that was responsible for keeping the four packaging lines humming during their shift. The team was performing well, but I was determined to make it the highest-performing group in the plant. To do so, I would often camp out on the packaging floor, walking between the lines and constantly asking the techs what they were doing and how we could do it better. And if there were problems, I was there—asking questions, doling out feedback, and pushing them to get a solution as soon as possible.

Sure, I was micromanaging, but things seemed to be going well. Performance started to tick up a bit.

About a month into the role, I arrived one afternoon after working the previous night, and I had a note to go speak to Darcie, the plant's HR manager. I worked well with Darcie and figured that there must be an HR issue with one of the technicians. As it turned out, the issue was with me.

Darcie told me that my entire team had stuck around after their shift ended at 6:00 that morning and waited at the plant until she arrived around 7:30. They then proceeded to inform her that my management style was unbearable and antithetical to the plant culture, and that they wanted me to be replaced. In their eyes, it was clear that my micromanagement wasn't driven by genuine concern for them but instead by my motivation to drive up performance to make myself look good and benefit my own career. I was taken aback, but I also defended my style and made the case that it was getting results. Darcie patiently listened (modeling behavior that I wasn't using in my own management), and then asked me if I had ever heard the term *new manager assimilation*. I had not.

She explained that to go through this process, my team would come in from 8:00 a.m. until noon on one of their Saturdays off. The company would give them breakfast and lunch and pay them overtime. I would be there, too. At the start of the session, Darcie would explain the purpose of the meeting—to improve the well-being and performance of the team. Then I would leave, and for the next two hours, she would listen to the techs and make notes of their feedback. Then I would join for the second two hours and we would talk through it all and agree to changes (if any) that I would make to improve my management effectiveness.

I've always been open to learning and self-improvement, so I thought this sounded like a good idea. I knew there would be criticism, but I also knew there would be opportunities to hear about the ways I had improved the team. In hindsight, I was clueless.

When the morning arrived, I went into the large meeting room and shared some niceties with the techs, and then Darcie walked in and went straight to the massive whiteboard that spanned the width of the front of the room. With a marker, she divided the board into three sections, and wrote START, STOP, and CONTINUE across the top of the sections. She explained to my team that I was open to this process and that I would leave and she would then ask them to voice their thoughts about what I should *start* doing, *stop* doing, and *continue* doing. I was then dismissed, and retreated to my desk to work for a couple of hours.

Two hours later, I reentered the room and looked immediately at the whiteboard.

I will never forget that sight.

The first section, about what I should *start* doing, was chock-full. The same goes for the middle board—what I needed to *stop* doing. In my memory, those two sections were so full with writing that Darcie had to write some comments sideways just to squeeze them all in. The third board? What I should *continue* doing? Empty. Nothing. Like a visual representation of crickets chirping. The team did not want me to continue one single thing that I was doing.

Recall that a common form of direct jolts is failure, and on this day, that type of jolt came for me. Any ego I had left at that point, any sense that I was a naturally great leader, melted to the floor. I knew these were professionals giving me this feedback—that it was valid. And right there on the board was their verdict. My leadership style wasn't working. Or worse, maybe I wasn't cut out to be a leader at all.

The next two hours changed the course of my career. If you've worked for a micromanager, you probably know the gist of my team's comments. The time I'd been spending with them was spent not actually *listening* to them but just trying to get them to work faster.* I wasn't seeing them as individuals. I hadn't shown them any trust or any respect, and what I

---

* Those of you who are students of the history of management would recognize this as classic scientific management, founded by Frederick Taylor. Such Taylorism can be good for performance but is often ruinous for worker well-being.

really needed to do was shut up, take a step back, and watch, listen, and learn.

And that's what I did. Over the remaining five months, I switched my style from micromanagement to supportive. Fortunately, I had an amazing role model in the team leader I was paired with. Michael had worked his way up from being an entry-level technician to being the most effective team leader in the plant. The biggest takeaway for me, from watching Michael and from the techs' feedback, was that management isn't all about doing; it's more often about listening. When I would do my rounds at the start of the shift, I would ask people about their equipment. Michael, on the other hand, would ask them how they were doing, and then listen to them tell him whatever was on their mind, personally or professionally. He's a genuinely good person, so I think he was mainly listening because it's who he is. But he was also being a good evidence-based manager. He was collecting data about how his employees were experiencing work and life. If a person was struggling personally, he'd think about how to help. If he picked up that they were getting a bit bored with their job, he'd think about how he could give them a new challenge or a development opportunity. *If they had been jolted, he would detect it in their responses.* Because of my micromanagement, on the occasions when I did ask the techs how they were doing, they would reply with answers about the manufacturing line, never opening up or giving clues as to the jolts they might be experiencing.

If you want to detect the jolts in the lives of those around you, you have to dedicate time to listen to them. When managers actively listen, workers feel supported, and managers gain insights about their employees' feelings, thoughts, and behaviors. This is a double win; in listening, we can better detect jolts in others, and it makes those around us feel supported and therefore more likely to proactively share experiences of jolts with us.

At that early stage of professional life, I had the bandwidth to spend time listening to my employees, showing concern for them, and learning from them. But as I advanced in my career, I found that my time slowly shrank. And looking back now, as that time shrank, so did my ability to pick up on jolts.

How Managers Spend Their Days, of Course . . .

As a manager, one of the most important aspects of the job is to support, engage, and develop those who work for you. Most managers will agree with that statement, and in most cases, part of their performance appraisal depends on how well they do it. And yet, when I talk to managers, spending quality time with their direct reports is one of the things they dedicate the least amount of their time to. This happens to us all outside of work as well. The identity bubble exercise in chapter 3 likely revealed to you at least some disconnect between the most important relationships in your life and where you dedicate your time and energy.

For organizations to help employees through jolts in ways that strengthen bonds rather than weaken them, there must be a mechanism in place that detects these events and assesses how they have affected employees. This mechanism is managers. Managers are in the key position to understand the personal and professional lives and experiences of their direct reports. To be clear, there are tools that can help managers in this role. Pulse surveys (i.e., a brief set of questions about how employees are feeling that are repeatedly asked over time) can give them some insight into how their employees are feeling. Peers and mentors can provide a source of support and understanding for employees. HR partners can make managers aware of external events that may jolt their employees and can provide extra assistance for engaging with employees through these events.

But on a day-in, day-out basis, it's my manager who is in a strong position to understand what I'm going through. To know a bit about my life outside of work. To understand how an external event may impact me or cause me to take a step back and reflect on life. To know that a certain change in company policy is not going to make a bit of difference to most employees, but it will jolt me.

But where are managers going to find this time? This is where the lessons I learned from Michael about listening started to fade away. As I got busier as a manager, one of the first things that started shrinking was the time I spent chatting and listening to my team members. This isn't a book on time management, but one premise of this book is that leaders either overlook the importance of events that kick off the turnover process or they don't even see them in the first place. There are no shortcuts to being attentive to these events in employees' lives, understanding them, and then dealing with their causes and effects. Being engaged in what happens to others is at the heart of management and leadership (and any close relationship, for that matter).

Here, I'll reiterate the thoughts of the late great strategy scholar Clayton Christensen, who observed that leaders are prone to allocating their time *toward* things that seem urgent and that give them a quick payback, and *away* from activities that don't provide an immediate solution and payback. He argued that this is backward, and the harmful consequences of this mis-investment of time often don't show up until it's too late to reverse them. Investing in human relationships (or neglecting them) doesn't provide a quick payback (or loss). During our days, we're bombarded with to-dos, big and small. There's a great deal of advice on how to manage these demands, with some of it suggesting that the small stuff should be handled right away, rather than letting it pile up. While well intentioned, the reality is that building and deepening relationships can't always be squeezed into one- or five-minute time segments. So, it gets deprioritized relative to the little stuff that can be quickly completed. Moreover, relationship building doesn't have a deadline associated with it, like most activities on our to-do lists. And of course, there are the big problems and projects that demand our attention. For many, each day brings a new batch of firefighting, and at the end of the workday, you silently chide yourself for not touching base with some of the people in your life.

So, between the small and the big, our attention to the most important relationships in our lives gets deprioritized and delayed. And our ability to detect jolts in others slips away as well.

In the case of managers, this means that the heart of business and management—the people—falls through the cracks. Now look, managers don't typically deliberately avoid dedicating time to their employees. Sure, there are toxic managers out there, but those bad apples make up just a small portion of the barrel. On the contrary, most managers find themselves in a bind when it comes to dedicating time and energy to their people versus their operational tasks. Research shows that as a manager's workload increases, *so does their tendency to prioritize technical tasks over people tasks*. This tendency is especially strong in settings where managers feel that their company mainly is focused on the bottom line and doesn't reward managers for supporting employees. On the flip side, in companies that emphasize and formally reward managers for focusing on people, managers tend to achieve a much better balance between investing in the technical and people sides of their jobs.

The takeaway for those at the top of organizations is clear. Managers' jobs should be designed such that they have time to dedicate to listening to their direct reports. Doing so puts managers in a position to detect jolts when they occur. Then, these leaders must make sure their managerial incentive programs don't emphasize business performance only, but employee well-being also. This recommendation probably won't go over well with many of today's business leaders, who seem to constantly call for shrinking the size of their managerial ranks. But the reality is that most of us want to work for someone who has the time and motivation to listen and respond to how we're experiencing work and life.

Of course, as great as having the time to listen to employees is, it won't always be enough to elicit their sharing of how they're truly experiencing work. Detecting jolts sometimes requires shifting from the passive to the active, and nudging workers to speak up.

Bring Me Problems

If you are interested in detecting jolts in those around you, then signaling that you want to hear about them will help you achieve that goal. For some managers, sending this signal may require rephrasing the saying "Don't bring me problems, bring me solutions." This much-beloved leader phrase is problematic for several reasons. First, finding good solutions to problems often requires the involvement of multiple parties—parties that managers are in the best position to round up. Forcing employees to develop solutions before voicing the problem can thus lead to inefficiency and suboptimal ideas. But on top of that, this phrase sends a strong signal to those it's directed toward—I don't want to hear your problems.

If you use this phrase and your employees follow it, it will likely save you from hearing about problems that they could and perhaps should have solved on their own. But it will also keep them from speaking up when there's a problem with their relationship with work and they're not sure if there's a solution to it.

Put another way, the phrase "don't bring me problems" will restrict your employees' sense that it's *psychologically safe* to talk about issues at work. Much has been written about the benefits of fostering psychological safety among employees, and for good reason. Psychological safety has a massive effect on whether employees will speak up or stay silent when they see a problem. In airplane cockpits, surgery theaters, and sports teams—when group members feel that it's safe to bring up problems, with or without accompanying solutions—they perform better and avoid preventable errors.

To foster psychological safety and get rid of the damage caused by the "don't bring me problems" mentality, companies have gone *radical*. At

Netflix, they call it *radical honesty*. At Bridgewater, it goes by the name *radical transparency*. And the person who wrote the book on it—Kim Scott—calls it *radical candor*. Regardless of the term, the "radical" notion at the core is the same. If you've got something to say, say it (respectfully).

What does it say about the state of organizations that policies allowing employees to speak freely when they have issues are dubbed "radical"? Well, it says that companies are chock-full of barriers to being yourself at work. All the earlier advice I gave about how to be politically savvy when speaking up was me providing you with evidence that if you're going to bring up a problem with your relationship with work, you have to be savvy about it to avoid being rejected or damaging your reputation. So, employees have to expend extra effort to craft their voice in a way that boosts its chances of success. As leaders, is that really where you want employees' finite energy to go?

In addition, it's well documented that employees differ in their level of political skill, and this individual difference affects the success or failure of their political behaviors, like bringing up problems in a socially smart manner. But do you really want something like political skill determining who's successful at your company?

The good news is, if you're open to your employees proactively bringing you problems so that you can help fix them, it's fairly easy to begin establishing a climate of psychological safety. It doesn't require a radical transformation of your leadership style. It just involves you displaying your openness to your employees' problems, ideas, and thoughts. That is, when it comes to building psychological safety, actions speak louder than words.

When managers display that they're open to suggestions—by doing things like listening, taking interest in employees' ideas and giving them real consideration, and occasionally acting on employees' ideas—it sends a strong signal of psychological safety to employees and spurs them to speak up and suggest improvements at work. Research has gone on to show that these effects of managerial openness on employee voice are strongest among the highest-performing employees.

If you want to catch jolts as they surface in those around you, then flip that tired idiom to "Please bring me your problems." Sure, that may lead some workers to bring up problems they should solve on their own. But part of good management is using those instances as coaching moments to show employees that they're empowered and capable to solve those issues. The upside, psychological safety, seems well worth the trade-off.

CHAPTER SEVENTEEN

SHAPE THE EFFECTS OF JOLTS

Time to act in response to the jolts that happen to those around you.

Share in the Ownership of Others' Jolts

In 2021, the CEO of a regional insurance company stopped by my university office, unannounced. He was an alum, on campus for some meetings. He enthusiastically told me about how, in the midst of the pandemic the prior year, he and his fellow executives realized that something in their employees had changed. Their people's connection with the company and with their work seemed to be drifting. In response, the leadership team rolled up their sleeves and worked tirelessly to connect with each of their employees, and to listen to their workers' experiences as they coped with the strains of the past year.

Shortly after his team began these efforts, he heard about the Great Resignation and immediately recognized my jolt-based explanation (though I didn't call it that at the time) as the cause of the drifting he was observing in his workforce. So, his team relabeled it within the company as the "Great Awakening" (he laughingly informed me that he liked his term better than mine) and began talking to his employees about it. As he and his executive team listened and learned, *they made small changes in response to each employee's concerns.* Then he got to the punch line. As a result of these efforts, unlike his competitors, his company didn't experience higher than usual turnover in 2021. Because of the leadership team's openness and responsiveness to the impact of the pandemic on their employees, the firm became stronger through one of the most challenging times that the modern world of work has seen.

This leader's actions contrasted with those of some other leaders I spoke with during that time. Rather than seeing that their workforce had been jolted and responding by dedicating time and energy to listening to employees and making changes based on what they heard, they told me that the wave of resignations was caused by factors beyond their control. Factors like: The current generation of workers isn't as loyal as those in the past; the government had been too generous with its stimulus checks and unemployment policies; remote work had made employees lazier; they were in an industry where "everyone" was experiencing similar turnover. These leaders were saying that the causes and solutions to their turnover issues were external. And in all cases, unlike the insurance exec who barged into my office, they were experiencing continued high turnover.

When I spoke with leadership teams from different companies in the same industry, this split in how they were reacting to the post-pandemic labor market kept appearing. Some executives looked internally, to themselves and their employees, for the solution to the disruptions that their business was experiencing. Others looked externally and concluded that the disruptions were out of their control. The self-fulfilling prophecy unfolded from there. Those who looked inside, listened to their employees, and made adjustments in response often didn't experience any Great Resignation, but told me they were confident they would have if they hadn't taken corrective action. Those who saw the problem as externally caused and therefore did nothing experienced higher turnover and the problems associated with it. Research findings from studies during the pandemic back up these divergent experiences. To the extent that workers had compassionate leaders, they responded to increased anxiety caused by the pandemic by more deeply engaging in their work and by increasing how much they helped their coworkers. Those with less caring leaders tended to withdraw from work and reduce engagement with their colleagues. Tough times call for leaders who not only listen, but who then *make whatever changes* are in their power to help employees cope with jolts.

Spend Time in Your Work Workshop

As mentioned in the last chapter, leaders at corporate giants have taken turns questioning the necessity of middle managers. Middle management gets a bad rap, and some of it is deserved. When they perform poorly, middle managers impede the effectiveness of their employees (those actually doing the work) and those above them (those steering the direction of the company). But when they excel, middle managers facilitate employee performance and well-being and bring to life the vision and strategy that the company's leaders lay out.

Middle managers often feel powerless, burdened by administrative duties and the demands coming at them from the top and bottom. No wonder it's a high burnout position. They often don't get the credit when things go well and get blamed when things go poorly.

But the reality is that these individuals often have more power than they realize, and executives should be giving them more power.

This hidden power has to do with how work is "designed." Recall that our jobs can be broken down into a bunch of small components, and a jolt may reveal that an aspect of our job is deficient and that we need to fix it or get away from it in order to have the career and life we want to have. *Managers' hidden power is that in many cases, they have control over the components of their employees' jobs.* This is the craft of management—not just sensing changes in employees and their work surroundings, but also *adjusting* their job components in response.

When you detect that someone has been jolted, simply listening to their concerns and letting them know that you're there for support if they need it may be enough for them to navigate the jolt on their own. But in many cases, some action needs to be taken, and this will often come in the form of tweaking some part of their job. This process happens all the time when it comes to safety concerns in the workplace. When a workplace hazard is revealed, action is taken to mitigate its risk. The same should go for when a manager learns that a jolt has opened an employee's eyes to a deficient aspect of their work. What action can they take to adjust a component of the employees' job, to fix the deficiency?

When the source of an employee's jolt involves their work tasks, managers often have more ability than they think to improve the situation. For example, employees vary in which aspects of the same jobs they do and don't like. Bob loves paperwork but hates sales calls, but his coworker Gina is the opposite. Employee jolts may reveal an opportunity to examine whether work tasks can be reallocated across the work group in ways that increase the well-being of multiple workers. By giving Gina more responsibility for sales calls and shifting her paperwork to Bob, the core of both workers' jobs becomes more satisfying. Of course, work tasks can also be outsourced and customized in many other ways, especially in the age of AI. The point here is that managers, and sometimes coworkers, often have the power to make these changes.

This power also extends to "the who" and "the where" of the job. Regarding the who, what do you do if your top producer has zero emotional intelligence and constantly doles out direct jolts to coworkers by treating them rudely? An intervention is needed. High performers who are disrespectful to others should actually not be called high performers. They're only good at half the job, and the other half of their job (being a good team member) needs to be corrected, or they need to be isolated from others or moved elsewhere (including perhaps out of the company). When managers detect direct and collateral jolts stemming from particular individuals, they typically have the power to insulate the rest of the team from these shocks.

And regarding "the where" of work, the past decade has shown us that where work takes place is much more flexible than imagined. Even wholly in-person work has aspects that can likely be done remotely. And even in jobs that cannot be done remotely, companies can give employees flexibility in how they use their time off, including the breaks within their workdays. As one example, GoPro encourages its employees to take midday breaks to hike or surf, with one employee taking the policy so far that he squeezes a skydive into his work breaks. Especially after employees experience jolts that emanate from the boundaries between work and home, like crossover jolts, managers can ask themselves and their workers if there are opportunities to make work more flexible, either temporarily or permanently, in a way that strengthens workers' relationship with their jobs.

The key lesson here is that when we detect that those around us, or working for us, have experienced a jolt, there is an opportunity to ask ourselves if we can redesign or change some aspect of their work, in order to improve their relationship with that work.

Be a Visionary for Those Stuck in Jolts

The negative effects of jolts, especially those that aren't navigated properly, can last for a long time. Right now, I bet you can think of someone in your life who is still struggling with the harmful effects of a past jolt. This may be for good reason; the effects of jolts that stem from tragedies may never (and perhaps should never) go away. But in other cases, we or those around us get stuck in a cycle of rumination about a jolt that happened in the past and how it has harmed us. In these cases, we may need someone else to help us take action to snap out of our jolt-caused funk. This is where being a visionary for others comes in. When someone close to us is stuck in a rut of thinking about a jolt and what it revealed about their relationship with work, we can help pull them out of the rut by opening their eyes to a path to the good life that they can't see.

Given that jolts cause us to question how much our jobs are contributing to our pursuit of *happiness* and *meaning* in our lives, the first step in helping others get through them is by calling their attention to the ways in which their current job does just that. This can be difficult to do when it comes to happiness. When a jolt has revealed an unfixable source of dissatisfaction with our jobs, there may be nothing that can be done about it. But the meaning we get from our jobs is a different story. We often lose sight of how our work benefits others, especially in the wake of a jolt. But that's exactly when we need to see it. Research conducted during the pandemic found that health-care workers who were able to keep the meaningfulness of their work top of mind were more able to stay engaged in their work amid the stream of jolts taking place at that time, especially in that industry.

Although managers may be in the best position to help workers see the positive impact of their work, all of us can channel our inner visionary and do the same. Far too often, visionary leadership—which provides a picture of how the company and its work changes the world for the better—is seen as something special that only executives do. And to be clear, it *is* in their job description. Ideally, executives invest the time to share their vision with middle managers and give them the bandwidth and power to make it a constant message for frontline workers. When this happens, our managers can help pull us out of the ruts that jolts can put us in. Unfortunately, company leaders sometimes fail in the vision department. The good news is that seeing how our work benefits others is something we all have the power to do. And so, when we see a friend, relative, or coworker caught in jolt-caused negative thinking, we may just need simply to give them a visionary pep talk. To remind them of all the ways that what they do—them, in particular—has a positive impact on their coworkers, customers, community members, and so forth.

Of course, the pep talk could reveal that your friend, or family member, or employee, finds no meaning and no happiness in their work. They're miscast in their job. Jolts sometimes reveal tough truths that we don't want to acknowledge—that we're in a bad relationship with our job and we need to make the tough decision to lean back or walk away from it. Although we're not ready to come to terms with it, it may be clear as day to those around us. They can see that we're in a quagmire of negative thinking stemming from a jolt in the past.

As a manager, colleague, friend, or spouse, we sometimes need to be the ones who help our close others realize that they need to make a change in their relationship with work. Simply bringing to the person's attention that they haven't been able to get over the jolt and offering to be a sounding board may be enough. In other cases, helping them craft a plan to lean out of work to help them develop other parts of their life that bring them more fulfillment may be what's needed. Or you may be the one who needs to encourage them to update their résumé and launch a new job search.

As discussed earlier, jolts are often unpleasant because they have high stakes and are often navigated alone. By being the person who helps others think through the pros and cons of carrying on, speaking up, leaning back, or walking away, you can increase the odds that the jolt will result in a positive change to the person's pursuit of the good life. Sometimes, this can be as simple as helping them keep calm as they carry on through the effects of the jolt. On the opposite end, it may involve helping them step back and rethink their life and career. This may involve asking the big, tough questions, like: As you look back on your career path up till now, what is the most salient "road not taken" for you?

This question can be quite powerful for those struggling to find the path to their good life. In asking this question of employees working in all sorts of professions across the US, researchers found that most people can easily point to a *forgone identity*. This identity is tied to a career or profession you dreamed of at some point earlier in your life. Most of us have dreams of doing other jobs, and in many cases, these dream jobs are ones we planned to pursue in some former life chapter. Participants in this study included a teacher who could have been a photographer. An HR professional who could have been a pastry chef. And a social worker who could have been a veterinarian. What's more, when the research team measured how much people still thought about and longed for these life paths not taken, a significant percentage (though not the majority) reported that in the past few weeks, they had yearned for them.

When we see the effects of a jolt but those who have been jolted don't, it's up to us to ask the tough questions that could help them realize a big change is needed. Of course, asking questions is only the start. You then need to copilot the big changes with them.

CHAPTER EIGHTEEN

CREATE A POSITIVE POST-JOLT RELATIONSHIP

Supporting others through the big changes caused by jolts can be tough, but it can also unlock long-term benefits for you and them.

Taking the Gut Punch with a Smile

> "My boss reacted awfully to my notice. They went on about how me leaving was the beginning of the end for the company, [how] other people . . . would now follow suit, how it was the worst year of his life, [how] I was making the wrong decision etc."

> "The agency partners who I work for now are normally great. They have good management styles and are respectful of boundaries . . . until someone resigns. Then it's like a switch is flipped, and all hell breaks loose."

> "It's almost a hallmark of poorly run companies that people are mistreated during their notice periods."

Think about the last time one of your friends at work told you they were leaving. Experiencing the collateral jolt caused by a close coworker quitting is no fun. This is especially true if you're a manager and the close coworker is your top employee. I'd argue that one of the least pleasant moments for any leader is when one of their top employees resigns. In many cases, managers are also friends with their team members, and the departure of an employee makes work less pleasant for them, too. Then of course there's the loss of that person's production and the work it will take to replace them. There's also the disruption to the work group with both the departure and the onboarding of a new team member. This disruption may be especially bad if the departing employee is going to work for a competitor, bringing the added threat of their stealing your business. Finally, especially for newer leaders, there's the feeling of failure and insecurity stemming from the old phrase "Workers don't leave jobs, they leave managers." Feelings like that can make you question your leadership ability. Altogether, it can feel like a gut punch.

We typically don't respond well to real or metaphorical gut punches. Our instinct is to go on the defensive and protect ourselves against further harm. That's why, if you listen to stories of employees quitting, you'll often hear tales like the ones above, about bosses who respond in dysfunctional ways.

Feeling betrayed, angry, sad, or insecure in response to a fellow employee's resignation isn't completely in your control. Remember our sociometer—that internal gauge of social acceptance or rejection? When an employee quits, it will often sound the alarm of social rejection. While your brain may recognize that it's "only business," your heart often doesn't. So having a wave of negative emotions is normal. You're human. But it *is* business, so you sometimes do have to rein in those emotions.

The moment after an employee makes their resignation known is a critical moment in which remaining workers, especially bosses, send powerful signals to leavers regarding whether it will be a pleasant or unpleasant end to this work relationship. When remainers respond to resignations constructively, it conveys that leavers can be open about their real reasons for quitting, that they'll be treated well during their final weeks on the job, and that their relationship with the company will continue after they depart. All these signals are good for the departing employee, the work group, and the company. When employees feel that it's safe for them to voice the real reason they're leaving, leaders can learn whether there are improvements they can make to reduce the negative effects of jolts in the future. When employees feel well treated during their notice period, they're less likely to badmouth the company to their remaining peers, thereby lessening the likelihood of collateral jolts becoming turnover contagion. And when leavers and their contributions to the company are properly celebrated as they exit, they're more likely to be positive ambassadors of the company even after they leave. I'm not saying that these positive outcomes will always happen, but by responding constructively to departing employees, remainers create the possibility of them occurring, rather than opening the door to disgruntled leavers, turnover contagion, and damage to the company's reputation.

Of course, when managers and other coworkers respond like the examples at the start of this chapter, it sends strong *negative* signals to the departing worker. That they'll have an uncomfortable notice period. That unless they want more negativity, they should hide their real reasons for leaving when asked. That their relationship with the company will be completely severed when they walk out the door for the last time.

The advice here is easy in theory and often hard in practice. Think back to the seven different resignation styles. When you learn of an employee's resignation, it may be via their telling you in advance (in the loop), telling you directly (by the book), your finding out from others or in an email (avoidant), or by their walking off the job (impulsive quitting) or disparaging you and the company as they resign (bridge burning). In all cases, your objective should be to respond constructively. That may mean that your initial reaction will involve a mix of showing your true feelings but also suppressing some others—showing genuine happiness for them and genuine disappointment over losing them as a colleague, but hiding the anger and frustration you may also feel. If they're someone you would like to retain, ask if there's anything you can do to keep them on. If not, express your appreciation for all they've done in their time with the company. Then, offer your intention and hope to work with them to craft a transition that will minimize their departure's disruption to the work group and will set them up for success in their new chapter. Even in the most difficult cases, such as when the departing employee is a quick quitter who just finished their expensive onboarding training, or when it's an avoidant, bridge burning, or impulsive quitting style of departure, there's nothing to be gained by reacting negatively. While sometimes difficult, taking a more positive approach will serve as a big step toward minimizing the disruptiveness of unexpected departures caused by jolts. And it will also increase the odds of turning your departing performers into future boomerangs.

Learn When and How to Throw a Boomerang

"I'm back."

On March 18, 1995, Michael Jordan famously released this two-word press release. Two years prior, after experiencing a series of jolts, including a golf buddy betraying him and writing an unflattering tell-all book and the disappearance and then tragic passing of his father, Jordan shocked the world by retiring from basketball. He then made a massive career pivot to baseball, spending two years playing in the minor leagues. But those two words announced that the greatest basketball player on earth was returning to the Chicago Bulls. Despite being stung by his departure, Jordan's coach, teammates, and fans celebrated the news. Understandably so. Starting in 1996, he and the Bulls went on to win three consecutive NBA Championships.

As the successful return of Jordan indicates, there's a serious upside to bringing great former employees back. And yet, some of us close our minds to rehiring those who were jolted into leaving, viewing them as disloyal and therefore not worthy of consideration for future job openings. The question begging to be answered is, then, aside from Michael Jordan, are boomerangs worth it?

To answer that question, let's stay in the NBA for a moment. Management professor Brian Swider and his colleagues studied NBA players who left their team for another club but then returned to their former team at some point later in their careers. Controlling for all other plausible explanations, the researchers found that boomerangs performed better when they returned than before they left, driven by experience gained in their time away.* These findings suggest that if someone was a good performer before they left, then they'll probably be a good performer when they return. Especially if they picked up some new skills while away.

Moving away from the court and into more traditional work settings, a study of over thirteen thousand new hires and boomerangs found that, initially, boomerangs tend to outperform new hires. It makes sense that these return employees are better able to contribute right away; they've done the job before. This performance boost was especially pronounced in jobs that required a great deal of teamwork. So if you have a big, immediate need on your team where a new hire will have to get up to speed and succeed right away, boomerangs are an especially attractive option. However, the performance advantage of boomerangs doesn't seem to last forever. In another study of almost thirty thousand external hires, boomerang hires, and internal promotions, another research team found that boomerangs tended to perform just as well when they returned as when they left, and all three groups performed similarly in their first year on the job. But after that first year, new external hires and those internally promoted outperformed boomerangs. Boomerangs were also more likely to quit than the other two groups of workers.†

From what we know about boomerangs, they're worth the risk only if they were pretty good employees when they left. If they have gained valuable experience in the interim, all the better. And if they're gone too long, these positive effects can fade. In some of my own research, we've

---

* Interestingly, these positive effects were reduced when the player returned to a different arena than the one they had previously played in for the team.
† Research has also revealed the resignation destinations that are most likely to yield boomerangs. They are most likely to occur when those who leave take a career break or switch to a different company in the same or similar industry. Those who resign to go work in a different industry rarely return.

found that the sweet spot for bringing boomerang employees back is often around the one-year anniversary of their departure.

Despite the potential upsides of embracing boomerang employment, many organizations put zero thought into setting up high-performing leavers to come back in the future. At minimum, this is a missed opportunity from a human standpoint. As we've discussed, the decision to quit in the wake of a jolt is tough, and so we sometimes get it wrong, and it would be in the best interest of all involved if we could return to our former jobs. But perhaps more compellingly to managers, at a time when almost every company is struggling to fill their job openings with highly qualified candidates, ignoring the boomerang potential of your leavers is a losing talent-management proposition. The alternative approach may seem a bit radical, but pioneering leaders are showing how to foster boomeranging and, in doing so, turn the negative of high performers leaving into a more positive event.

The best resignation experience I ever had began with me telling my dean that I had accepted a job at another university. She put her head down and muttered an expletive, which made me laugh. She then noted that I had used the past tense when I said "accepted" and she took that to mean that there was nothing she could do to change my mind. I confirmed. At this point, her mood and tone immediately shifted from disappointed and surprised to developmental and future-thinking. She told me some nice things about my potential and gave me some astute advice about how to navigate the process of switching between schools. And then she did something that should be in every manager's playbook. She said she was not going to accept my resignation; instead, she was going to give me a one-year leave of absence. That way, if I found that my new job wasn't what I hoped, I could return without missing a beat in my service or dealing with any cumbersome HR issues or policies related to rehiring.

Every few months during the following year, she and a fellow leader would email me and ask how I was liking the new gig. I *was* liking it, and they expressed genuine happiness about that. But they also mentioned that if those positive feelings faded, to let them know so I could return. At the end of the year, they gave me one last chance to change my mind, which caused me to do one last "check-in" with my current relationship with work. Concluding it was healthy, I pulled up my old resignation letter, updated the date, and turned it in. Even though I didn't become a boomerang, to this day I am a vocal fan of that institution, partly because of how well they treated me on my way out.

Fast-forward a year, and I was speaking with the HR executive team at a large organization about the importance of both retention and keeping strong ties with former employees. The executives agreed that there was more they could be doing but said that one practice they had recently begun was extending one-year leaves of absence to high-performing employees when they quit. It was working. The company had already brought back a few stars who, shortly after they left for another company, had experienced honeymoon jolts. As the innovation of this company and my former boss shows, you can take action right now to increase the odds that the departures of your high performers will be temporary leavers.

Even when jolts lead employees to sever their relationship with their employer, how those who remain (especially managers) respond to the resignations has significant implications for whether the departure is a loss for both parties versus simply the start of a new chapter between them.

Leaving but Staying Together Forever

A coworker or employee leaving is seen by some as the ultimate sign of professional disloyalty. In the cases of bridge-burning resignations, that view may be correct. But, of course, in almost all cases, resigning isn't a sign of disloyalty but of someone leaving to pursue what they hope will be a better situation for them. To improve their relationship with work and their progress on the road to the good life.

Treating resignations as acts of betrayal isn't only inaccurate; it also harms the potential for the remaining work group to grow stronger through the transition. By labeling departing employees as disloyal, managers blame the leavers as the problem and let themselves off the hook for not learning the actual cause of the resignation. It's a classic example of what my colleague Mark Bolino calls *lazy management*—attributing problems to the traits of workers ("She's a disloyal person") and not considering that the problem is actually within the manager's control, or is the manager themselves. Even in cases where a colleague's resignation really stings, it's just another organizational disruption that deserves a root cause analysis, the same way you would handle a safety or quality issue. What went wrong, if anything? Can we prevent this from happening in the future? This learning will simply not happen if managers lazily chalk up the cause of the departure to disloyalty.

Approaching the reason for a colleague's departure with curiosity, as an open question, sets a different process in motion. It signals to the leaver, and to those who remain, not only that you hope the leaver finds what they're looking for but that you would like to learn from the departure and improve the work lives of those who remain. In seeking to understand the cause and consequences of an employee's resignation, managers can then talk to their remaining team members about how to improve. In having these conversations, managers may learn more about different aspects of the departure. But even if they don't learn anything, they'll still strengthen communication with current employees, thereby mitigating the potential for turnover contagion.

In addition, treating all who resign as disloyal forgoes the opportunity to strengthen the company's reputation in the talent marketplace. Companies' employer brands are partly shaped by the experiences and testimonials of former employees. One of the most visible ways this shows up is on platforms such as Glassdoor, which allow current and former workers to anonymously share their experiences as members of a given organization. Employer brand matters to job seekers. It affects their initial impressions of a potential employer and the likelihood that they'll be attracted to it and seek a job there. Treating former employees well, both as they depart and once they become alumni, increases the likelihood that they will retain positive feelings toward their former employer, and share these feelings when given the opportunity to talk about the company.

Finally, when a worker quits, remaining employees watch it unfold in real time, and see firsthand whether there's alignment between what the company says about how they view their workers and what they actually do. Most organizations convey that they care about their employees as *humans*, not just as cogs in a machine. That they care about their employees' well-being beyond the workplace. Some go so far as to call employees their partners, or even family. When companies communicate these sorts of bonds with their employees, and then act in ways that conflict with that messaging, employees lose trust. One example of this comes from Salesforce, whose CEO long stated that the company is a family and that employees are all family members. That was before the company ever had a layoff. Enter 2023, when almost every tech company was laying off employees, some via multiple rounds. Salesforce cut 10 percent of its workforce, around seven thousand of its "family members." As observed by many pundits, this move damaged the credibility of the message that the company is one big family. The analogy of companies as families is inherently flawed; they're two very different entities, and the notion of family doesn't conjure fond feelings for everyone. But that's beside the point. To ring true, leaders' claims that they see their employees as not just workers but as humans or family members have to align with their actions. And one way to do that is to invest in caring for workers *even when they are no longer employees.*

Forward-thinking companies have done away with the mentality that departing employees are disloyal workers, and they also have done away with the notion that former employees are no longer connected to the company. Instead, they view former employees as company alumni. Former employees didn't quit, they *graduated*. By labeling them as alumni, these companies give former employees a living, positive identity associated with the company. I should note here that Salesforce does an extraordinarily good job at this.

Going back one final time to the identity bubble exercise, some of you may have listed being an alum of the places where you went to school. It's a valued role in your life. Corporate alumni programs have the same goal. Rather than letting a jolt ultimately end the relationship between a worker and their former employer, alumni programs keep the tie alive, in a way that benefits the company, its current employees, and its alums. Of course, you don't need to make a major investment in building an alumni program to get the benefits of it. Each of us, managers or not, can do our part to keep in touch with our valued friends and colleagues who have moved on to greener pastures. I bet you can think of one of those people you've been meaning to reach out to right now. There's no time like the present.

EPILOGUE

Most of us recognize how work can contribute to our pursuit of the good life. That it can be a source of happiness and meaning in our lives. But our relationship with work is changing. It's becoming less stable, as jolts become more frequent and impactful. Is this change and instability a good thing or a bad thing? By now you know my answer. It depends.

Although jolts often stem from negative events, they almost always contain silver linings. At certain points in our lives, we need jolts. At one time or another, all of us get complacent and need a jolt to get us out of autopilot. The problem is, it can be hard to tell when a jolt should spur us into a major change, a medium change, a minor change, or no change at all. Life gives us more than the binary options of quit or stay. But too often, we overly narrow down the options to: stick with the status quo or make a huge change. To stay on the road we're on, or to take the road less traveled.

We can do better. As workers, leaders, and humans, we can take actions that will allow us and others to navigate jolts in ways that bring us closer to the good life, rather than constantly setting us back and leading us astray.

In the next week, the next month, or the next year, you will be jolted. It's part of life. Jolts are coming, for us and those around us. And when they arrive, we'll be ready for them.

ACKNOWLEDGMENTS

This book would not have happened if not for Arianne Cohen, the amazing journalist and author who immediately recognized the importance of the Great Resignation prediction and amplified it. Arianne would never have contacted me had it not been for Adam Grant, the embodiment of prosociality, who also pointed me in the right direction when I began to consider writing a book. As a result, I found Katherine Flynn, literary agent extraordinaire, who believed in me and this book from start to finish, and who showed unending patience and incredible wisdom as I navigated this process as a first-time author. Arianne, Adam, and Katherine, thank you!

I had the great fortune of working with an outstanding editorial team on both sides of the pond. I am immensely grateful to Rick Kot and Drummond Moir, who took a chance on me and shepherded me through the early ideating and writing stages. Emily Wunderlich and Géraldine Collard were incredible editorial partners. Emily's ability to keep me focused on "the stakes" and her creativity in structuring the story were transformational. Géraldine's keen eye for the big and little pieces that weren't fitting quite right, and how to fix them, took the book to a new level. The wonderful writing skills of Kassie Brabaw elevated and sharpened the readability of every section of the book.

I am so grateful for Carlos Zayas-Pons, who piloted the manuscript through production with immense professionalism, positivity, and skill.

Thanks to Carlos, the administrative side of this process was seamless, easy, and even fun. In addition, the fact that you're reading this book is at least partly due to the masterful publicity and marketing work of Ivy Cheng, Rachel Wainz, Bridget Gilleran, and Britney Bioh. This dynamite team's talent and initiative had a transformative effect on the book's reach and impact. I also deeply appreciate the work of the many other pros who contributed to this book behind the scenes at Viking and Ebury. Finally, Sarah Khahil and the entire team at Calligraph provided me with incredible support every step of the way. Thank you!

I owe a massive debt of gratitude to a few folks who read rough versions of the book and provided incredible feedback, edits, and suggestions. Brian Swider found countless ways to bring the writing to life while also keeping it firmly and faithfully grounded in the academic literature. Nitya Chawla and Rahul Prabhakaran were a dynamic duo of insight, highlighting the sections that really worked and those that were misfits, and helping me think through the different ways to structure the book. Kaitlin Maasdam opened my eyes to the loose threads in the manuscript and how to tie them up in ways that enhanced the storyline's clarity.

I deeply appreciate the help of friends who served as sounding boards as I developed the ideas in the book. In particular, John Grose, Emeline Therias, Thiago Catao Abrantes, and Colin Fisher provided critical support and feedback at key moments of my writing process.

Many ideas in this book were shaped by conversations with, and learning from, friends and colleagues at Creighton University, the University of Oklahoma, Oregon State University, Texas A&M University, and UCL School of Management. You know who you are, and I'm grateful for you.

This book would never have happened had it not been for my wonderful friend and adviser Mark Bolino, who was open-minded and supportive enough to allow me to pursue my dissertation on the topic of resignations, even though doing so meant more work for him. No one has had a greater or more positive impact on how I think about the psychology of work than Mark.

My understanding of how to manage jolts has been shaped by working for and alongside an incredible set of leaders. I've learned so much thanks to the good fortune of working with Michael Frongillo, Darcie Karol, Ramon Gallardo, Mike Noble, Mike Corbin, Nikki Gasaway, Jay Kamin, Aaron Harris, Andre St. Amour, Tony Wiese, Ilene Kleinsorge, Mitzi Montoya, Don Neubaum, Jim Coakley, Wendy Boswell, and Davide Ravasi.

This book-writing process turned out to be quite a journey, and through its twists and turns I was grateful for the support of my family. Especially my mom and dad, Maureen and Chris. In addition, Sharifa, Andy, Coover, Mark, Julie, Jeanne, Steve, Joey, Melina, Kevin, and Becky were always there with positivity and encouragement when I needed it.

Finally, there is a small section in this book that discusses the unique, positive effects that come from long-term relationships, and I definitely experienced those positive effects as I worked on this book. As she has been for the past three decades, Michelle was the perfect partner to have throughout this process. From lifting my spirits to challenging my thinking to endlessly proofreading to helping me keep everything in perspective, Michelle was always there with the support I needed, when I needed it.

RESOURCES

Many ideas in this book were inspired by, or grounded in, the research of fellow organizational psychologists who study employee turnover and careers. For anyone seeking to learn more about these topics, I recommend reading and following the work of these outstanding researchers.

Jos Akkermans	Timothy M. Gardner	Anthony Nyberg
David Allen	Barry Gerhart	Rebecca Paluch
Blake Ashforth	Rodger Griffeth	Jenna R. Pieper
Talya Bauer	Brad Harris	Robert Ployhart
Wendy Boswell	John Hausknecht	Caitlin Porter
John Boudreau	Brooks Holtom	Alex Rubenstein
Joel Brockner	Peter Hom	Sima Sajjadiani
Matthew Call	Herminia Ibarra	Scott Seibert
Michael A. Campion	Kohyar Kiazad	Jason Shaw
David G. Collings	Maria Kramer	Abbie Shipp
Samantha Conroy	Carol Kulik	Brian Swider
Serge da Motta Veiga	Tom Lee	Charlie Trevor
Alison M. Dachner	Dong Liu	Connie Wanberg
Annie Duke	Carl Maertz, Jr.	Ryan Zimmerman
Marion Eberly	Erin Makarius	
Jie (Jasmine) Feng	Terence Mitchell	
Allison Gabriel	Fred Morgeson	

NOTES

INTRODUCTION

3 **on May 10, 2021:** Arianne Cohen, "How to Quit Your Job Flawlessly," *Daily Republic*, March 31, 2021, dailyrepublic.com/state-nation-world/how-to-quit-your-job-flawlessly/article_be024d14-2190-531f-81a3-58e29a3edd50.html.

3 **"Professor's Prediction Goes Viral":** "Professor's Prediction Goes Viral: 'The Great Resignation Is Coming.' Here Are His Tips for Quitting Your Job Post-Pandemic," *Entrepreneur*, May 10, 2021, entrepreneur.com/business-news/professors-prediction-goes-viral-the-great-resignation/371521.

5 **bad for our mental health:** David B. Newman and John B. Nezlek, "Private Self-Consciousness in Daily Life: Relationships Between Rumination and Reflection and Well-Being, and Meaning in Daily Life," *Personality and Individual Differences* 136 (2019): 184–89, doi.org/10.1016/j.paid.2017.06.039.

CHAPTER ONE

13 **because "no one wants to work anymore":** Kerry Breen and Rima Abdelkader, "'We All Quit': Burger King Staff Leaves Message to Management on Viral Sign," *Today*, July 13, 2021, today.com/food/we-all-quit-burger-king-staff-leaves-message-management-t225263; Emily Hofstaedter, "Monsters: Those 'Nobody Wants to Work' Signs," *Mother Jones*, December 24, 2021, motherjones.com/politics/2021/12/monsters-those-nobody-wants-to-work-signs.

13 **that enters the workforce:** CBS Sacramento, "Folsom Taqueria Posts Sign Blaming Government Assistance for Slow Service," CBS News, July 11, 2021, cbsnews.com/sacramento/news/folsom-taqueria-sign-government-assistance; Hannah Epstein, "How Come 'No One Wants to Work Anymore?'" *Marist Circle*, April 16, 2024, maristcircle.com/citynational-news/2024/4/16/how-come-no-one-wants-to-work-anymore.

13 **cold water on the *anymore* part:** *Stockton Review and Rooks County Record*, April 27, 1894, newspapers.com/newspage/379643726.

14 **force for good in workers' lives:** Gallup, *State of the Global Workplace: 2024 Report* (2024), gallup.com/workplace/349484/state-of-the-global-workplace.aspx.

14 **(GSS) in the US:** Scott Highhouse et al., "Would You Work If You Won the Lottery? Tracking Changes in the American Work Ethic," *Journal of Applied Psychology* 95, no. 2 (2010): 349–57, doi.org/10.1037/a0018359; NORC, "The General Social Survey," gss.norc.org.

15 **survey on a global scale:** International Social Survey Programme, issp.org.

16 **17 million more workers:** Based on size of US workforce in November 2024, bls.gov/news.release/pdf/empsit.pdf.

17 **from the UK to Japan:** Jon Boys, "The Great Resignation—Fact or Fiction?" CIPD, February 21, 2022, cipd.org/uk/views-and-insights/thought-leadership/cipd-voice/great-resignation-fact-fiction; Stefan Ellerbeck, "This Country Has the Highest Number of People Planning to Quit Their Jobs," World Economic Forum, August 11, 2022, weforum.org/agenda/2022/08/jobs-work-quit-great-resignation; Julia Horowitz, "The Great Resignation Is Taking Root Around the World," CNN Business, March 30, 2022, edition.cnn.com/2022/03/30/economy/great-resignation-uk-australia-europe/index.html.

17 **for over a century:** Thomas W. Lee et al., "On the Next Decade of Research in Voluntary Employee Turnover," *Academy of Management Perspectives* 31, no. 3 (2017): 201–21, doi.org/10.5465/amp.2016.0123.

17 **when we leave our jobs:** Peter W. Hom et al., "One Hundred Years of Employee Turnover Theory and Research," *Journal of Applied Psychology* 102, no. 3 (2017): 530–45, doi.org/10.1037/apl0000103.

18 **"say 'yes' at that time":** Jack Kelly, "Why the 'Great Resignation' Is Greatly Exaggerated," *Forbes*, June 8, 2021, forbes.com/sites/jackkelly/2021/06/08/why-the-great-resignation-is-greatly-exaggerated.

18 **good alternatives frequently quit:** Aditya Makik, "How to Reverse the 'Quit Work' Movement," Forbes, January 8, 2025, forbes.com/councils/forbestechcouncil/2025/01/08/how-to-reverse-the-quit-work-movement.

19 **external events shake companies:** Alan Meyer, "Adapting to Environmental Jolts," *Administrative Science Quarterly* 27, no. 4 (1982): 515–37, doi.org/10.2307/2392528.

19 **hundreds of new ventures:** Albert Shapero, "The Displaced, Uncomfortable Entrepreneur," *Psychology Today* 9 (1975): 83–88, papers.ssrn.com/sol3/papers.cfm?abstract_id=1506368.

20 **likely to become entrepreneurs:** Albert Shapero and Lisa Sokol, "The Social Dimensions of Entrepreneurship," in *Encyclopedia of Entrepreneurship*, ed. K. H. Vesper, D. L. Sexton, and C. A. Kent (Prentice-Hall, 1982): 72–90.

20 **of quitting, in 1994:** Thomas W. Lee and Terence R. Mitchell, "An Alternative Approach: The Unfolding Model of Voluntary Employee Turnover," *Academy of Management Review* 19, no. 1 (1994): 51–89, doi.org/10.5465/amr.1994.9410122008.

20 **cases involved a jolt:** Thomas W. Lee et al., "An Unfolding Model of Voluntary Employee Turnover," *Academy of Management Journal* 39, no. 1 (1996): 5–36, doi.org/10.5465/256629.

21 **in workers' personal lives:** Thomas W. Lee et al., "The Unfolding Model of Vol-

untary Turnover: A Replication and Extension," *Academy of Management Journal* 42, no. 4 (1999): 450–62, doi.org/10.5465/257015.
21 **studies around the globe:** Kevin Morrell, "Towards a Typology of Nursing Turnover: The Role of Shocks in Nurses' Decisions to Leave," *Journal of Advanced Nursing* 49, no. 3 (2005): 315–22, doi.org/10.1111/j.1365-2648.2004.03290.x.
21 **an Australian marketing firm:** Carol T. Kulik et al., "Shocks and Final Straws: Using Exit-Interview Data to Examine the Unfolding Model's Decision Paths," *Human Resource Management* 51, no. 1 (2012): 25–46, doi.org/10.1002/hrm.20466.
21 **"than accumulated job dissatisfaction":** Brooks C. Holtom et al., "Shocks as Causes of Turnover: What They Are and How Organizations Can Manage Them," *Human Resource Management* 44, no. 3 (2005): 337–52, doi.org/10.1002/hrm.20074.
22 **between the ages of eighteen:** Bureau of Labor Statistics, "Baby Boomers Born from 1957 to 1964 Held an Average of 12.7 Jobs from Ages 18 to 56," US Department of Labor, January 3, 2024, bls.gov/opub/ted/2024/baby-boomers-born-from-1957-to-1964-held-an-average-of-12-7-jobs-from-ages-18-to-56.htm.
24 **"found out until he got home":** Dave Schilling, "The 9 Best Jokes from Chris Rock's New Netflix Special," *Vulture*, February 14, 2018, vulture.com/2018/02/chris-rock-tamborine-best-jokes-netflix.html.
25 **term *rage applying* went viral:** Claudia Guthrie, "What Is 'Rage Applying,' and Does It Actually Work?," *Muse*, February 4, 2023, themuse.com/advice/rage-applying.
26 **of [usually online] platform:** Robert H. Moorman et al., "Driving the Extra Mile in the Gig Economy: The Motivational Foundations of Gig Worker Citizenship," *Annual Review of Organizational Psychology and Organizational Behavior* 11 (2024): 363–91, doi.org/10.1146/annurev-orgpsych-111821-033012.
26 **well-being and sustained productivity:** Kira Schabram et al., "Recover, Explore, Practice: The Transformative Potential of Sabbaticals," *Academy of Management Discoveries* 9, no. 4 (2023): 441–68, doi.org/10.5465/amd.2021.0100.
27 **who regrets doing so:** Meike Sons and Cornelia Niessen, "Cross-Lagged Effects of Voluntary Job Changes and Well-Being: A Continuous Time Approach," *Journal of Applied Psychology* 107, no. 9 (2022): 1600–27, doi.org/10.1037/apl0000940; Emi Nietfeld, "There's a Good Chance You'll Regret Quitting Your Job," *Atlantic*, March 11, 2023, theatlantic.com/ideas/archive/2023/03/great-resignation-quit-job-regret/673346.
27 **actively search for other jobs:** Jason R. Faberman et al., "Job Search Behavior Among the Employed and Non-Employed," *Econometrica* 90, no. 4 (2022): 1743–79, doi.org/10.3982/ECTA18582.

CHAPTER TWO

29 **season would be his last:** James Carroll, "Jürgen Klopp Extended Interview: Why I've Made the Decision to Leave Liverpool," Liverpool Football Club, January 26, 2024, liverpoolfc.com/news/jurgen-klopp-extended-interview-why-ive-made-decision-leave-liverpool.
30 **each episode in writing:** Daniel Kahneman et al., "A Survey Method for

Characterizing Daily Life Experience: The Day Reconstruction Method," *Science* 306, no. 5702 (2004): 1776–80, doi.org/10.1016/j.tbs.2025.101028.

32 **every aspect of our well-being:** Christopher M. Barnes and Nathaniel F. Watson, "Why Healthy Sleep Is Good for Business," *Sleep Medicine Reviews* 47 (2019): 112–18, doi.org/10.1016/j.smrv.2019.07.005.

34 **how we respond to events:** Howard M. Weiss and Russell Cropanzano, "Affective Events Theory: A Theoretical Discussion of the Structure, Causes and Consequences of Affective Experiences at Work," in *Research in Organizational Behavior: An Annual Series of Analytical Essays and Critical Reviews* 18 (1996), 1–74.

35 **how strong they are:** Frederick P. Morgeson et al., "Event System Theory: An Event-Oriented Approach to the Organizational Sciences," *Academy of Management Review* 40, no. 4 (2015): 515–37, doi.org/10.5465/amr.2012.0099.

36 **Oprah pointed to that event:** Lynette Rice, "Oprah Winfrey Says She Quit 60 Minutes Because 'I Have Too Much Emotion in My Name,'" *Entertainment Weekly*, April 30, 2019, ew.com/tv/2019/04/30/oprah-winfrey-quit-60-minutes; Lacey Rose, "Oprah Talks Apple Plans, '60 Minutes' Exit, 'Leaving Neverland' Backlash and Mayor Pete 'Buttabeep, Buttaboop,'" *Hollywood Reporter*, April 30, 2019, hollywoodreporter.com/tv/tv-features/oprah-winfrey-talks-apple-plans-60-minutes-split-2020-election-1205311.

37 **often unfolds during crises:** Karl E. Weick, *Sensemaking in Organizations* (SAGE Publications, 1995).

38 **spike in negative emotions:** Carl P. Maertz and Michael A. Campion, "Profiles in Quitting: Integrating Process and Content Turnover Theory," *Academy of Management Journal* 47, no. 4 (2004): 566–82, doi.org/10.5465/20159602.

39 **makes you want to leave:** Ellen Scott, "Career Cushioning Is the Next Big Work Trend—but Should You Be Doing It?," *Stylist*, 2022, stylist.co.uk/life/careers/career-cushioning-work-trend/736067.

39 **and put up with it:** Romano Santos, "What Is 'Fuck You Money' and Do You Have Enough of It?," *Vice*, March 7, 2022, vice.com/en/article/xgdmg4/how-quit-job-early-invest-money-retire.

39 **we set for ourselves:** Peter M. Gollwitzer, "Implementation Intentions: Strong Effects of Simple Plans," *American Psychologist* 54, no. 7 (1999): 493–503, doi.org/10.1037/0003-066X.54.7.493.

39 **"of making quitting easier":** Annie Duke, *Quit: The Power of Knowing When to Walk Away* (2022, Portfolio).

40 **higher well-being and career success:** Helena D. Cooper-Thomas et al., "The Relative Importance of Proactive Behaviors and Outcomes for Predicting Newcomer Learning, Well-Being, and Work Engagement," *Journal of Vocational Behavior* 84, no. 3 (2014): 318–31, doi.org/10.1016/j.jvb.2014.02.007; S. E. Seibert et al., "What Do Proactive People Do? A Longitudinal Model Linking Proactive Personality and Career Success," *Personnel Psychology* 54, no. 4 (2001): 845–74, doi.org/10.1111/j.1744-6570.2001.tb00234.x.

41 **a "psychologically ready" state:** Erik Dane, "Promoting and Supporting Epiphanies in Organizations: A Transformational Approach to Employee Development," *Organizational Behavior and Human Decision Processes* 180 (2024): 104295, doi.org/10.1016/j.obhdp.2023.104295.

CHAPTER THREE

43 **Championships in Malta:** PA Media, "Lottery Winner to Represent England at Pool After Buying Table with Winnings," *Guardian*, October 23, 2023, theguardian.com/uk-news/2023/oct/23/lottery-winner-represent-england-pool-championships-table-winnings-neil-jones.

43 **how she handled it:** James Cox, "Youngest Lotto Winner Callie Rogers Says She Regrets Spending Her Millions on Cocaine, Cars and Plastic Surgery," *news.com.au*, August 20, 2018, news.com.au/lifestyle/real-life/true-stories/youngest-lotto-winner-callie-rogers-says-she-regrets-spending-her-millions-on-cocaine-cars-and-plastic-surgery/news-story/34ccd576569b34858678d941af7be8e5.

44 **frequently cited lottery study:** Philip Brickman et al., "Lottery Winners and Accident Victims: Is Happiness Relative?," *Journal of Personality and Social Psychology* 36, no. 8 (1978): 917–27, doi.org/10.1037/0022-3514.36.8.917.

44 **in their country's lottery:** Erik Lindqvist et al., "Long-Run Effects of Lottery Wealth on Psychological Well-Being," *Review of Economic Studies* 87, no. 6 (2020): 2703–26, doi.org/10.1093/restud/rdaa006; Shirin Ali, "Why Lottery Winnings Don't Always Lead to Happiness," *Hill*, July 27, 2022, thehill.com/changing-america/well-being/mental-health/3576632-why-lottery-winnings-dont-always-lead-to-happiness.

45 **break and then returning:** Richard D. Arvey et al., "Work Centrality and Post-Award Work Behavior of Lottery Winners," *Journal of Psychology* 138, no. 5 (2004): 404–20, doi.org/10.3200/JRLP.138.5.404-420.

45 **"retain the ability to function":** F. Scott Fitzgerald, "The Crack-Up," *Esquire*, February 1, 1936, classic.esquire.com/article/share/97a6b0a8-ba1c-4b7b-aa64-0d08dd9fb952.

48 **distilled into two halves:** Richard M. Ryan and Edward L. Deci, "On Happiness and Human Potentials: A Review of Research on Hedonic and Eudaimonic Well-Being," *Annual Review of Psychology* 52 (2001): 141–66, doi.org/10.1146/annurev.psych.52.1.141.

49 **measure in workers—job satisfaction:** Howard M. Weiss et al., "An Examination of the Joint Effects of Affective Experiences and Job Beliefs on Job Satisfaction and Variations in Affective Experiences over Time," *Organizational Behavior and Human Decision Processes* 78, no. 1 (1999): 1–24, doi.org/10.1006/obhd.1999.2824.

50 **in other attainable jobs:** Frank L. Schmidt and John Hunter, "General Mental Ability in the World of Work: Occupational Attainment and Job Performance," *Journal of Personality and Social Psychology* 86, no. 1 (2004): 162–73, doi.org/10.1037/0022-3514.86.1.162.

50 *is meaningful to me*: Gretchen M. Spreitzer, "Psychological Empowerment in the Workplace: Dimensions, Measurement, and Validation," *Academy of Management Journal* 38, no. 5 (1995): 1442–65, doi.org/10.5465/256865.

50 *broader scheme of things*: Jacqueline R. Idaszak and Fritz Drasgow, "A Revision of the Job Diagnostic Survey: Elimination of a Measurement Artifact," *Journal of Applied Psychology* 72, no. 1 (1987): 69–74, doi.org/10.1037/0021-9010.72.1.69.

51 **immigration officer made headlines:** Katie Grant, "Postscript: Chris Holmes aka 'Mr Cake,'" *Independent*, July 11, 2015, independent.co.uk/news/people/postscript-chris-holmes-aka-mr-cake-10382164.html.

258 | NOTES

52 **likely you will be to quit:** A. L. Kristof-Brown, "Perceived Applicant Fit: Distinguishing Between Recruiters' Perceptions of Person-Job and Person-Organization Fit," *Personnel Psychology* 53, no. 3 (2000): 643–71, doi.org/10.1111/j.1744-6570.2000.tb00217.x.

53 **gave a name to this internal system:** Mark R. Leary and Roy F. Baumeister, "The Nature and Function of Self-Esteem: Sociometer Theory," *Advances in Experimental Social Psychology* (Academic Press, 2000): 1–62.

54 **them in a different job:** Studs Terkel, *Working: People Talk About What They Do All Day and How They Feel About What They Do* (New Press, 1974).

55 **surveys and quantitative analyses:** Richard J. Hackman and Greg R. Oldham, "Development of the Job Diagnostic Survey," *Journal of Applied Psychology* 60, no. 2 (1975): 159–70, doi.org/10.1037/h0076546; Hackman and Oldham, "Motivation Through the Design of Work: Test of a Theory," *Organizational Behavior and Human Performance* 16, no. 2 (1976): 250–79, doi.org/10.1016/0030-5073(76)90016-7.

56 **lives of other people:** Adam M. Grant, "Relational Job Design and the Motivation to Make a Prosocial Difference," *Academy of Management Review* 32, no. 2 (2007): 393–417, doi.org/10.5465/amr.2007.24351328.

58 **are one with it:** Fred Mael and Blake E. Ashforth, "Alumni and Their Alma Mater: A Partial Test of the Reformulated Model of Organizational Identification," *Journal of Organizational Behavior* 13, no. 2 (1992): 103–23, doi.org/doi.org/10.1002/job.4030130202.

58 **at work more meaningful:** Rolf van Dick et al., "Interactive Effects of Work Group and Organizational Identification on Job Satisfaction and Extra-Role Behavior," *Journal of Vocational Behavior* 72, no. 3 (2008): 388–99, doi.org/10.1016/j.jvb.2007.11.009.

59 **"I'm putting a man on the moon":** Andrew M. Carton, "'I'm Not Mopping the Floors, I'm Putting a Man on the Moon': How NASA Leaders Enhanced the Meaningfulness of Work by Changing the Meaning of Work," *Administrative Science Quarterly* 63, no. 2 (2018): 323–69, doi.org/10.1177/0001839217713748.

59 **call this *construal level*:** Batia M. Wiesenfeld et al., "Construal Level Theory in Organizational Research," *Annual Review of Organizational Psychology and Organizational Behavior* 4 (2017): 367–400, doi.org/10.1146/annurev-orgpsych-032516-113115.

60 **switch between levels:** Merlijn Venus et al., "Seeing the Big Picture: A Within-Person Examination of Leader Construal Level and Vision Communication," *Journal of Management* 45, no. 7 (2019): 2666–84, doi.org/10.1177/0149206318761576.

61 **assigned a new boss:** Robert Iger, *The Ride of a Lifetime: Lessons in Creative Leadership from 15 Years as CEO of the Walt Disney Company* (Random House, 2019).

CHAPTER FOUR

62 **experiences and new beginnings:** Shigehiro Oishi and Erin C. Westgate, "A Psychologically Rich Life: Beyond Happiness and Meaning," *Psychological Review* 129, no. 4 (2022): 790–811, doi.org/10.1037/rev0000317.

63 **of support or disapproval:** Megan Tatum, "#Quittok: Why Young Workers Are Live-Quitting on Tiktok," BBC, March 27, 2023, bbc.com/worklife/article/20230321-quittok-why-young-workers-are-live-quitting-on-tiktok.

63 **to quit into reality:** Ryan D. Zimmerman and Todd C. Darnold, "The Impact of Job Performance on Employee Turnover Intentions and the Voluntary Turnover Process," *Personnel Review* 38, no. 2 (2009): 142–58, doi.org/10.1108/00483480910931316.

64 **Census started tracking it:** Richard Fry, "For Today's Young Workers in the U.S., Job Tenure Is Similar to That of Young Workers in the Past," Pew Research Center, December 2, 2022, pewresearch.org/short-reads/2022/12/02/for-todays-young-workers-in-the-u-s-job-tenure-is-similar-to-that-of-young-workers-in-the-past.

65 **"individual can become stuck":** Terence R. Mitchell et al., "Why People Stay: Using Job Embeddedness to Predict Voluntary Turnover," *Academy of Management Journal* 44, no. 6 (2001): 1102–21, doi.org/10.5465/3069391.

65 **comes from three places:** Kohyar Kiazad et al., "Job Embeddedness: A Multifoci Theoretical Extension," *Journal of Applied Psychology* 100, no. 3 (2015): 641–59, doi.org/10.1037/a0038919.

66 **to perform well:** Mark C. Bolino et al., "The Implications of Turning Down an International Assignment: A Psychological Contracts Perspective," *International Journal of Human Resource Management* 28, no. 13 (2017): 1816–41, doi.org/10.1080/09585192.2015.1130735; Manfred F. R. Kets de Vries, "Are You Ready to Lead Overseas?," INSEAD, November, 10, 2014, knowledge.insead.edu/leadership-organisations/are-you-ready-lead-overseas.

67 **researchers call *reluctant stayers*:** Peter W. Hom et al., "Reviewing Employee Turnover: Focusing on Proximal Withdrawal States and an Expanded Criterion," *Psychological Bulletin* 138, no. 5 (2012): 831–58, doi.org/10.1037/a0027983.

67 **from her work life:** Michelle Obama, *Becoming* (Crown, 2018).

69 ***goodwill* you have at work:** Paul S. Adler and Seok-Woo Kwon, "Social Capital: Prospects for a New Concept," *Academy of Management Review* 27, no. 1 (2002): 17–40, doi.org/10.5465/amr.2002.5922314.

70 **will champion our careers:** Scott E. Seibert et al., "A Social Capital Theory of Career Success," *Academy of Management Journal* 44, no. 2 (2001): 219–37, doi.org/10.5465/3069452.

70 **of couples in old age:** Anna Rabelová et al., "Beyond Success: Understanding the Characteristics of Long-Term Relationships in Older Age," *Journal of Family Psychology* 38, no. 1 (2024): 17–25, doi.org/10.1037/fam0001157.

71 **"through the difficult times":** Ellen D. B. Riggle et al., "'The Secret of Our Success': Long-Term Same-Sex Couples' Perceptions of Their Relationship Longevity," *Journal of GLBT Family Studies* 12, no. 4 (2016): 319–34, doi.org/10.1080/1550428X.2015.1095668.

71 **professional lives more predictable:** Edgar H. Schein, "Coming to a New Awareness of Organizational Culture," *Sloan Management Review* 25, no. 2 (1984): 3–16.

72 **it's also our emotions:** Arlie Russell Hochschild, *The Managed Heart: The Commercialization of Human Feeling* (University of California Press, 1983).

73 **actually feel, at work:** Alicia A. Grandey, "Emotional Regulation in the Workplace: A New Way to Conceptualize Emotional Labor," *Journal of Occupational*

Health Psychology 5, no. 1 (2000): 95–110, doi.org/10.1037/1076-8998.5.1.95; Alicia A. Grandey and Allison S. Gabriel, "Emotional Labor at a Crossroads: Where Do We Go from Here?," *Annual Review of Organizational Psychology and Organizational Behavior* 2, no. 2 (2015): 323–49, doi.org/10.1146/annurev-orgpsych-032414-111400.

73 **emotional labor exhaust us:** Allison S. Gabriel et al., "Are Coworkers Getting into the Act? An Examination of Emotion Regulation in Coworker Exchanges," *Journal of Applied Psychology* 105, no. 8 (2020): 907–29, doi.org/10.1037/apl0000473.

74 **problem in our relationship with work:** Merve Alabak et al., "More Than One Strategy: A Closer Examination of the Relationship Between Deep Acting and Key Employee Outcomes," *Journal of Occupational Health Psychology* 25, no. 1 (2020): 32–45, doi.org/10.1037/ocp0000152.

75 **have very positive experiences:** Ute R. Hülsheger and Anna F. Schewe, "On the Costs and Benefits of Emotional Labor: A Meta-Analysis of Three Decades of Research," *Journal of Occupational Health Psychology* 16, no. 3 (2011): 361–89, doi.org/10.1037/a0022876.

CHAPTER FIVE

79 **height of its popularity:** "Chappelle's Story," Oprah.com, February 3, 2006, oprah.com/oprahshow/chappelles-story/all; Amos Barshad, "On the Skit That 'Killed' Chappelle's Show," *Fader*, July 29, 2016, thefader.com/2016/07/29/skit-that-killed-chappelles-show.

79 **"my head almost exploded":** C. J. Farley, "Dave Speaks," *Time*, May 14, 2005, content.time.com/time/printout/0,8816,1061512,00.html.

79 **making the same mistake twice:** Miriam Muethel et al., "Erring Professionals as Second Victims: Grappling with Guilt and Identity in the Aftermath of Error," *Academy of Management Journal* 67, no. 2 (2024): 407–36, doi.org/10.5465/amj.2021.1132.

80 **an opportunity for learning:** Amy C. Edmondson, *Right Kind of Wrong: The Science of Failing Well* (Simon and Schuster, 2023).

82 **work *on a weekly basis*:** Christine Porath and Christine Pearson, "The Price of Incivility," *Harvard Business Review* 91, no. 1/2 (2013): 114–21, hbr.org/2013/01/the-price-of-incivility; Trevor Foulk et al., "Catching Rudeness Is Like Catching a Cold: The Contagion Effects of Low-Intensity Negative Behaviors," *Journal of Applied Psychology* 101, no. 1 (2016): 50–67, doi.org/10.1037/apl0000037.

82 **in a male-dominated profession:** Lilia M. Cortina et al., "What's Gender Got to Do with It? Incivility in the Federal Courts," *Law & Social Inquiry* 27, no. 2 (2002): 235–70, doi.org/10.1111/j.1747-4469.2002.tb00804.x.

83 **linked to lower job performance:** Soojung Hong et al., "A Meta-Analysis Integrating 20 Years of Workplace Incivility Research: Antecedents, Consequences, and Boundary Conditions," *Journal of Organizational Behavior* 43, no. 3 (2022): 497–523, doi.org/10.1002/job.2568.

83 **Shannon Taylor and his colleagues:** Shannon G. Taylor et al., "Developing and

Testing a Dynamic Model of Workplace Incivility Change," *Journal of Management* 43, no. 3 (2017): 645–70, doi.org/10.1177/0149206314535432.
83 **to the organization:** Dana Kabat-Farr et al., "The Emotional Aftermath of Incivility: Anger, Guilt, and the Role of Organizational Commitment," *International Journal of Stress Management* 25, no. 2 (2018): 109–28, doi.org/10.1037/str0000045.
84 **offer ample evidence of this:** A. E. Colbert et al., "Flourishing Via Workplace Relationships: Moving Beyond Instrumental Support," *Academy of Management Journal* 59, no. 4 (2016): 1199–223, doi.org/10.5465/amj.2014.0506.
85 **colder when they're ostracized:** Matt C. Howard et al., "The Antecedents and Outcomes of Workplace Ostracism: A Meta-Analysis," *Journal of Applied Psychology* 105, no. 6 (2020): 577–96, doi.org/10.1037/apl0000453.
85 **harassment is more harmful:** Jane O'Reilly et al., "Is Negative Attention Better Than No Attention? The Comparative Effects of Ostracism and Harassment at Work," *Organization Science* 26, no. 3 (2015): 774–93, doi.org/10.1287/orsc.2014.0900.
87 **up to ten times per day:** Alicia A. Grandey et al., "The Customer Is Not Always Right: Customer Aggression and Emotion Regulation of Service Employees," *Journal of Organizational Behavior* 25, no. 3 (2004): 397–418, doi.org/doi.org/10.1002/job.252.
87 **worse mood the next morning:** Mo Wang et al., "Can't Get It Out of My Mind: Employee Rumination After Customer Mistreatment and Negative Mood in the Next Morning," *Journal of Applied Psychology* 98, no. 6 (2013): 989–1004, doi.org/10.1037/a0033656.
87 **over the prior month:** Danielle D. van Jaarsveld et al., "Unpacking the Relationship Between Customer (in) Justice and Employee Turnover Outcomes: Can Fair Supervisor Treatment Reduce Employees' Emotional Turmoil?," *Journal of Service Research* 24, no. 2 (2021): 301–19, doi.org/10.1177/1094670519883949.

CHAPTER SIX

91 **searching and quitting are contagious:** Caitlin M. Porter and James R. Rigby, "The Turnover Contagion Process: An Integrative Review of Theoretical and Empirical Research," *Journal of Organizational Behavior* 42, no. 2 (2021): 212–28, doi.org/10.1002/job.2483; Donald Hale et al., "A Two-Phase Longitudinal Model of a Turnover Event: Disruption, Recovery Rates, and Moderators of Collective Performance," *Academy of Management Journal* 59, no. 3 (2016): 906–29, doi.org/10.5465/amj.2013.0546.
91 **at work are more engaged:** Marcus Buckingham and Curt Coffman, *First, Break All the Rules* (Gallup Press, 2016).
92 **effects of disruptive work events:** Yang Chen et al., "Workplace Events and Employee Creativity: A Multistudy Field Investigation," *Personnel Psychology* 74, no. 2 (2021): 211–36, doi.org/10.1111/peps.12399.
92 **everyone else on the team:** Will Felps et al., "How Coworkers' Job Embeddedness

and Job Search Behaviors Influence Quitting," *Academy of Management Journal* 52, no. 3 (2009): 545–61, doi.org/10.5465/amj.2009.41331075.

92 **us into thinking about leaving:** Lyonel Laulié and Frederick P. Morgeson, "The End Is Just the Beginning: Turnover Events and Their Impact on Those Who Remain," *Personnel Psychology* 74, no. 3 (2021): 387–409, doi.org/10.1111/peps.12422.

93 **leave after their manager does:** Gary A. Ballinger et al., "Leader–Member Exchange and Turnover Before and After Succession Events," *Organizational Behavior and Human Decision Processes* 113, no. 1 (2010/09/01/ 2010): 25–36, doi.org/10.1016/j.obhdp.2010.04.003.

93 **turnover within the affected work group:** Huisi Li et al., "Initial and Longer-Term Change in Unit-Level Turnover Following Leader Succession: Contingent Effects of Outgoing and Incoming Leader Characteristics," *Organization Science* 31, no. 2 (2020): 458–76, doi.org/10.1287/orsc.2019.1295.

93 **their job searching and turnover:** Scott E. Seibert et al., "Even the Best Laid Plans Sometimes Go Askew: Career Self-Management Processes, Career Shocks, and the Decision to Pursue Graduate Education," *Journal of Applied Psychology* 98, no. 1 (2013): 169–82, doi.org/10.1037/a0030882.

93 **of layoffs (i.e., survivor guilt):** Joel Brockner et al., "Layoffs, Equity Theory, and Work Performance: Further Evidence of the Impact of Survivor Guilt," *Academy of Management Journal* 29, no. 2 (1986): 373–84, doi.org/10.5465/256193.

93 **those who were let go:** Joel Brockner et al., "Survivors' Reactions to Layoffs: We Get By with a Little Help for Our Friends," *Administrative Science Quarterly* 32, no. 4 (1987): 526–41, doi.org/10.2307/2392882.

94 **1,500 stores over two years:** Sima Sajjadiani et al., "Who Is Leaving and Why? The Dynamics of High-Quality Human Capital Outflows," *Academy of Management Journal* 66, no. 6 (2023): 1929–53, doi.org/10.5465/amj.2021.1327.

95 **on our well-being—savoring:** Remus Ilies et al., "Crafting Well-Being: Employees Can Enhance Their Own Well-Being by Savoring, Reflecting Upon, and Capitalizing on Positive Work Experiences," *Annual Review of Organizational Psychology and Organizational Behavior* 11 (2024): 63–91, doi.org/10.1146/annurev-orgpsych-110721-045931.

96 **you experienced it firsthand:** Lindsay Y. Dhanani and Matthew L. LaPalme, "It's Not Personal: A Review and Theoretical Integration of Research on Vicarious Workplace Mistreatment," *Journal of Management* 45, no. 6 (2019): 2322–51, doi.org/10.1177/0149206318816162.

96 **burnout, and even physical illness:** Kathi Miner-Rubino and Lilia M. Cortina, "Beyond Targets: Consequences of Vicarious Exposure to Misogyny at Work," *Journal of Applied Psychology* 92, no. 5 (2007): 1254–69, doi.org/10.1037/0021-9010.92.5.1254.

96 **that we could be next:** Emily M. David et al., "Am I Next? Men and Women's Divergent Justice Perceptions Following Vicarious Mistreatment," *Journal of Applied Psychology* 109, no. 7 (2024): 1039–58, doi.org/10.1037/apl0001109.

96 **less trusting of our managers:** Michelle K. Duffy et al., "The Social Context of Undermining Behavior at Work," *Organizational Behavior and Human Decision Processes* 101, no. 1 (2006): 105–26, doi.org/10.1016/j.obhdp.2006.04.005; Benjamin B. Dunford et al., "Be Fair, Your Employees Are Watching: A Relational

Response Model of External Third-Party Justice," *Personnel Psychology* 68, no. 2 (2015): 319–52, doi.org/10.1111/peps.12081.

96 **in workers' plans to quit:** Marjan Houshmand et al., "Escaping Bullying: The Simultaneous Impact of Individual and Unit-Level Bullying on Turnover Intentions," *Human Relations* 65, no. 7 (2012): 901–18, doi.org/10.1177/0018726712445100.

96 **stigmatized for having done so:** James K. Summers et al., "A Typology of Stigma within Organizations: Access and Treatment Effects," *Journal of Organizational Behavior* 39, no. 7 (2018): 853–68, doi.org/10.1002/job.2279.

96 **behave badly with no repercussions:** Trevor A. Foulk et al., "Heavy Is the Head That Wears the Crown: An Actor-Centric Approach to Daily Psychological Power, Abusive Leader Behavior, and Perceived Incivility," *Academy of Management Journal* 61, no. 2 (2018): 661–84, doi.org/10.5465/amj.2015.1061.

CHAPTER SEVEN

98 **"of the ride-sharing business":** Kara Swisher and Johana Bhuiyan, "Uber President Jeff Jones Is Quitting, Citing Differences over 'Beliefs and Approach to Leadership,'" *Vox*, March 19, 2017, vox.com/2017/3/19/14976110/uber-president-jeff-jones-quits.

99 **a new job within a year:** LinkedIn News, "Move Over Quiet Quitting," LinkedIn News, 2023, linkedin.com/posts/linkedin-news_move-over-quiet-quitting-these-days-its-activity-6983137627528908802-dfBF.

99 **within the first ninety days:** "Job Seeker Nation Study: Researching the Candidate-Recruiter Relationship," Jobvite, 2018, jobvite.com/wp-content/uploads/2018/04/2018_Job_Seeker_Nation_Study.pdf.

99 **"difficulty adjusting to the job":** Peter W. Hom et al., "One Hundred Years of Employee Turnover Theory and Research," *Journal of Applied Psychology* 102, no. 3 (2017): 530–45, doi.org/10.1037/apl0000103.

99 **in the prior year alone:** George Anders, "Forget 'Quiet Quitting'—Many Workers Are Still Outright Quitting Their Jobs as Quickly as Possible," LinkedIn News, 2022, linkedin.com/pulse/forget-quiet-quitting-many-workers-still-outright-jobs-george-anders/?trackingId=O%2FokFyKJQiekbI5gcif3Gw%3D%3D.

100 **say and what we do:** Leon Festinger, *A Theory of Cognitive Dissonance* (Row, Peterson, 1957).

100 **can harm your employability:** Ruth Umoh, "Leaving a Job in the First 15 Months Is Like Erasing Years of Experience from Your Resume," *CNBC Make It*, May 22, 2018, cnbc.com/2018/05/21/how-leaving-a-job-within-15-months-hurts-future-hiring-chances.html.

100 **has become the Great Regret:** Gene Marks, "Turns Out the Great Resignation May Be Followed by the Great Regret," *Guardian*, March 20, 2022, theguardian.com/business/2022/mar/20/great-resignation-great-regret-employees-quitting; Jessica Stillman, "The Great Resignation Is Turning into the Great Regret. Employers Are Joining in Too," *Inc.*, August 5, 2022, inc.com/jessica-stillman/hiring-great-resignation-great-regret.html.

101 **almost immediately after resigning:** Anthony C. Klotz, "Is Breaking Up Hard to Do? An Exploration of the Resignation Process," University of Oklahoma, 2013, proquest.com/dissertations-theses/is-breaking-up-hard-do-exploration-resignation/docview/1347340588/se-2?accountid=14511.

101 **happened in their new jobs:** "Job Seeker Nation Study," 2018, jobvite.com/wp-content/uploads/2018/04/2018_Job_Seeker_Nation_Study.pdf.

103 **between themselves and their organization:** Denise M. Rousseau, "Psychological and Implied Contracts in Organizations," *Employee Responsibilities and Rights Journal* 2, no. 2 (1989): 121–39, doi.org/10.1007/BF01384942; Rousseau, "New Hire Perceptions of Their Own and Their Employer's Obligations: A Study of Psychological Contracts," *Journal of Organizational Behavior* 11, no. 5 (1990): 389–400, doi.org/10.1002/job.4030110506; Rousseau, *Psychological Contracts in Organizations: Understanding Written and Unwritten Agreements* (SAGE Publications, 1995).

104 **after they made a job change:** Wendy R. Boswell et al., "The Relationship Between Employee Job Change and Job Satisfaction: The Honeymoon-Hangover Effect," *Journal of Applied Psychology* 90, no. 5 (2005): 882–92, doi.org/10.1037/0021-9010.90.5.882.

105 **they began their new jobs:** Wendy R. Boswell et al., "Changes in Newcomer Job Satisfaction Over Time: Examining the Pattern of Honeymoons and Hangovers," *Journal of Applied Psychology* 94, no. 4 (2009): 844–58, doi.org/10.1037/a0014975.

105 **seen in international assignments:** Nancy J. Adler, "Re-Entry: Managing Cross-Cultural Transitions," *Group & Organization Studies* 6, no. 3 (1981): 341–56, doi.org/10.1177/105960118100600310.

105 **bit of a honeymoon period:** Meike Sons and Cornelia Niessen, "Cross-Lagged Effects of Voluntary Job Changes and Well-Being: A Continuous Time Approach," *Journal of Applied Psychology* 107, no. 9 (2022): 1600–27, doi.org/10.1037/apl0000940.

106 **who were never laid off:** Paul R. Davis et al., "Creating a More Quit-Friendly National Workforce? Individual Layoff History and Voluntary Turnover," *Journal of Applied Psychology* 100, no. 5 (2015): 1434–55, doi.org/10.1037/apl0000012.

107 **strong emotional reactions in us:** Connie R. Wanberg et al., "The Job Search Grind: Perceived Progress, Self-Reactions, and Self-Regulation of Search Effort," *Academy of Management Journal* 53, no. 4 (2010): 788–807, doi.org/10.5465/amj.2010.52814599.

107 **posted and others are eliminated:** Serge P. da Motta Veiga et al., "From the Unfolding Process to Self-Regulation in Job Search: Integrating Between-and Within-Person Approaches," in *Research in Personnel and Human Resources Management*, ed. M. Ronald Buckley, Anthony R. Wheeler, and Jonathon R. B. Halbesleben, Research in Personnel and Human Resources Management series (Emerald Publishing Limited, 2018), 241–72.

108 **decisions, it's our emotions:** Rajagopal Raghunathan and Michel Tuan Pham, "All Negative Moods Are Not Equal: Motivational Influences of Anxiety and Sadness on Decision Making," *Organizational Behavior and Human Decision Processes* 79, no. 1 (1999): 56–77, doi.org/10.1006/obhd.1999.2838.

109 **acting, to some degree:** Bartleby, "How to Get the Lying out of Hiring," *Economist*, October 30, 2023, economist.com/business/2023/10/30/how-to-get-the-lying-out-of-hiring.

109 **those who are recruiting them:** Aleksander P. J. Ellis et al., "The Use of Impression Management Tactics in Structured Interviews: A Function of Question Type?," *Journal of Applied Psychology* 87, no. 6 (2002): 1200–08, doi.org/10.1037/0021-9010.87.6.1200; Chad H. Van Iddekinge et al., "Antecedents of Impression Management Use and Effectiveness in a Structured Interview," *Journal of Management* 33, no. 5 (2007): 752–73, doi.org/10.1177/0149206307305563.

109 **jobs when they're offered:** Kang Yang Trevor Yu et al., "Winning Applicants and Influencing Job Seekers: An Introduction to the Special Issue on Employer Branding and Talent Acquisition," *Human Resource Management* 61, no. 5 (2022): 515–24, doi.org/10.1002/hrm.22140.

109 **them than their competitors:** Daniel M. Cable and Daniel B. Turban, "The Value of Organizational Reputation in the Recruitment Context: A Brand-Equity Perspective," *Journal of Applied Social Psychology* 33, no. 11 (2003): 2244–66, doi.org/10.1111/j.1559-1816.2003.tb01883.x.

CHAPTER EIGHT

111 **Nazi-occupied France to safety:** Malcolm Gladwell, "The Gift of Doubt: Albert O. Hirschman and the Power of Failure," *New Yorker*, June 17, 2013, newyorker.com/magazine/2013/06/24/the-gift-of-doubt.

111 **customer receiving bad service:** Albert O. Hirschman, *Exit, Voice, and Loyalty: Responses to Decline in Firms, Organizations, and States* (Harvard University Press, 1970).

114 **Counterfactual thinking tends to lead:** Neal J. Roese and Kai Epstude, "The Functional Theory of Counterfactual Thinking: New Evidence, New Challenges, New Insights," in *Advances in Experimental Social Psychology*, ed. James M. Olson (Academic Press, 2017), 1–79.

115 **branch performance was higher:** James R. Detert et al., "Voice Flows to and Around Leaders: Understanding When Units Are Helped or Hurt by Employee Voice," *Administrative Science Quarterly* 58, no. 4 (2013): 624–68, doi.org/10.1177/0001839213510151.

116 **those negative vibes around:** Michael D. Baer et al., "Pacification or Aggravation? The Effects of Talking About Supervisor Unfairness," *Academy of Management Journal* 61, no. 5 (2018): 1764–88, doi.org/10.5465/amj.2016.0630.

116 **critiquing the status quo:** Jian Liang et al., "Psychological Antecedents of Promotive and Prohibitive Voice: A Two-Wave Examination," *Academy of Management Journal* 55, no. 1 (2012): 71–92, doi.org/10.5465/amj.2010.0176.

116 **unnecessary turnover of good workers:** Mark C. Noort et al., "Speaking Up to Prevent Harm: A Systematic Review of the Safety Voice Literature," *Safety Science* 117 (2019): 375–87, doi.org/10.1016/j.ssci.2019.04.039; Alex Ning Li and Subrahmaniam Tangirala, "How Employees' Voice Helps Teams Remain Resilient in the Face of Exogenous Change," *Journal of Applied Psychology* 107, no. 4 (2022): 668–92, https://doi.org/10.1037/apl0000874.

117 **up in a supportive manner:** Ethan R. Burris, "The Risks and Rewards of Speaking Up: Managerial Responses to Employee Voice," *Academy of Management Journal* 55, no. 4 (2012): 851–75, doi.org/10.5465/amj.2010.0562.

- 117 **challenging voice does the opposite:** Melissa Chamberlin et al., "A Meta-Analysis of Voice and Its Promotive and Prohibitive Forms: Identification of Key Associations, Distinctions, and Future Research Directions," *Personnel Psychology* 70, no. 1 (2017): 11–71, doi.org/10.1111/peps.12185.
- 117 **higher energy and subsequent performance:** Hudson Sessions et al., "I'm Tired of Listening: The Effects of Supervisor Appraisals of Group Voice on Supervisor Emotional Exhaustion and Performance," *Journal of Applied Psychology* 105, no. 6 (2020): 619–36, doi.org/10.1037/apl0000455.
- 118 **supportive versus challenging voice:** David T. Welsh et al., "The Social Aftershocks of Voice: An Investigation of Employees' Affective and Interpersonal Reactions After Speaking Up," *Academy of Management Journal* 65, no. 6 (2022): 2034–57, doi.org/10.5465/amj.2019.1187.
- 118 **"than doing the eulogy":** *I'm Telling You for the Last Time*, written by Jerry Seinfeld, directed by Marty Callner, aired August 9, 1998, on HBO.
- 119 **positively to employee voice:** Steven W. Whiting et al., "Effects of Message, Source, and Context on Evaluations of Employee Voice Behavior," *Journal of Applied Psychology* 97, no. 1 (2012): 159–82, doi.org/10.1037/a0024871.
- 120 **benefit our company and coworkers:** Timothy D. Maynes and Philip M. Podsakoff, "Speaking More Broadly: An Examination of the Nature, Antecedents, and Consequences of an Expanded Set of Employee Voice Behaviors," *Journal of Applied Psychology* 99, no. 1 (2014): 87–112, doi.org/10.1037/a0034284.
- 120 **effect of voice disappeared:** Adam M. Grant et al., "Getting Credit for Proactive Behavior: Supervisor Reactions Depend on What You Value and How You Feel," *Personnel Psychology* 62, no. 1 (2009): 31–55, doi.org/10.1111/j.1744-6570.2008.01128.x.
- 120 **on the culture you're in:** Erin Meyer, *The Culture Map: Breaking Through the Invisible Boundaries of Global Business* (Public Affairs, 2014).
- 120 **than supportive voice alone:** Ethan R. Burris et al., "Mixed Messages: Why Managers (Do Not) Endorse Employee Voice," *Organizational Behavior and Human Decision Processes* 172 (2022): 104185, doi.org/10.1016/j.obhdp.2022.104185.
- 121 **its odds of being granted:** Chak Fu Lam et al., "Challenging the Status Quo in a Non-Challenging Way: A Dominance Complementarity View of Voice Inquiry," *Personnel Psychology* 77, no. 3 (2024): 1235–64, doi.org/10.1111/peps.12625.
- 121 **you've got political skill:** Gerald R. Ferris et al., "Development and Validation of the Political Skill Inventory," *Journal of Management* 31, no. 1 (2005): 126–52, doi.org/10.1177/0149206304271386.
- 121 **high or low political skill:** Shuhua Sun and Hetty I. J. van Emmerik, "Are Proactive Personalities Always Beneficial? Political Skill as a Moderator," *Journal of Applied Psychology* 100, no. 3 (2015): 966–75, doi.org/10.1037/a0037833.

CHAPTER NINE

- 125 **spending with his family:** Anthony Breznican, "Chris Hemsworth Changed His Life After an Ominous Health Warning," *Vanity Fair*, November 17, 2022, vanityfair.com/hollywood/2022/11/chris-hemsworth-exclusive-interview-alzheimers-limitless.

127 **your friends and family members:** Ana Isabel Sanz-Vergel et al., "The Thin Line Between Work and Home: The Spillover and Crossover of Daily Conflicts," *Journal of Occupational and Organizational Psychology* 88, no. 1 (2015): 1–18, doi.org/10.1111/joop.12075.

127 **their partners in the evening:** Helen Pluut et al., "How Social Stressors at Work Influence Marital Behaviors at Home: An Interpersonal Model of Work–Family Spillover," *Journal of Occupational Health Psychology* 27, no. 1 (2022): 74–88, doi.org/10.1037/ocp0000298.

128 **after the event has occurred:** Christoph Nohe and Karlheinz Sonntag, "Work–Family Conflict, Social Support, and Turnover Intentions: A Longitudinal Study," *Journal of Vocational Behavior* 85, no. 1 (2014): 1–12, doi.org/10.1016/j.jvb.2014.03.007.

128 **make a career change:** Scott E. Seibert et al., "Developing Career Resilience and Adaptability," *Organizational Dynamics* 45, no. 3 (2016): 245–57, doi.org/10.1016/j.orgdyn.2016.07.009.

128 **value, in another domain:** Belle Rose Ragins et al., "Life Spillovers: The Spillover of Fear of Home Foreclosure to the Workplace," *Personnel Psychology* 67, no. 4 (2014): 763–800, doi.org/10.1111/peps.12065.

128 **worse mood at work:** Mahira L. Ganster et al., "Retreating or Repairing? Examining the Alternate Linkages Between Daily Partner-Instigated Incivility at Home and Helping at Work," *Journal of Applied Psychology* 108, no. 5 (2023): 826–49, doi.org/10.1037/apl0001048.

128 **your mood and ability to concentrate:** Shawn T. McClean et al., "Stumbling Out of the Gate: The Energy-Based Implications of Morning Routine Disruption," *Personnel Psychology* 74, no. 3 (2021): 411–48, doi.org/10.1111/peps.12419.

129 **one of my all-time favorites:** Linn Van Dyne and Jennifer B. Ellis, "Job Creep: A Reactance Theory Perspective on Organizational Citizenship Behavior as Overfulfillment of Obligations," in *The Employment Relationship: Examining Psychological and Contextual Perspectives*, ed. Jacqueline A. M. Coyle-Shapiro, Lynn M. Shore, M. Susan Taylor, and Lois E. Tetrick (Oxford University Press, 2004), 181–205.

131 *over their job performance:* Dennis W. Organ, "A Reappraisal and Reinterpretation of the Satisfaction-Causes-Performance Hypothesis," *Academy of Management Review* 2, no. 1 (1977): 46–53, doi.org/10.5465/amr.1977.4409162.

131 **BEYOND their required duties:** Dennis W. Organ, "The Roots of Organizational Citizenship," in *The Oxford Handbook of Organizational Citizenship Behavior*, ed. Philip M. Podsakoff, Scott B. Mackenzie, and Nathan P. Podsakoff (Oxford University Press, 2018), 7–18.

132 **to higher company performance:** Thomas S. Bateman and Dennis W. Organ, "Job Satisfaction and the Good Soldier: The Relationship Between Affect and Employee 'Citizenship,'" *Academy of Management Journal* 26, no. 4 (1983): 587–95, doi.org/10.5465/255908.

132 **to support Organ's prediction:** Dennis W. Organ et al., *Organizational Citizenship Behavior: Its Nature, Antecedents, and Consequences* (SAGE Publications, 2005).

132 **higher firm performance:** Nathan P. Podsakoff et al., "Individual- and Organizational-Level Consequences of Organizational Citizenship Behaviors: A Meta-Analysis," *Journal of Applied Psychology* 94, no. 1 (2009): 122–41, doi.org/

10.1037/a0013079; Scott B. Mackenzie et al., "Individual- and Organizational-Level Consequences of Organizational Citizenship Behaviors," in *The Oxford Handbook of Organizational Citizenship Behavior*, eds. Philip M. Podsakoff, Scott B. Mackenzie, and Nathan P. Podsakoff (Oxford University Press, 2018), 105–48.

132 **double-edged sword for employees:** Mark C. Bolino et al., "The Unintended Consequences of Organizational Citizenship Behaviors for Employees, Teams, and Organizations," in *The Oxford Handbook of Organizational Citizenship Behavior*, eds. Philip M. Podsakoff, Scott B. Mackenzie, and Nathan P. Podsakoff (Oxford University Press, 2018), 185–202.

133 **fights with family members:** Mark C. Bolino and William H. Turnley, "The Personal Costs of Citizenship Behavior: The Relationship Between Individual Initiative and Role Overload, Job Stress, and Work-Family Conflict," *Journal of Applied Psychology* 90, no. 4 (2005): 740–48, doi.org/10.1037/0021-9010.90.4.740.

133 **engagement in family activities:** Jonathon R. B. Halbesleben et al., "Too Engaged? A Conservation of Resources View of the Relationship Between Work Engagement and Work Interference with Family," *Journal of Applied Psychology* 94, no. 6 (2009): 1452–65, doi.org/10.1037/a0017595.

133 **had a significant commute:** Charles Calderwood and Tanya Mitropoulos, "Commuting Spillover: A Systematic Review and Agenda for Research," *Journal of Organizational Behavior* 42, no. 2 (2021): 162–87, doi.org/10.1002/job.2462.

134 **what it was in 2019:** Jose Maria Barrero et al., "Why Working from Home Will Stick," *National Bureau of Economic Research Working Paper 28731* (2021), wfhresearch.com/wp-content/uploads/2024/06/WFHResearch_updates_September2025.pdf.

134 **by eliminating their commute:** Cevat Giray Aksoy et al., "Time Savings When Working from Home," *AEA Papers and Proceedings* 113 (2023): 597–603, doi.org/10.1257/pandp.20231013.

134 **or frustrating day at work:** Keren Turgeman-Lupo and Michal Biron, "Make It to Work (and Back Home) Safely: The Effect of Psychological Work Stressors on Employee Behaviour While Commuting by Car," *European Journal of Work and Organizational Psychology* 26, no. 2 (2017): 161–70, doi.org/10.1080/1359432X.2016.1228628; Charles Calderwood and Phillip L. Ackerman, "Modeling Intra-Individual Variation in Unsafe Driving in a Naturalistic Commuting Environment," *Journal of Occupational Health Psychology* 24, no. 4 (2019): 423–37, doi.org/10.1037/ocp0000127.

134 **relationships get more negative:** Calderwood and Mitropoulos, "Commuting Spillover."

135 **and less anxiety at home:** Madelon L. M. van Hooff, "The Daily Commute from Work to Home: Examining Employees' Experiences in Relation to Their Recovery Status," *Stress and Health* 31, no. 2 (2015): 124–37, doi.org/10.1002/smi.2534.

135 **before their commute to work:** Jon M. Jachimowicz et al., "Between Home and Work: Commuting as an Opportunity for Role Transitions," *Organization Science* 32, no. 1 (2021): 64–85, doi.org/10.1287/orsc.2020.1370.

CHAPTER TEN

137 **top players in the league:** Paul Zimmerman, "Dr. Z's All-Pro Team," *Sports Illustrated*, 2001, vault.si.com/vault/2001/01/08/dr-zs-all-pro-team.

137 **"haven't done a damn thing":** Pat Tillman Foundation, "Pat's Story," 2024, pattillmanfoundation.org/the-foundation/pats-story.

138 **"It's no longer important":** Mia Smith, "Pat Tillman: More Than an Incredible Athlete," myhero.com, June 10, 2018, myhero.com/pat-tillman-more-than-an-incredible-athlete.

138 **watch less news:** Seoin Yoon et al., "Working through an 'Infodemic': The Impact of Covid-19 News Consumption on Employee Uncertainty and Work Behaviors," *Journal of Applied Psychology* 106, no. 4 (2021): 501–17, doi.org/10.1037/apl0000913.

139 **originally planned to do so:** Heather C. Vough et al., "Going Off Script: How Managers Make Sense of the Ending of Their Careers," *Journal of Management Studies* 52, no. 3 (2015): 414–40, doi.org/10.1111/joms.12126.

140 **fear of death affects humans:** Ernest Becker, *The Denial of Death* (Simon and Schuster, 1997).

141 **that will last beyond death:** Tom Pyszczynski et al., "Thirty Years of Terror Management Theory: From Genesis to Revelation," in *Advances in Experimental Social Psychology*, ed. James M. Olson and Mark P. Zanna (Academic Press, 2015), 1–70.

141 **standards of that worldview:** Brian L. Burke et al., "Two Decades of Terror Management Theory: A Meta-Analysis of Mortality Salience Research," *Personality and Social Psychology Review* 14, no. 2 (2010): 155–95, doi.org/10.1177/1088868309352321.

142 **other parts of their lives:** Michael T. Sliter et al., "Don't Fear the Reaper: Trait Death Anxiety, Mortality Salience, and Occupational Health," *Journal of Applied Psychology* 99, no. 4 (2014): 759–69, doi.org/10.1037/a0035729.

143 **and enrich our lives:** Adam M. Grant and Kimberly A. Wade-Benzoni, "The Hot and Cool of Death Awareness at Work: Mortality Cues, Aging, and Self-Protective and Prosocial Motivations," *Academy of Management Review* 34, no. 4 (2009): 600–22, doi.org/10.5465/amr.34.4.zok600; Jeff Greenberg et al., "Toward a Dual-Motive Depth Psychology of Self and Social Behavior," in *Efficacy, Agency, and Self-Esteem*, ed. Michael H. Kernis (Springer US, 1995), 73–99.

143 **think about our legacy:** Zhenyu Yuan et al., "Memento Mori: The Development and Validation of the Death Reflection Scale," *Journal of Organizational Behavior* 40, no. 4 (2019): 417–33, doi.org/10.1002/job.2339.

143 **generative reflections about death:** Ruodan Shao et al., "Employees' Reactions Toward Covid-19 Information Exposure: Insights from Terror Management Theory and Generativity Theory," *Journal of Applied Psychology* 106, no. 11 (2021): 1601–14, doi.org/10.1037/apl0000983.

143 **and their intentions to quit:** Minya Xu et al., "Covid-19 and the Great Resignation: The Role of Death Anxiety, Need for Meaningful Work, and Task Significance," *Journal of Applied Psychology* 108, no. 11 (2023): 1790–811, doi.org/10.1037/apl0001102.

143 **traditional employees—bus drivers:** Yehuda Baruch et al., "Career and Work Attitudes of Blue-Collar Workers, and the Impact of a Natural Disaster Chance

Event on the Relationships Between Intention to Quit and Actual Quit Behaviour," *European Journal of Work and Organizational Psychology* 25, no. 3 (2016): 459–73, doi.org/10.1080/1359432X.2015.1113168.

145 **"receive significant media attention":** Angelica Leigh and Shimul Melwani, "#Blackemployeesmatter: Mega-Threats, Identity Fusion, and Enacting Positive Deviance in Organizations," *Academy of Management Review* 44, no. 3 (2019): 564–91, doi.org/10.5465/amr.2017.0127.

146 **in a set of studies:** Angelica Leigh and Shimul Melwani, "'Am I Next?' The Spillover Effects of Mega-Threats on Avoidant Behaviors at Work," *Academy of Management Journal* 65, no. 3 (2022): 720–48, doi.org/10.5465/amj.2020.1657.

147 **suggest this is the case:** Natalie Gontcharova, "And So I Quit: Tired of the Grind, Parents Are Creating New Work-Life Balance for Themselves," *Parents*, July 5, 2022, parents.com/parenting/work/how-parents-are-reshaping-their-work-life-balance; Faith Karimi, "She Packed Her Bags, Quit Her Job in Law Enforcement and Moved to Mexico After George Floyd's Death," CNN, August 4, 2020, edition.cnn.com/2020/08/04/us/demetria-brown-law-enforcement-mexico-trnd/index.html.

149 **into pain-avoiding mode:** Weilin Su and Yinan Zhang, "Supervisor Negative Feedback, Subordinate Prevention Focus and Performance: Testing a Mediation Model," *Current Psychology* 42, no. 28 (2023): 24613–22, doi.org/10.1007/s12144-022-03494-0.

149 **a happiness-seeking mode:** Jaclyn Koopmann et al., "Daily Shifts in Regulatory Focus: The Influence of Work Events and Implications for Employee Well-Being," *Journal of Organizational Behavior* 37, no. 8 (2016): 1293–316, doi.org/10.1002/job.2105.

149 **to enact their own bad behavior:** Fadel K. Matta et al., "Significant Work Events and Counterproductive Work Behavior: The Role of Fairness, Emotions, and Emotion Regulation," *Journal of Organizational Behavior* 35, no. 7 (2014): 920–44, doi.org/10.1002/job.1934.

CHAPTER ELEVEN

151 **"bold print" in our lives:** Dan P. McAdams, "Personality, Modernity, and the Storied Self: A Contemporary Framework for Studying Persons," *Psychological Inquiry* 7, no. 4 (1996): 295–321, doi.org/10.1207/s15327965pli0704_1.

152 **positive-negative asymmetry effect:** Guido Peeters and Janusz Czapinski, "Positive-Negative Asymmetry in Evaluations: The Distinction Between Affective and Informational Negativity Effects," *European Review of Social Psychology* 1, no. 1 (1990): 33–60, doi.org/10.1080/14792779108401856; John J. Skowronski and Donal E. Carlston, "Negativity and Extremity Biases in Impression Formation: A Review of Explanations," *Psychological Bulletin* 105, no. 1 (1989): 131–42, doi.org/10.1037/0033-2909.105.1.131.

152 **reactions to bad versus good:** Roy F. Baumeister et al., "Bad Is Stronger Than Good," *Review of General Psychology* 5, no. 4 (2001): 323–70, doi.org/10.1037/1089-2680.5.4.323.

152 **deeply when they're negative:** James P. David et al., "Differential Roles of Neuroticism, Extraversion, and Event Desirability for Mood in Daily Life: An Integrative Model of Top-Down and Bottom-Up Influences," *Journal of Personality and Social Psychology* 73, no. 1 (1997): 149–59, doi.org/10.1037/0022-3514.73.1.149; John B. Nezlek and Shelly L. Gable, "Depression as a Moderator of Relationships Between Positive Daily Events and Day-to-Day Psychological Adjustment," *Personality and Social Psychology Bulletin* 27, no. 12 (2001): 1692–704, doi.org/10.1177/01461672012712012.

152 **that are equally positive:** Joyce E. Bono et al., "Building Positive Resources: Effects of Positive Events and Positive Reflection on Work Stress and Health," *Academy of Management Journal* 56, no. 6 (2013): 1601–27, doi.org/10.5465/amj.2011.0272.

153 **make us feel bad afterward:** Daniel T. Gilbert et al., "Immune Neglect: A Source of Durability Bias in Affective Forecasting," *Journal of Personality and Social Psychology* 75, no. 3 (1998): 617–38, doi.org/10.1037/0022-3514.75.3.617.

153 **tend to narrow our focus:** Barbara L. Fredrickson, "The Role of Positive Emotions in Positive Psychology: The Broaden-and-Build Theory of Positive Emotions," *American Psychologist* 56, no. 3 (2001): 218–26, doi.org/10.1037/0003-066X.56.3.218.

153 **nature makes us feel good:** Anthony C. Klotz, "Creating Jobs and Workspaces That Energize People," *MIT Sloan Management Review* 61, no. 4 (2020): 74–78, sloanreview.mit.edu/article/creating-jobs-and-workspaces-that-energize-people.

153 **for the rest of the day:** Pok Man Tang et al., "From Natural to Novel: The Cognition-Broadening Effects of Contact with Nature at Work on Creativity," *Journal of Management* 50, no. 7 (2024): 2490–533, doi.org/10.1177/01492063231172182.

154 **presence of positive emotions:** Erik Dane, "Suddenly Everything Became Clear: How People Make Sense of Epiphanies Surrounding Their Work and Careers," *Academy of Management Discoveries* 6, no. 1 (2020): 39–60, doi.org/10.5465/amd.2018.0033.

155 **committed to our organization:** Alan Benson and Ben A. Rissing, "Strength from Within: Internal Mobility and the Retention of High Performers," *Organization Science* 31, no. 6 (2020): 1475–96, doi.org/10.1287/orsc.2020.1362; Matthew Bidwell, "Paying More to Get Less: The Effects of External Hiring Versus Internal Mobility," *Administrative Science Quarterly* 56, no. 3 (2011): 369–407, doi.org/10.1177/0001839211433562; Paula Phillips Carson et al., "Promotion and Employee Turnover: Critique, Meta-Analysis, and Implications," *Journal of Business and Psychology* 8, no. 4 (1994): 455–66, doi.org/10.1007/BF02230960; Karen S. Lyness and Michael K. Judiesch, "Are Female Managers Quitters? The Relationships of Gender, Promotions, and Family Leaves of Absence to Voluntary Turnover," *Journal of Applied Psychology* 86, no. 6 (2001): 1167–78, doi.org/10.1037/0021-9010.86.6.1167.

155 **after they've been promoted:** Charlie O. Trevor et al., "Voluntary Turnover and Job Performance: Curvilinearity and the Moderating Influences of Salary Growth and Promotions," *Journal of Applied Psychology* 82, no. 1 (1997): 44–61, doi.org/10.1037/0021-9010.82.1.44.

155 **company, the *employability paradox*:** Jill Nelissen et al., "Employee Development and Voluntary Turnover: Testing the Employability Paradox," *Human Resource Management Journal* 27, no. 1 (2017): 152–68, doi.org/10.1111/1748-8583.12136; Jay H. Hardy III et al., "After Shocks: The Effects of Internal Sourcing on Voluntary Turnover," *Journal of Applied Psychology* (2025): Online First, doi.org/10.1037/apl0001274.

155 **than those that did not:** Daniel B. Sands, "Double-Edged Stars: Michelin Stars, Reactivity, and Restaurant Exits in New York City," *Strategic Management Journal* 46, no. 1 (2025): 148–76, doi.org/10.1002/smj.3651.

156 **might feel jealous or annoyed:** Irene Scopelliti et al., "You Call It 'Self-Exuberance'; I Call It 'Bragging': Miscalibrated Predictions of Emotional Responses to Self-Promotion," *Psychological Science* 26, no. 6 (2015): 903–14, doi.org/10.1177/0956797615573516.

156 **a bump of good feelings:** Trevor Watkins, "Workplace Interpersonal Capitalization: Employee Reactions to Coworker Positive Event Disclosures," *Academy of Management Journal* 64, no. 2 (2021): 537–61, doi.org/10.5465/amj.2018.1339.

157 **are common across workers:** Jenny M. Hoobler et al., "Self-Ambivalence: Naming a Contemporary Work-Family Problem That Has No Name," *Journal of Organizational Behavior* 45, no. 2 (2024): 252–65, doi.org/doi.org/10.1002/job.2750.

158 **"physical spaces" can do to us:** Herminia Ibarra and Otilia Obodaru, "Betwixt and Between Identities: Liminal Experience in Contemporary Careers," *Research in Organizational Behavior* 36 (2016): 47–64, doi.org/10.1016/j.riob.2016.11.003.

159 **forty-fifth birthday:** Natalie Stone, "Why Portia De Rossi Decided to Quit Acting—Then Came Back for 'Arrested Development,'" *People*, May 16, 2018, people.com/tv/portia-de-rossi-why-she-quit-acting.

159 **"It was now or never":** Albert Shapero and Lisa Sokol, "The Social Dimensions of Entrepreneurship," in *Encyclopedia of Entrepreneurship*, ed. K. H. Vesper, D. L. Sexton, and C. A. Kent (Prentice-Hall, 1982), 72–90.

159 **make big life decisions:** Adam L. Alter and Hal E. Hershfield, "People Search for Meaning When They Approach a New Decade in Chronological Age," *Proceedings of the National Academy of Sciences* 111, no. 48 (2014): 17066–70, doi.org/doi:10.1073/pnas.1415086111.

159 **ages that end in nine:** Talya Miron-Shatz et al., "Milestone Age Affects the Role of Health and Emotions in Life Satisfaction: A Preliminary Inquiry," *PLOS ONE* 10, no. 8 (2015): e0133254, doi.org/10.1371/journal.pone.0133254.

159 **"temporal landmarks" in their lives:** Jinhyung Kim et al., "Thinking About a New Decade in Life Increases Personal Self-Reflection: A Replication and Reinterpretation of Alter and Hershfield's (2014) Findings," *Journal of Personality and Social Psychology* 117, no. 2 (2019): e27–e34, doi.org/10.1037/pspp0000199.

159 **few weeks, they fade:** Jessica de Bloom et al., "Vacation (after-) Effects on Employee Health and Well-Being, and the Role of Vacation Activities, Experiences and Sleep," *Journal of Happiness Studies* 14, no. 2 (2013): 613–33, doi.org/10.1007/s10902-012-9345-3.

160 **employees' likelihood of leaving:** John W. Lounsbury and Linda L. Hoopes, "A Vacation from Work: Changes in Work and Nonwork Outcomes," *Journal of Applied Psychology* 71, no. 3 (1986): 392–401, doi.org/10.1037/0021-9010.71.3.392.

160 **or negatively, is common:** Charlotte Fritz and Sabine Sonnentag, "Recovery, Well-Being, and Performance-Related Outcomes: The Role of Workload and Vacation Experiences," *Journal of Applied Psychology* 91, no. 4 (2006): 936–45, doi.org/10.1037/0021-9010.91.4.936.

161 **than just a role model:** Julie Bosman et al., "In and Out of the Courtroom, O'Connor Inspired a Generation of Women," *New York Times*, December 2, 2023, nytimes.com/2023/12/02/us/sandra-day-oconnor-women-legacy.html.

162 **abruptly quit their jobs:** Tae Heon Lee et al., "Understanding Voluntary Turnover: Path-Specific Job Satisfaction Effects and the Importance of Unsolicited Job Offers," *Academy of Management Journal* 51, no. 4 (2008): 651–71, doi.org/10.5465/amr.2008.33665124.

162 **by an unexpected offer:** Lee et al., "Understanding Voluntary Turnover," 651–71.

CHAPTER TWELVE

164 **dissatisfying romantic relationship:** Caryl E. Rusbult et al., "Exit, Voice, Loyalty, and Neglect: Responses to Dissatisfaction in Romantic Involvements," *Journal of Personality and Social Psychology* 43, no. 6 (1982): 1230–42, doi.org/10.1037/0022-3514.43.6.1230.

165 **fourth one showed up again:** Caryl E. Rusbult et al., "Determinants and Consequences of Exit, Voice, Loyalty, and Neglect: Responses to Dissatisfaction in Adult Romantic Involvements," *Human Relations* 39, no. 1 (1986): 45–63, doi.org/10.1177/001872678603900103.

165 **and more flexible schedules:** Morgan Smith, "Professor Who Predicted the 'Great Resignation' Says Quits Will Plateau in 2023—Here's Why," *CNBC Make It*, February 1, 2023, cnbc.com/2023/02/01/professor-who-coined-great-resignation-anthony-klotz-says-quits-will-plateau-in-2023.html.

167 **"work has to be your life":** Zaid Leppelin, "On Quiet Quitting," TikTok, 2022, tiktok.com/@zaidleppelin/video/7124414185282391342?lang=en.

168 **Amy Wrzesniewski and Jane Dutton:** Amy Wrzesniewski et al., "Turn the Job You Have into the Job You Want," *Harvard Business Review* (June 2010): 114–17, hbr.org/2010/06/managing-yourself-turn-the-job-you-have-into-the-job-you-want; Justin M. Berg et al., "Job Crafting and Meaningful Work," in *Purpose and Meaning in the Workplace* (American Psychological Association, 2013), 81–104; Amy Wrzesniewski and Jane E. Dutton, "Crafting a Job: Revisioning Employees as Active Crafters of Their Work," *Academy of Management Review* 26, no. 2 (2001): 179–201, doi.org/10.5465/amr.2001.4378011.

169 **higher satisfaction and performance:** Cort W. Rudolph et al., "Job Crafting: A Meta-Analysis of Relationships with Individual Differences, Job Characteristics, and Work Outcomes," *Journal of Vocational Behavior* 102 (2017): 112–38, doi.org/10.1016/j.jvb.2017.05.008.

169 **company what you owe it:** Mark C. Bolino and Anthony C. Klotz, "How to Motivate Employees to Go Beyond Their Jobs," in *HBR Guide to Motivating People* (Harvard Business Review Press, 2019), 125–29.

170 **exhaustion during the workday:** Hongjai Rhee and Sudong Kim, "Effects of Breaks on Regaining Vitality at Work: An Empirical Comparison of 'Conventional' and 'Smart Phone' Breaks," *Computers in Human Behavior* 57 (2016): 160-67, doi.org/10.1016/j.chb.2015.11.056.

170 **balance between work and life:** Jana Kühnel et al., "Take a Break! Benefits of Sleep and Short Breaks for Daily Work Engagement," *European Journal of Work and Organizational Psychology* 26, no. 4 (2017): 481–91, doi.org/10.1080/1359432X.2016.1269750.

170 **all have clearly positive effects:** Zhanna Lyubykh et al., "Role of Work Breaks in Well-Being and Performance: A Systematic Review and Future Research Agenda," *Journal of Occupational Health Psychology* 27, no. 5 (2022): 470–87, doi.org/10.1037/ocp0000337.

171 **did some work, or socialized:** John P. Trougakos et al., "Lunch Breaks Unpacked: The Role of Autonomy as a Moderator of Recovery During Lunch," *Academy of Management Journal* 57, no. 2 (2014): 405–21, doi.org/10.5465/amj.2011.1072.

172 **other player in the league:** Brian Windhorst, "Cavaliers Are Surviving in the Playoffs Despite the Dilemma of Lebron James' Rest," ESPN, May 3, 2018, espn.com/nba/story/_/id/23384071/lebron-james-plays-rests-keep-cleveland-cavaliers-hopes-alive.

172 **fatigue you will experience:** Patricia Albulescu et al., "'Give Me a Break!' A Systematic Review and Meta-Analysis on the Efficacy of Micro-Breaks for Increasing Well-Being and Performance," *PLOS ONE* 17, no. 8 (2022): e0272460, doi.org/10.1371/journal.pone.0272460.

172 **when the workday ends:** Sooyeol Kim et al., "Daily Microbreaks in a Self-Regulatory Resources Lens: Perceived Health Climate as a Contextual Moderator Via Microbreak Autonomy," *Journal of Applied Psychology* 107, no. 1 (2022): 60–77, doi.org/10.1037/apl0000891.

CHAPTER THIRTEEN

179 **and difficult to navigate:** Anthony C. Klotz et al., "The Paths from Insider to Outsider: A Review of Employee Exit Transitions," *Human Resource Management* 60, no. 1 (2021): 119–44, doi.org/10.1002/hrm.22033.

179 **in your next professional chapter:** Herminia Ibarra and Roxana Barbulescu, "Identity as Narrative: Prevalence, Effectiveness, and Consequences of Narrative Identity Work in Macro Work Role Transitions," *Academy of Management Review* 35, no. 1 (2010): 135–54, doi.org/10.5465/amr.35.1.zok135.

179 **cause changes in our identity:** Blake E. Ashforth, *Role Transitions in Organizational Life: An Identity-Based Perspective* (Lawrence Erlbaum Associates Publishers, 2001).

179 **actually give their notice:** Anthony C. Klotz, "Is Breaking Up Hard to Do? An Exploration of the Resignation Process," University of Oklahoma, 2013, proquest.com/dissertations-theses/is-breaking-up-hard-do-exploration-resignation/docview/1347340588/se-2?accountid=14511.

181 **reason they left their job:** Emily Neaves, "It's Not You, It's Me: An Inductive Exploration of Employee Accounts for Quitting," Honors College Thesis, Oregon

State University, 2017, ir.library.oregonstate.edu/concern/honors_college_theses/gf06g480c.
183 **they gave five reasons:** Klotz, "Is Breaking Up Hard to Do?"
184 **reacted with outright shock:** Klotz, "Is Breaking Up Hard to Do?"
185 **as we plan to depart:** Ethan R. Burris et al., "Quitting Before Leaving: The Mediating Effects of Psychological Attachment and Detachment on Voice," *Journal of Applied Psychology* 93, no. 4 (2008): 912–22, doi.org/10.1037/0021-9010.93.4.912.
185 **they were going to quit:** Timothy M. Gardner et al, "If You've Got Leavin' on Your Mind: The Identification and Validation of Pre-Quitting Behaviors," *Journal of Management* 44, no. 8 (2018): 3231–57, doi.org/10.1177/0149206316665462.
187 **management scholar Ben Tepper:** Bennett J. Tepper et al., "Abusive Supervision, Intentions to Quit, and Employees' Workplace Deviance: A Power/Dependence Analysis," *Organizational Behavior and Human Decision Processes* 109, no. 2 (2009): 156–67, doi.org /10.1016/j.obhdp.2009.03.004.
188 **the maxim "power corrupts":** Tyler Burns, "A Tale of Two Quotes: When Power 'Corrupts' and When It Triggers 'Great Responsibility,'" University of Georgia, 2020, proquest.com/dissertations-theses/tale-two-quotes-when-power-corrupts-triggers/docview/2411647041/se-2?accountid=14511.
188 **say that power *reveals*:** Adam D. Galinsky et al., "Power: Past Findings, Present Considerations, and Future Directions," in *APA Handbook of Personality and Social Psychology 3: Interpersonal Relations,* APA Handbooks in Psychology (American Psychological Association, 2015), 421–60.
188 **act on our impulses:** Joris Lammers et al., "Power and Morality," *Current Opinion in Psychology* 6 (2015): 15–19, doi.org/10.1016/j.copsyc.2015.03.018.

CHAPTER FOURTEEN

189 **company's treatment of customers:** Greg Smith, "Why I Am Leaving Goldman Sachs," *New York Times,* March 14, 2012, nytimes.com/2012/03/14/opinion/why-i-am-leaving-goldman-sachs.html?_r 0.
189 **energy to damage control:** Liz Rappaport and David Enrich, "Goldman Plays Damage Control," *Wall Street Journal,* March 14, 2012, wsj.com/articles/SB10001424052702304692804577281252012689294.
189 **they deliver the news:** Megan Tatum, "#Quittok: Why Young Workers Are Live-Quitting on Tiktok," BBC *Worklife,* March 27, 2023, bbc.com/worklife/article/20230321-quittok-why-young-workers-are-live-quitting-on-tiktok.
190 **ways people quit their jobs:** Anthony C. Klotz and Mark C. Bolino, "Saying Goodbye: The Nature, Causes, and Consequences of Employee Resignation Styles," *Journal of Applied Psychology* 101, no. 10 (2016): 1386–404, doi.org/10.1037/apl0000135.
192 **and posted on YouTube:** Emanuella Grinberg, "'Joey' Becomes Recession Hero After Using Marching Band to Quit Job," CNN, October 24, 2011, edition.cnn.com/2011/10/24/living/marching-band-resignation/index.html.
193 **walked off the set:** Mark Harris, "Jack Paar's 'Tonight Show' Exit," *Entertainment Weekly,* February 7, 1992, ew.com/article/1992/02/07/jack-paars-tonight-show-exit.

194 **respond to any company communication:** Carl P. Maertz and Michael A. Campion, "Profiles in Quitting: Integrating Process and Content Turnover Theory," *Academy of Management Journal* 47, no. 4 (2004): 566–82, doi.org/10.5465/20159602; Carl P. Maertz and Kayla R. Kmitta, "Integrating Turnover Reasons and Shocks with Turnover Decision Processes," *Journal of Vocational Behavior* 81, no. 1 (2012): 26–38, doi.org/10.1016/j.jvb.2012.04.002.

198 **emotions, including even regret:** Odile Guinot, "From 'Great Resignation' to 'Great Regret': A Qualitative Analysis of Regret Post Resignation," University of Florida, 2024, dissertation.

198 **during your notice period:** Anthony C. Klotz, "You've Quit Your Job. How Do You Manage the Time Before You Actually Leave?," *Wall Street Journal*, September 22, 2001, wsj.com/lifestyle/careers/quit-job-notice-period-11632244422.

PART V INTRODUCTION

203 **favorite was one entitled:** Leena Sidat, "10 Ways to Know If Your Partner Has Won the Lottery and Is Keeping It a Secret," *Stoke Sentinel*, January 27, 2022, stokesentinel.co.uk/special-features/know-partner-won-lottery-secret-6559215.

203 **share the riches with them:** Niamh Spence, "Lottery Winner Who Kept Win Secret from Wife Has Been Ordered to Give Her Part of the Winnings," *Unilad*, June 2, 2024, unilad.com/news/money/lottery-winner-forced-money-husband-divorce-185904-20240602; r/AskWomen, Reddit, "Would You Tell Your Partner If You Won the Lottery and What's the First Thing That You Would Do?," reddit.com/r/AskWomen/comments/pt9m3m/would_you_tell_your_partner_if_you_won_the/?force_seo=1.

203 **disclosing it to those around them:** Anthony C. Klotz, "Is Breaking Up Hard to Do? An Exploration of the Resignation Process," University of Oklahoma, 2013, proquest.com/dissertations-theses/is-breaking-up-hard-do-exploration-resignation/docview/1347340588/se-2?accountid=14511.

204 **look for many work situations:** Phillip S. Thompson and Mark C. Bolino, "Negative Beliefs About Accepting Coworker Help: Implications for Employee Attitudes, Job Performance, and Reputation," *Journal of Applied Psychology* 103, no. 8 (2018): 842–66, doi.org/10.1037/apl0000300.

204 **helping them deal with jolts:** Adam M. Grant, "Leading with Meaning: Beneficiary Contact, Prosocial Impact, and the Performance Effects of Transformational Leadership," *Academy of Management Journal* 55, no. 2 (2012): 458–76, doi.org/10.5465/amj.2010.0588.

CHAPTER FIFTEEN

208 **tend to trigger turnover:** Scott E. Seibert et al., "Even the Best Laid Plans Sometimes Go Askew: Career Self-Management Processes, Career Shocks, and the Decision to Pursue Graduate Education," *Journal of Applied Psychology* 98, no. 1 (2013): 169–82, doi.org/10.1037/a0030882; Scott E. Seibert et al., "Awakening the Entre-

preneur Within: Entrepreneurial Identity Aspiration and the Role of Displacing Work Events," *Journal of Applied Psychology* 106, no. 8 (2021): 1224–38, doi.org/10.1037/apl0000823; J. Daniel Kim, "Startup Acquisitions as a Hiring Strategy: Turnover Differences Between Acquired and Regular Hires," *Strategy Science* 9, no. 2 (2024/06/01 2023): 118–34, doi.org/10.1287/stsc.2022.0026.

208 **if he wasn't reinstated:** Chris Vallance et al., "OpenAI Staff Demand Board Resign over Sam Altman Sacking," *BBC Worklife*, November 20, 2023, bbc.co.uk/news/business-67470876.

208 **try to collectively make sense:** Jenna R. Pieper et al., "Collective Turnover Response over Time to a Unit-Level Shock," *Journal of Applied Psychology* 108, no. 6 (2023): 1001–26, doi.org/10.1037/apl0001052.

209 **make sense of those disruptions:** Ray A. Smith, "You've Heard of Quiet Quitting. Now Companies Are Quiet Cutting," *Wall Street Journal*, August 27, 2023, wsj.com/lifestyle/careers/youve-heard-of-quiet-quitting-now-companies-are-quiet-cutting-ba2c326d.

209 **asked about their departure:** S. Foy, "PwC Asks for Silence from Departing Staff in Programme of UK Job Cuts," *Financial Times* (2024), ft.com/content/c1c1eaab-0eda-46da-b530-cf3d42c351eb.

210 **being treated unfairly:** Jason A. Colquitt et al., "Justice at the Millennium, a Decade Later: A Meta-Analytic Test of Social Exchange and Affect-Based Perspectives," *Journal of Applied Psychology* 98, no. 2 (2013): 199–236, doi.org/10.1037/a0031757; Jason A. Colquitt and Kate P. Zipay, "Justice, Fairness, and Employee Reactions," *Annual Review of Organizational Psychology and Organizational Behavior* 2 (2015): 75–99, doi.org/10.1146/annurev-orgpsych-032414-111457.

212 **(e.g., temporary pay cuts):** Joshua D. Margolis and Andrew Molinsky, "Navigating the Bind of Necessary Evils: Psychological Engagement and the Production of Interpersonally Sensitive Behavior," *Academy of Management Journal* 51, no. 5 (2008): 847–72, doi.org/10.5465/amj.2008.34789639.

212 **communication in stark terms:** Jerald Greenberg, "Employee Theft as a Reaction to Underpayment Inequity: The Hidden Cost of Pay Cuts," *Journal of Applied Psychology* 75, no. 5 (1990): 561–68, doi.org/10.1037/0021-9010.75.5.561.

213 **to prevent future problems:** Brian P. Niehoff and Robert H. Moorman, "Justice as a Mediator of the Relationship Between Methods of Monitoring and Organizational Citizenship Behavior," *Academy of Management Journal* 36, no. 3 (1993): 527–56, doi.org/10.5465/256591.

215 **life of an employee:** Chris Platts, "Realistic Job Preview: 7 Great Examples to Inspire You," *ThriveMap*, November 20, 2020, thrivemap.io/realistic-job-preview.

215 **jolts and associated turnover:** David R. Earnest et al., "Mechanisms Linking Realistic Job Previews with Turnover: A Meta-Analytic Path Analysis," *Personnel Psychology* 64, no. 4 (2011): 865–97, doi.org/10.1111/j.1744-6570.2011.01230.x.

215 **to become high performers:** Robert D. Bretz Jr. and Timothy A. Judge, "Realistic Job Previews: A Test of the Adverse Self-Selection Hypothesis," *Journal of Applied Psychology* 83, no. 2 (1998): 330–37, doi.org/10.1037/0021-9010.83.2.330.

216 **they are eventually unmet:** M. Ronald Buckley et al., "Investigating Newcomer Expectations and Job-Related Outcomes," *Journal of Applied Psychology* 83, no. 3 (1998): 452–61, doi.org/10.1037/0021-9010.83.3.452.

CHAPTER SIXTEEN

217 **ownership over their work:** Kyoung Yong Kim et al., "High Performance Work Systems and Employee Mental Health: The Roles of Psychological Empowerment, Work Role Overload, and Organizational Identification," *Human Resource Management* 62, no. 6 (2023): 791–810, doi.org/10.1002/hrm.22160.

220 **employees' feelings, thoughts, and behaviors:** Jeffrey Yip and Colin M. Fisher, "Listening in Organizations: A Synthesis and Future Agenda," *Academy of Management Annals* 16, no. 2 (2022): 657–79, doi.org/10.5465/annals.2020.0367.

222 **immediate solution and payback:** Clayton M. Christensen, "How Will You Measure Your Life?," *Harvard Business Review* 88, no. 7/8 (2010), hbr.org/2010/07/how-will-you-measure-your-life.

222 **than letting it pile up:** David Allen, *Getting Things Done: The Art of Stress-Free Productivity* (Penguin, 2015).

223 **technical tasks over people tasks:** Elad N. Sherf et al., "Too Busy to Be Fair? The Effect of Workload and Rewards on Managers' Justice Rule Adherence," *Academy of Management Journal* 62, no. 2 (2019): 469–502, doi.org/10.5465/amj.2016.1061.

223 **of their managerial ranks:** Jack Kelly, "If Companies Follow the Lead of Elon Musk and Mark Zuckerberg, Middle Managers Are the Next Layoff Victims," *Forbes*, February 6, 2023, forbes.com/sites/jackkelly/2023/02/06/if-companies-follow-the-lead-of-elon-musk-and-mark-zuckerberg-middle-managers-are-the-next-layoff-victims.

224 **the best position to round up:** Sabina Nawaz, "The Problem with Saying 'Don't Bring Me Problems, Bring Me Solutions,'" *Harvard Business Review*, September 1, 2017, hbr.org/2017/09/the-problem-with-saying-dont-bring-me-problems-bring-me-solutions.

224 **employees, and for good reason:** Amy C. Edmondson, *The Fearless Organization: Creating Psychological Safety in the Workplace for Learning, Innovation, and Growth* (John Wiley & Sons, 2018).

225 **call it *radical honesty*:** Ray Dalio, *Principles* (Simon and Schuster, 2018).

225 **the name *radical transparency*:** Reed Hastings and Erin Meyer, *No Rules Rules: Netflix and the Culture of Reinvention* (Penguin, 2020).

225 **calls it *radical candor*:** Kim Scott, *Radical Candor: Be a Kick-Ass Boss Without Losing Your Humanity* (St. Martin's Press, 2019).

225 **a socially smart manner:** Kenneth J. Harris et al., "The Impact of Political Skill on Impression Management Effectiveness," *Journal of Applied Psychology* 92, no. 1 (2007): 278–85, doi.org/10.1037/0021-9010.92.1.278.

225 **suggest improvements at work:** James R. Detert and Ethan R. Burris, "Leadership Behavior and Employee Voice: Is the Door Really Open?," *Academy of Management Journal* 50, no. 4 (2007): 869–84, doi.org/10.5465/amj.2007.26279183; Phillip S. Thompson and Anthony C. Klotz, "Led by Curiosity and Responding with Voice: The Influence of Leader Displays of Curiosity and Leader Gender on Follower Reactions of Psychological Safety and Voice," *Organizational Behavior and Human Decision Processes* 172 (2022): 104170, doi.org/10.1016/j.obhdp.2022.104170.

CHAPTER SEVENTEEN

228 **they helped their coworkers:** Jia Hu et al., "The Mind, the Heart, and the Leader in Times of Crisis: How and When Covid-19-Triggered Mortality Salience Relates to State Anxiety, Job Engagement, and Prosocial Behavior," *Journal of Applied Psychology* 105, no. 11 (2020): 1218–33, doi.org/10.1037/apl0000620.

231 **skydive into his work breaks:** Joe Berkowitz, "Forget Quiet Vacationing. GoPro Says Midday Breaks Have Employees More Engaged," *Fast Company*, June 7, 2024, fastcompany.com/91134156/forget-quiet-vacationing-gopro-says-midday-breaks-have-employees-more-engaged.

232 **especially in that industry:** Dong Liu et al., "Tackling the Negative Impact of Covid-19 on Work Engagement and Taking Charge: A Multi-Study Investigation of Frontline Health Workers," *Journal of Applied Psychology* 106, no. 2 (2021): 185–98, doi.org/10.1037/apl0000866.

232 **community members, and so forth:** Adam M. Grant, "How Customers Can Rally Your Troops," *Harvard Business Review* 89, no. 6 (2011): 97–103, hbr.org/2011/06/how-customers-can-rally-your-troops.

233 **path to their good life:** Rachel Burgess et al., "Longing for the Road Not Taken: The Affective and Behavioral Consequences of Forgone Identity Dwelling," *Academy of Management Journal* 65, no. 1 (2022): 93–118, doi.org/10.5465/amj.2019.0746.

CHAPTER EIGHTEEN

235 **"making the wrong decision etc.":** Anxious_Agent98, "Handed in My Notice and Boss Reacted Badly," Reddit, reddit.com/r/TrueOffMyChest/comments/15ckuvp/handed_in_my_notice_and_boss_reacted_badly.

235 **"and all hell breaks loose":** Alison Green, "My Company Is Incredibly Weird When People Resign," *Ask a Manager*, August 11, 2020, askamanager.org/2020/08/my-company-is-incredibly-weird-when-people-resign.html.

235 **"mistreated during their notice periods":** Alison Green, "My Boss Is Handling My Resignation Badly," *Ask a Manager*, May 16, 2023, askamanager.org/2023/05/my-boss-is-handling-my-resignation-badly.html.

236 **who respond in dysfunctional ways:** Alison Green, "Let's Discuss Deranged Things Your Employer Did When You Resigned," *Ask a Manager*, January 25, 2024), askamanager.org/2024/01/lets-discuss-deranged-things-your-employer-did-when-you-resigned.html.

236 **end to this work relationship:** Ingrid Smithey Fulmer et al., "You Can Check Out Any Time You Like, but Can You Ever Leave? A Theory of Firm Value Capture from Alumni," *Organization Science* 35, no. 4 (2024): 1427–42, doi.org/10.1287/orsc.2019.13061.

238 **by retiring from basketball:** David Aldridge, "When Michael Jordan Walked Away from Basketball in 1993, the Recoil Was Seismic," *New York Times*, October 8, 2023, nytimes.com/athletic/4905700/2023/10/06/michael-jordan-retirement-anniversary-1993-bulls.

239 **gained in their time away:** Brian W. Swider et al., "Employees on the Rebound: Extending the Careers Literature to Include Boomerang Employment," *Journal of Applied Psychology* 102, no. 6 (2017): 890–909, doi.org/10.1037/apl0000200.

239 **a great deal of teamwork:** JR Keller et al., "In With the Old? Examining When Boomerang Employees Outperform New Hires," *Academy of Management Journal* 64, no. 6 (2021): 1654–84, doi.org/10.5465/amj.2019.1340.

239 **other two groups of workers:** John D. Arnold et al., "Welcome Back? Job Performance and Turnover of Boomerang Employees Compared to Internal and External Hires," *Journal of Management* 47, no. 8 (2021): 2198–225, doi.org/10.1177/0149206320936335.

240 **anniversary of their departure:** Anthony C. Klotz et al., "The Promise (and Risk) of Boomerang Employees," *Harvard Business Review*, March 15, 2023, hbr.org/2023/03/the-promise-and-risk-of-boomerang-employees.

242 **is the manager themselves:** Mark C. Bolino and Anthony C. Klotz, "Don't Let Lazy Managers Drive Away Your Top Performers," *Harvard Business Review*, November 21, 2018, hbr.org/2018/11/dont-let-lazy-managers-drive-away-your-top-performers.

242 **different process in motion:** Anthony C. Klotz and Mark C. Bolino, "Do You Really Know Why Employees Leave Your Company?," *Harvard Business Review*, July 31, 2019, hbr.org/2019/07/do-you-really-know-why-employees-leave-your-company.

242 **potential for turnover contagion:** Anthony C. Klotz, "Quitting Can Be Contagious at a Company. Here's How to Stop It," *Wall Street Journal*, February 19, 2022, wsj.com/articles/turnover-contagion-quitting-can-be-contagious-heres-how-to-stop-it-11645219806.

243 **talk about the company:** Ingrid Smithey Fulmer et al., "You Can Check Out Any Time You Like, but Can You Ever Leave? A Theory of Firm Value Capture from Alumni," *Organization Science* 35, no. 4 (2024): 1427–42, doi.org/10.1287/orsc.2019.13061.

243 **company is one big family:** Tom Dotan and Katherine Bindley, "At Marc Benioff's Salesforce, It's One Big Family—Until Trouble Hits," *Wall Street Journal*, February 28, 2023, wsj.com/articles/salesforce-layoffs-marc-benioff-ohana-culture-8b3e82c.

244 **good job at this:** careers.salesforce.com/en/life-at-salesforce/alumni.

244 **and its alums:** Erin E. Makarius et al., "You Say Goodbye, and I Say Hello: The Alumni–Organization Relationship and Post-Separation Value," *Academy of Management Review* 50, no. 2 (2025): 251–71, doi.org/10.5465/amr.2022.0242; Rebecca M. Paluch et al., "A Cross-Level Theory of Alumni–Organization Relationships," *Academy of Management Review* (2024), doi.org/10.5465/amr.2021.0523.

INDEX

Academy of Management (AOM), 89
active listening, 220
affective events theory, 34
Altman, Sam, 208
Alzheimer's disease, 125
Aniston, Jennifer, 63
avoidant resignations, 193–96, 237

Becker, Ernest, 140–41
Becoming (Obama), 67
behaviors
   citizenship, 132–33, 169
   customers displaying bad, 87–88
   deviant, 87
   organizational, 210
   political, 225
   during pre-resignation period, 185–86, 198
   rude, 81–83, 85–88, 128
Beyoncé, 63
birthdays, 158–60
Bolino, Mark, 242
Boomerang employees, 238–41
Boswell, Wendy, 104–5
"Break My Soul" (song), 63
bridge burning resignations, 177, 192, 195–96, 238, 241–42
Brooklyn Nine-Nine (television), 84
burnout, of employees, 83, 127

Burris, Ethan, 117
butterfly effect, 138
bystanders, 95–97
by-the-book resignation, 190–91, 194, 237

careers, 24–28, 44–45
career cushioning, 38
career success, 62
   goodwill for, 70
   long-term, 107
   organizational culture for, 71
carrying on, 8, 65–67
challenging voice, 117–18, 121–22
Chappelle, Dave, 79, 81
Chappelle's Show (television), 79
China, 18–19
Christensen, Clayton, 222
citizenship behaviors, 132–33, 169
citizenship crafting process, 169–70
Coe, David Allan, 62
collateral jolts, 89–97, 156–57
collective turnover, 208
communications
   employee resignation understanding through, 242–43
   employment checking-in benefits in, 40–41
   resignation and how to, 182, 193

communications (*cont.*)
  resignation and when to, 182–83
  resignation process using, 183–84, 193–94
  resignations via written, 193
  rude behaviors expressed through, 81–83
  technology influencing, 24–25, 190
  written, 193
commuting
  mental detachment while, 135–36
  time saving in, 134
  in work life, 133–36
company
  forward-thinking, 243–44
  negative information sharing about, 216
  solutions benefiting, 119–20
  staffing, 210
compensation, 49
conflict, speaking up and, 114
construal levels, 59–61
contentment, 48–51
counterfactual thinking, 114
counteroffers, 184
COVID-19 pandemic, 24
  quitting work desire increases during, 16–17
  terror management event of, 143
  vaccines for, 1–2
  workforce during, 68
coworkers
  abusive, 74–75
  boss abusive toward, 36
  collateral jolts as departures of, 90–95
  credit-claiming by, 34–35
  departures of, 90–95
  disrespect of, 95–97
  employee belittled by, 5–6
  employment with added work from, 91–93
  former, 199
  good things happening to, 156–57
  goodwill built with, 69
  involuntary departures of, 93–95
  malicious intent of, 82
  problems discussed by, 115–16
  socializing with, 170–71
  speaking up to boss or, 8, 113
  vicarious mistreatment of, 96
  well-being influenced by, 52
crossover jolts, 125–36, 157–60
The Culture Map (Meyer), 120
culture shock, 105
customers
  are always right, 86
  retail workers abused by, 87–88
  rude behaviors to, 87–88

Dane, Erik, 41, 154
death
  anxiety, 143
  awareness, 139, 144
  generativity perspective on, 143
decision-making
  about careers, 24–28, 44–45
  emotional reactions interfering with, 25, 107–8
  fairness of, 210–13
  feeling-thinking-acting process in, 148–49
  happiness and meaning in, 232–33
  if-then plans in, 39
  jolts causing, 6, 240
  during milestone years, 159
  during notice period, 182–83
  onboarding process and, 103–4
  organizational changes influencing, 207–9
  perfunctory resignations, 191, 194–95
  ponderer path in, 42
  post-quitting regret and, 101
  power surge influencing, 186–88
  push and pull factors in, 181
  quitting and, 18, 23, 63–64

remote jolts in, 147, 149–50
sensemaking in, 37
unfairness and injustice from, 196, 210–14
unsolicited job offers influencing, 162
work break, 171–72
work relationships in, 61–62
deep acting, 73–75
DeFrancesco, Joey, 192
The Denial of Death (Becker), 140
departures
  collateral jolts from coworker, 90–95
  coworkers involuntary, 93–95
  disruption by, 92–93
  negative signals sent during, 237
Detert, Jim, 115
deviant behaviors, 87
direct jolts, 79–88
disengagement problem, 166–67
disloyalty, 238
disruptive events
  departures as, 92–93
  emotional reaction to, 36–37
  leadership facing, 228–29
doom scrolling, 24
Duke, Annie, 39
Dutton, Jane, 168

Eat, Pray, Love (Gilbert), 63
economy
  gig, 26
  resignations influenced by, 2
  sluggish, 166
emotional labor, 73
emotional reactions
  affective events theory with, 34
  decision-making interference by, 25, 107–8
  to disruptive events, 36–37
  exhaustion from, 75, 149
  to negative events, 5
  to positive events, 5, 153–54
  to resignations, 237–38

employability, 100, 155
employees
  burnout of, 83, 127
  changes made to help, 228–29
  citizenship behaviors of, 132–33
  coworker belittling, 5–6
  crossover jolts with costs of good, 128–33
  dissatisfied, 132
  employment relationship of, 4–5
  Great Resignation by, 3
  identity as, 57
  incivility, 83
  job embeddedness of, 65–67
  job satisfaction of, 17–18
  job search of, 27–28
  loyalty, 23–24, 64, 71
  management and quitting of top, 235–36
  moment after resignation of, 236–37
  productivity from happy, 130–31
  quitting over fixable situations, 113
  rational and calculated quitting by, 18
  realistic solutions offered by, 119
  rehiring of, 238–39
  resignation communications about, 242–43
  turnover of, 17
employer branding, 109, 242–43
employment
  career-limiting move in, 97
  COVID-19 pandemic influencing, 1–2
  coworker's departure causing more work in, 91–93
  desirable alternatives to, 66–67
  dignity from, 54–55
  employee's relationship with, 4–5
  failures during, 79–80
  good deeds beyond required duties in, 131
  hostility experienced during, 80

employment (*cont.*)
  management decision-making during, 204–5, 210–13
  no one wants to work anymore and, 13–14
  pay and status from, 46–47
  staying put for, 68–72
  toxic elements in, 74–75
  ways of leaving, 190–94
  work relationship check-in, 39–41
energy levels
  day-to-day mental, 46
  pockets of, 172–73
entrepreneurship, 19–20
environmental jolts, 19
epiphanies, 41, 153–54, 158
events
  acknowledging and engaging with, 31–32
  balancing act after, 45–47
  behavior response to, 34–35
  bystander experiencing, 95–97
  construal levels in, 60–61
  disruptive, 36–37, 92–93, 228–29, 242
  nuclear, 151
  one-off, 19
  proactive preparations for, 38
  push and pull from, 17–24
  quitting work from, 64
  resignations caused by, 6–7
  sensemaking of, 37, 46–47
  smart resilience to, 75
  unexpected, 19–20
  work-family ought, 157
  work relationships influenced by, 32
evidence-based manager, 220
exhaustion, emotional, 75, 149
expectations, reality not meeting, 99, 102–5
extroverts, 33

failures, 79–80
fairness, of decision-making, 210–13
f-ck you money, 38–39
feedback sandwich, 120
feeling-thinking-acting process, 35, 37–38, 148–49
Field, Marshall, 86
fight-or-flight response, 38
financial crisis (2008), 128
financial freedom, 4, 44
Fitzgerald, F. Scott, 45
flexible work, 26, 133–34
Floyd, George, 146–47
foreclosures, home, 128
forgone identity, 233–34
Friedan, Betty, 157
frontline workers, 2
functional turnover, 166

General Social Survey (GSS), 14–17
generativity perspective on death, 143
gig economy, 26
Gilbert, Elizabeth, 63
Glassdoor, 243
Goldman Sachs, 189–90, 192
good citizen, 130
good deeds, beyond work tasks, 131
good life
  calculus, 49
  well-being and, 48
  work getting in way of, 72
goodwill, 69–70
Grant, Adam, 120
grateful goodbye resignation, 191, 194–95
Great Awakening, 227–28
Great Regret, 100
Great Resignation
  employees quitting in, 3
  as Great Awakening, 227–28
  as Great Regret, 100
  prediction of, 143, 207

resignations increase during, 16–17
worker shortages from, 13–14
groups
　disruptions to, 236
　membership in, 56–58
　negative events of social, 145–47
　not included in, 84–85
　work tasks allocated across, 230–31
GSS. *See* General Social Survey

Hackman, Richard, 55
happiness, 44, 245. *See also*
　　meaningfulness; well-being
　day-to-day, 49
　decision-making for, 232–33
　good life for, 48
　meaningfulness and, 48–51
　mindset for seeking, 149–50
　pain reduction for, 148–50
　pursuit of, 231–32
　work relationships influencing,
　　53–54
　from work tasks, 51–52
harassment
　ostracism and, 85–86
　well-being influenced by, 85–86
　at work, 80
healthy boundaries, from work, 129–30
help, asking for, 203–4
Hemsworth, Chris, 125–26, 139
Hermant, Albert. *See* Hirschman,
　　Albert Otto
high-performance work systems, 217
high performers
　leadership and, 217–18
　resignations by, 94–95
hiring process, 108, 110
Hirschman, Albert Otto, 111–12,
　　164–66
Hochschild, Arlie Russell, 72
holidays, 158–60
Holmes, Chris, 51
Holtom, Brooks, 21

honeymoon jolts
　hangover effect in, 105
　job previews reducing, 215
　job searches in, 106–8
　from negative events, 98–99
　positive events in, 161–62
　reality not meeting expectations in,
　　99, 102–5
hustle culture, 167
hybrid work, 17

identity
　as employees, 57
　forgone, 233–34
　sense of self in, 57–58
　work tasks and, 58
if-then plans, 38–39
Iger, Bob, 61–62
Ignatius of Loyola, 142
impulsive quitting resignations, 38,
　　193–96, 238
infodemic, 24
in-person resignations, 190
International Social Survey
　　Programme, 15
in-the-loop resignations, 192, 194–95
introverts, 33
involuntary departures, 93–95

Jaarsveld, Danielle van, 87
James, LeBron, 172
jobs
　crafting, 168–70
　creep, 129
　embeddedness, 65–67
　preview, 215
　problems with satisfaction at, 31
　satisfaction from, 17–18, 49, 105
　unsolicited offers for, 162
job searches
　of employees, 27–28
　of grad students, 89–91
　hiring process and, 110

job searches (*cont.*)
  in honeymoon jolts, 106–8
  recruitment process and, 214–16
job seekers, 107–8, 215–16, 243
jolts. *See also* events
  collateral, 90–97, 156–57, 237
  crossover, 126–33, 157–60
  decision-making caused by, 240
  decisions caused by, 6
  direct, 79–88
  environmental, 19
  honeymoon, 102–8, 161–62, 215
  looking for signs of, 204–5
  loyalty response to, 165
  organizational changes signaling, 207–9
  positive, 151–54, 156–61
  remote, 137–45, 147, 149–50, 160–61
  shared ownership of, 227–29
jolts-response process, 186
Jones, Jeff, 98–99
Jones, Neil, 43–44
Jordan, Michael, 238

Kahneman, Daniel, 30
Kennedy, John F., 59
Klopp, Jürgen, 29–31, 45–47

layoffs, 93–94, 208, 211–12
lazy management, 242
leadership
  disruptive events faced by, 228–29
  high-performance workers and, 217–18
  poor communications from, 211–12
  visionary, 231–34
leaning back, 8, 167–68, 170–73
Leary, Mark, 53
leave of absence, 240–41
Lee, Thomas, 20, 38, 41
Leigh, Angelica, 145–48
life satisfaction, 44
life spillovers, 128

life stories
  common threads in, 151
  positive changes in, 154
  positive possibilities for, 8, 151
liminal space, 158–59, 179–84
Limitless (series), 125
listening, active, 220
long-term career success, 107
long-term relationships, 70–72
long-term well-being, 27
Lorenz, Edward, 138
Lottery Question
  continue or quit working in, 14–15
  keep working from, 3–4, 14–15
  people still want to work, 15–16
lottery winning, 44–45
loyalty
  disloyalty and, 238
  of employees, 71
  employees couldn't quit because of, 23–24, 64
  jolt response of, 165
  resignation and, 241–43
"Lunch Breaks Unpacked" (article), 171

The Managed Heart (Hochschild), 72
management. *See also* boss; leadership
  bringing up problems to, 116
  decision-making of, 204–5, 210–13
  evidence-based, 220
  incentive programs from, 223–24
  lazy, 242
  middle, 229–31
  problems brought up to, 224–26
  scientific, 219
  top employee quits and, 235–36
  toxic, 196, 223
matched sample approach, 44
McAdams, Dan, 151
meaningfulness
  happiness and, 48–51
  mortality and work lacking, 142

negative events with reflections of, 147
pursuit of, 231–32
from work, 59, 245
from work relationships, 56–58
from work tasks, 54–56
mega-threats, 145, 147
Melwani, Shimul, 145–48
mental detachment, 135–36
mental energy, 46
Meyer, Alan, 19
Meyer, Erin, 120
Michelin star, 155–56
microbreaks, 172
micromanagement, 218–20
middle managers, 229–31
milestone age years, 159
Mitchell, Terence, 20, 38, 41
mortality
  death awareness and, 139, 144
  remote jolts from, 139–45
  salience, 141–42, 145, 147
  work not meaningful and, 142

naked resignations, 18–19
National Football League (NFL), 137
negative reasons, for quitting work, 181
neglect, 165
network, of goodwill, 69–70
new job
  job satisfaction dropping with, 105
  negative events at, 98–99
  workers quitting, 99
new manager assimilation, 218
NFL. *See* National Football League
9/11 attacks, 137
no one wants to work anymore, 13–14
notice period
  decision-making during, 182–83
  in resignations, 197–99
nuclear events, 151

Obama, Michelle, 67–68
O'Connor, Sandra Day, 160–61

Office Space (film), 63
Oldham, Greg, 55
onboarding process, 103–4
one-off events, 19
OpenAI, 208–9
open-minded approach, 148
operational tasks, 223
O'Reilly, Jane, 85
Organ, Dennis, 131–32
organizations
  citizens of, 130–32
  culture of, 71
  disruptions to, 242
  harassment mishandled by, 80
  jolts signaled by changes in, 207–9
ostracism, 85–86
outside job offers, 162

Paar, Jack, 193
pain-avoiding mindset, 148–50
pain spiral, 148–50
partnership, 61
pauser path, 41–42
pay and status, in decision-making, 46–47
Paycheck, Johnny, 62–64
pep talks, 232–33
perfunctory resignations, 191, 194–95
permacrisis, 144
personal life
  good citizen in, 130
  professional life disruption of, 126–27, 129
  work disrupting, 127–28
person-job fit, 52
planning, by management, 208
political behaviors, 225
political skills, 121–22
pondered path, 42
positive emotions, 31
positive jolts, 151–63
positive-negative asymmetry effect, 152
power balance, 186–87

power surge, 186–88
prepper path, 38
pre-resignation period
  behaviors during, 185–86, 198
  high-risk strategies during, 192
  power shifts in, 186–88
  of resignation, 179–84
proactive preparations, 38
professional life, 126–27, 129
promotions, 155–56
psychological contract, 102–6, 108–10
psychological safety, 224–25
psychological needs, 84
psychology, organizational, 185
pulse surveys, 221
push and pull factors, 17–24, 181

quick quitting, 99, 101, 214
quiet quitting, 165–68, 185–86
Quit (Duke), 39
quit-friendly workforce, 106
"Quitting Before Leaving" (study), 185
quitting work
  attention given to, 63–64
  best way to, 22–23
  COVID-19 increases desire to, 16–17
  decision-making on, 63–64
  employees extra work from, 91–93
  employees with fixable situations, 113
  employees with lowered bar for, 26–27
  employees with rational and calculated, 18
  impulsive, 38
  keep working and, 3–4, 14–15
  Lottery Question and, 14–15
  loyalty and not being able to, 23–24, 64
  in new jobs, 99
  pause and ponder paths to, 41–42
  regret about, 101
  risk involved in, 27
  sticking around and, 67–68
  what happens after decision to, 18, 23

racial injustice, 2
radical honesty, 225
radical transparency, 225
rage applying, 25
realistic job preview, 214–15
reality, expectations not met by, 99, 102–5
reality shock, 216
recruitment process, 110, 214–16
refugees, becoming entrepreneurs, 20
regret, 101, 104–5, 114
regulatory focus theory, 148
rehiring, of employees, 238–39
relationships
  employment, 4–5
  employment check-ins on, 39–41
  events influencing work, 32
  happiness influenced by work, 53–54
  long-term, 70–72
  meaningfulness from work, 56–58
  with work, 61–62
reluctant stayers, 67–68
remote jolts, 137–50
remote work, 2, 17, 133–34
resignations. *See also* departures; quit working
  avoidant, 193–96, 237
  boomerangs from, 239
  bridge burning, 177, 192, 195–96, 238, 241–42
  by-the-book, 190–91, 194, 237
  naked, 18–19
  communications how-to on, 182
  communications process for, 183–84, 193–94
  confiding in others about, 180–81
  economy influencing, 2
  emotional reactions to, 237–38

employee communications for understanding of, 242–43
events playing role in, 6–7
grateful goodbye, 191, 194–95
Great Resignation increase in, 16–17
by high performers, 94–95
honesty about, 181–82
impulsive quitting, 193–96, 238
information for transparency in, 181–82
in-person, 190
in-the-loop, 192, 194–95
leave of absence instead of, 240–41
loyalty and, 241–43
management of notice period in, 197–99
moment after employee, 236–37
perfunctory, 191, 194–95
in person, 190
poorly executed, 22–23
pre-resignation period of, 179–84
public, 189–90
research of, 7–9
when to communicate, 182–83
via written communications, 193
resilience, 75
résumé gaps, 26
retail workers, 87
retirement, early, 139
return-to-office mandates, 162–63
revenge bedtime procrastination, 24
reverse culture shock, 105
Ride of a Lifetime (Iger), 61
rightsizing, 168
risk
  bringing up problems to management as, 116
  during pre-resignation period, 192
  quitting work with, 27
  thoughtful resignations with, 177–78
Ritz, César, 86
Rock, Chris, 24
Rogers, Callie, 43–44

Rossi, Portia de, 158
rude behaviors, 81–83
Rusbult, Caryl, 164
Russia, 165

sabotage, 177
sacrifice, 65–66
Sajjadiani, Sima, 93–94
salaries, increasing, 17
Salesforce, 243–44
Sands, Daniel, 155
scientific management, 219
Scott, Kim, 225
Seinfeld, Jerry, 118
self-employment, 19
sensemaking, of events, 37, 45–47
sense of self, 57–58
service workers, 87–88
severance packages, 209
Shapero, Albert, 19–20, 152, 159
shocks. *See* jolts
silent layoffs, 208
silver linings, to negative events, 245
60 Minutes (television), 35–36, 101
sleep quality, 32–33
smart resilience, 75
Smith, Greg, 189–90, 192
social capital, 70
social groups, 145–47
socializing, with coworkers, 170–71
social media, 63, 170, 189
social networks, 53–54, 65–67
sociometer, 53–54, 236
Sokol, Lisa, 19–20, 159
speaking up, 111–22
staffing company, 210
staying put, for employment, 68–72
sticking around, 67–68
supportive voice, 117–18
Supreme Court, US, 160
surface acting, 73–74
Swider, Brian, 238

Taylor, Frederick, 219
Taylor, Shannon, 83
teamwork, 239
tech industry, 211–12
technology, 24–25, 126, 190
temporal landmarks, 159
"10 Ways to Know If Your Partner Has Won the Lottery and Is Keeping It a Secret" (article), 203
Tepper, Ben, 187
Terkel, Studs, 54–55
terminations, 93–95
terror management theory, 141–45
theft rates, 213
thinking, disruptions to, 82–83
TikTok, 167
Tillman, Patrick, 137–38, 142
Tonight Show (television), 193
toxic elements, in employment, 74–75
toxic management, 196, 223
trust, breach of, 214
turnover
  collective, 208
  of employees, 17
  functional, 166
  ingredients for, 93
  outside job offers causing, 162
  voluntary, 104, 166
two-week notice, 190–91

Uber (ride-sharing company), 98–99
Ukraine, 165
unexpected events, 19–20
unfairness, from decision-making, 196, 210–14
Unfolding Model of Turnover, 20–22, 38
unsolicited job offer, 162

vacations, 159–60
vaccines, for COVID-19 pandemic, 1–2
vicarious mistreatment, 96
visionary leadership, 231–34
voice. *See* speaking up
voluntary quitting, 94
voluntary turnover, 104, 166
volunteering, 50

walking away, 8
Weick, Karl, 37
well-being
  coworkers influencing, 52
  good life and, 48
  harassment influencing, 85–86
  long-term, 27
  reluctant stayers and influence on, 68
  sleep quality influencing, 32–33
  speaking up good for, 112
  thoughts of work and, 41
  vacations for, 159–60
whistleblowers, 96
"Why the 'Great Resignation' Is Greatly Exaggerated" (article), 18
Winfrey, Oprah, 35–36, 101
work
  community, 51
  decisions based on relationships at, 61–62
  flexible, 26
  good life obstructed by, 72
  harassment at, 80
  healthy boundaries from, 129–30
  hybrid, 17
  meaning and purpose from, 59, 245
  mortality and meaningful, 142
  negative events and reflections about, 147
  no one wants to, 13–14
  people still want to, 15–16
  personal life disrupted by, 127–29
  quitting work creating employees extra, 91–93

remote, 2, 17, 133–34
rude behaviors experienced at, 81–83
social networks at, 65–67
well-being and thoughts of, 41
work breaks, 170–73
worker shortages, 13–14
work-family ought events, 157
workforce, quit-friendly, 106
Working (Terkel), 54–55

work tasks
emotional feelings toward, 72–73
good deeds beyond required, 131
happiness from, 51–52
identifying with, 58
job crafting of, 168–70
management of, 230–31
meaningfulness from, 54–56
Wrzesniewski, Amy, 168

ABOUT THE AUTHOR

Anthony Klotz is a professor of organizational behavior at the UCL School of Management in London. He is best known for predicting a global pandemic–related labor shift and dubbing it the Great Resignation. An award-winning teacher and a leading scholar on the psychology of work, Klotz has written for *Harvard Business Review* and *The Wall Street Journal*, and his research is regularly published in the leading academic journals in management. He has discussed the current and future state of work with media outlets, including NBC News, Bloomberg Businessweek, CNN, CNBC, *Today*, *The New York Times*, Financial Times, BBC, and NPR, and with executive teams at numerous Fortune 100 firms.

anthonyklotz.com
LinkedIn: AKlotz